CERAMICS IN THE ENVIRONMENT

AN INTERNATIONAL REVIEW

大脚人家
Big Feet People

CERAMICS IN THE ENVIRONMENT

AN INTERNATIONAL REVIEW

JANET MANSFIELD

A&C Black • London

American Ceramic Society • Ohio

Nino Caruso with Janet Mansfield at the inauguration of the Shigaraki Park, Shigaraki, Japan, at which time Caruso's pavilion was also officially opened.

First published in Great Britian 2005
A& C Black (publishers) Limited
Alderman House
37 Soho Square
London WID 2QX
www.acblack.com

ISBN-10 0-7136-6851-2
ISBN-13 978-0-7136-6851-3

Published simultaneously in the USA by
The American Ceramic Society
735 Ceramic Place, Suite 100
Westerville, Ohio 43081
www.ceramics.org

ISBN-10: 1-57498-270-2
ISBN-13: 9-781-75498-270-5

Book design: Linda Yeates and Penny & Tony Mills
Cover design: Sutchinda Rangsi Thompson
Editor/Project manager: Alison Stace

COVER (FRONT): (top) *The Light for Life*, by Zhu Le Geng, (bottom left) *Capistrano* by
Barbara Sorenson, (bottom right) *Vertical Blue* by Bernard Dejonghe.
COVER (BACK): (top) *River Riders* by Ann Roberts, (middle) *Foyer, St George Building Society* by
Joan Campbell, (bottom) *Clearing, Drawn by Nature* by Gina Bobrowski.
FRONTISPIECE: Hsu Yung-Hsu, *Big Feet People*, 2000. Dimensions: 83 x 82 x 319 cm
(33 x 32 x 124 in.).

Printed and bound by Tien Wah Press

A & C Black uses paper produced with elemental chlorine-free pulp, harvested from
managed sustainable forests.

CONTENTS

Preface

WITH THE RESURGENCE OF the use of ornamental, celebrative and contemplative artworks in the built and natural environments, this book is a timely reminder of the appropriateness of the use of clay for such work as well as the near universality of its usage. The range of work presented in *Ceramics in the Environment: An International Review* reflects both the myriad applications of clay as well as its ability to express a multitude of ideas in the hands of talented ceramists. These works communicate powerfully with their specific environments and with the reader in a way that transcends differences in geography and language. The works of more than 100 ceramicists from around the world are represented in this book and they reinforce the universal importance of clay as an abundant utilitarian as well as magical material that is able to be processed into works of expressive power.

The almost 2600 year-old Ishtar gate from ancient Babylon with its reliefs of animals modelled and glazed and used as bricks built into the structural fabric of the architecture speaks well of the durability and versatility of ceramics. The achievements of Nebuchadnezzar, dimly remembered from primary school history classes, those graceful and stately lions, bulls and dragons remain indelibly imprinted on my mind, and gave us a summary image of the achievements of the Assyrians. Such was the nature of the use of ceramics in particular historical environments. I cannot think of a better-placed person to write on the contemporary use of ceramics in this context than Janet Mansfield. Janet is internationally renowned as a ceramicist, an important author and publisher and collector of ceramics and, combined with her tireless travelling, she has access to the work of practitioners across the world. The breadth of coverage in *Ceramics in the Environment: An International Review* gives this impressive book an authoritative and vital place in the library of anyone with an interest in the field.

Michael Keighery
Head of Fine Arts, University of Western Sydney

C H A P T E R   O N E

Introducing Sculpture in a Specific Environment

ONE OF THE REASONS FOR WRITING THIS BOOK was the need, as I saw it, to draw attention to the work of ceramic artists who make large-scale works for placement in public or private environments. These works are usually made on commission, often in collaboration with an architect, and with a specific place in mind. The client for whom the work is made, as a rule, also has a say in the final outcome for the project. The idea for the book came to me when I was organising an event in Gulgong in 1995, which I called ClaySculpt. This event was also a result of my wanting to see, as well as encourage, the idea that ceramics be placed in a 'sculpture park' setting. I invited 22 ceramic artists, who were internationally known, to come to Australia to make and install work in a rural area. This project attracted 400 artists, teachers and students of ceramics to assist the sculptors over a ten-day period. Gulgong is a small country town in New South Wales, Australia; the surrounding rolling countryside is farming land for cattle, sheep and crops. ClaySculpt, however, was just the germ of the idea for the book because the more I studied the work of the invited artists, the more I realised what other major projects they had been commissioned to make that enhance the environment. This led me to other artists and the more I travelled and researched, the more ceramic artists I discovered who were involved in public works. During the intervening ten years, the material for the book gathered and the numbers of large-scale projects undertaken by artists using the ceramic medium seemed immense. This book refers to the work of more than 100 ceramic artists, yet I know there are many more. This text will concentrate on the contemporary application of the use of ceramics in environmental settings, acknowledging the fact that,

CAMPBELL

McGRATH

WISSINGER

MUSEN

LAUNDER

OPPOSITE: *Chuck Wissinger,* **Dinosaur's Backbone**. *Gulgong NSW, Australia.*

Joan Campbell,
Shower of Sunflowers, 1995.
Gulgong, NSW, Australia.

OPPOSITE
Joan Campbell, ***Bathers' Beach***
Construction. *Ceramic, wood.*
Fremantle, Western Australia.

historically, ceramic materials have been used over the centuries: to clad porous building materials to make them fire- and waterproof; to decorate walls; to tell a story or provide ornamentation; to form complete sculptures to enrich an area or honour a personage. Some of these sculptures make a social comment about contemporary life and culture.

In this book I have divided the artists and their work into chapters with nominated headings, including them where I thought they would fit best according to their artistic intentions. These chapter headings are meant as a general classification and the artists could be seen to fit into or overlap a number of categories. The artists themselves have supplied the illustrations, and the text has been taken from interviews, written statements or reviews about their work garnered from a number of sources such as books, magazines and newspaper articles. I saw myself primarily as an editor reviewing research material, however, I have included some remarks of my own about why their work is significant both from a contemporary stance and an aesthetic point of view.

The artists invited to Gulgong came from many different countries. They arrived early enough to wander over the countryside, selecting sites, clarifying their thoughts as to the projects they had in mind and wished to build. Their particular stories will appear throughout the text. However, as a foretaste to the book and its purpose I outline in this chapter some of the ClaySculpt projects and describe how they were resolved. This is best achieved by introducing some of the invited artists.

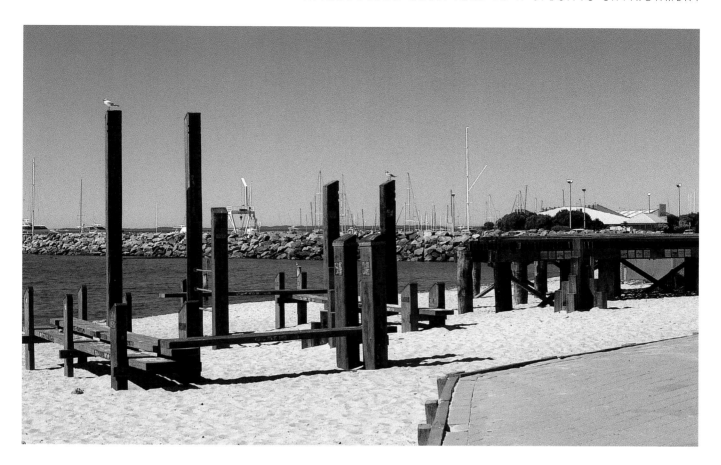

JOAN CAMPBELL (1926-1997), from Fremantle in Western Australia, always had a special respect for the land. Writing for Campbell's final exhibition, Crescendo, at the University of Western Australia in 1997, Vice-Chancellor Fay Gale noted Campbell's affinity with clay and the joy its use could bring, saying: 'Joan Campbell's love of the Australian landscape with its enormous diversity was reflected in her work; she was constantly changing, adapting, adding or eliminating, refining her ceramics to achieve a gentle quiet understanding of existence. One of the many qualities which attracted people to Campbell's work was her disregard for people's expectations, her belief in knowing herself and her work, and looking beyond what the rest of the world is thinking or doing.' Referring to one of Campbell's many commissions, a special piece for the University of Western Australia, made in 1982, she wrote: 'It is an integral part of the University's School of Music's garden. The rock-like forms follow the contours of the landscape and blend with the surroundings, maintaining the ambience of the space rather than imposing an unrelated dominant form.'

Joan Campbell spent a lifetime working with clay. Some of her major architectural commissions include the mural installed at the Art Gallery of Western Australia and a fountain for the foyer of the St George Society headquarters in Sydney. Curator for the Crescendo exhibition Anne Gray wrote,

> It was not just her facility with clay or her freedom of expression which made Joan Campbell an outstanding artist, it was also her affinity with the environment, her rootedness in nature. Like so many Australian painters, the source of her work was the landscape around her. But hers was a three-dimensional expression of place. She believed that if we want to know about form we must go to nature. She observed and listened to the rhythms of life in the land, sea and sky, and sought to capture these in her work – to convey the life force underlying all creation. And she did so with ceramic sculptures.

Full of energy, Campbell wrote and talked about life and its continuity:

Our span of life force is limited, but our contribution is important. I have always lived within the sight and sound of the sea. There is a rhythm on the beach, there is freshness. My studio on Bathers' Beach looks out to the sea and I can hear the moods and the different energies being played. My forms are abstracted to fulfil the sculptural needs of three-dimensional expression: balancing the curves, overcoming the difficulties of working in the round so that harmony and contradiction are all faced. For me, the consideration of line, balance, dynamic tension and texture are part of the making process.

Glenda King, Curator of Craft and Design at the Queen Victoria Museum and Art Gallery, Launceston, Tasmania, writing in *Ceramics: Art and Perception 27* examined Campbell's life and work, in particular her community involvement, her architectural commissions and the influence she has had on those working with her.

Working without an inherited ceramic tradition, Campbell sought to create works which reflected the influences of her environment around Fremantle and the Western Australian landscape within her personal aesthetic concerns. These sites have been a constant reference for the forms, colours and textures in her work. From the beginning she sought to challenge the traditional applications of her processes, firstly with the scale of her work and secondly with the technical adaptations that have been required in the firing to produce large work. The tactility of making has remained an integral component of the creative process for Campbell because she has been challenged to work in a wide range of techniques in both pottery and public works.

Since 1981, Campbell has undertaken large-scale art commissions for public buildings and community-based projects. This involved the employment and training of assistants who have contributed to many of her major projects. Critical to this aspect of her work is her concern for the way in which individuals react to and interact with art in the spaces they use.

Her philosophy for creating work for public spaces centres on making work that not only has a sense of connection to the location and function of the site, but that also relates to the people who will use it. In an interview with June Moorhouse in 1991, quoted by Glenda King, Campbell explains her ideas in relation to public art and how more 'user-friendly' communities can be developed. She stresses the importance of play as

both a form of attitude and a physical release from the pressures of everyday life: 'I have been concerned for some time about what we have lost in our society . . . what we have lost is the area of play, the area in which we were all part of community life, the small intimate parks that you consider to be the neighbourhood park.'

Campbell's viewpoint, and her successfully completed interactive sculptural installation and playground project on the waterfront at Bather's Beach, implies a different way of thinking about the manner in which our communities are built. It is a way of working that challenges urban planners to consider a far more interventionist role from the residents and users of such spaces. Joan Campbell was recognised as a leading figure in Australian ceramics, gaining awards and distinctions for her work. Mostly self-taught and certainly self-motivated, she took on challenges of both techniques and self-expression in ceramic art. Working with raku techniques and then glazed earthenware, her creations, like her ideas, were always large-scale. Her raku pieces were often larger than she was, and her environmental art filled foyers, office walls, private gardens and public places. Her sense of community found her representing artists on various boards and committees, and her ability as a public speaker meant that she was in constant demand to put the case of the artist. Exhibitions, commissions and teaching were all challenges that she met through her life as a ceramic artist.

VINCENT MCGRATH, now living in Tasmania and head of the Academy of the Arts, University of Tasmania, Launceston, was also one of the artists invited to come to Gulgong. Landscape has been his focus in art for many years, both as a positive inspiration and as a reminder that we have a responsibility not to desecrate its beauty. In an article by Gudrun Klix, 'Aspects of Landscape', *Ceramics: Art and Perception 17,* McGrath's work is cited as re-establishing a relationship with the earth:

Having grown up on a sheep farm, Vincent McGrath, throughout his life, has witnessed the ongoing misuse of

OPPOSITE
Joan Campbell, **Foyer, St George Building Society**. *Ceramic, steel, water. Sydney, Australia.*

*Vincent McGrath, **Markers**, 1995. Firing the works in situ. Gulgong NSW, Australia.*

the Australian landscape and has chosen to deal with this in his work. While living in the Northern Territory, he explored man's intrusion into the land in a vivid and graphic style, utilising narrative and images from his tropical surroundings. On moving to Tasmania in 1984, his work has become more sombre. His structures of clay, both two and three dimensional, appear ripped, torn and scarred like the landscape itself, devastated by the numerous mining companies intent on taking what riches were there to be had. In his work McGrath explores how the debris left behind through these activities is being reintegrated into the earth through the natural processes of decay.

A later article by Terry Davies in *Ceramics: Art and Perception 30*, describes McGrath's work from the 1970s, relating it to the ownership and management of land in 'a series of large narrative murals whose painterly and sculptural concerns illustrated historical tales concerning European settlement, agricultural and mining incursions. With the move to Tasmania, the figural element vanished from his images of the island's deserted mine workings and yet retained a haunting human presence which punctuated the sense of the loneliness of the European in Australia's vastness. The

artist invariably invites viewers to embroider their own ideas on the work.'

In a further body of work, *Heartlands*, McGrath also investigated the impact of the European presence in the Australian landscape seeking to record the achievements, successes and failures of European endeavours in the landscape. Davies continues:

> Not only are the outcomes about aspects of national identity evident but issues of self are equally important. McGrath makes a painterly use of ceramic. The crusty thick impasto is spread with gusto, creating a rich palette aided by a patina of texture and line. His shards look as if they were literally sliced off rock faces or dug up from the ground's surface. The flaky layer effect with its fissured and cracked elements is literally the mud clay of Australia, which, via the ceramic processes, is dried and baked, not by sun but by the ceramicist's kiln. McGrath plays many roles such as that of an explorer, cartographer, surveyor, shaman and animist while outlining his concerns. This collection of ceramic references, grid maps and snapshots of the terrain is searching for truth and understanding so as to embrace the spirit and texture of this land.

Many of Vincent McGrath's works could be seen as

aerial views, or at least views from a distance taking in wide sweeps of landscape. This was evident in the work he made for ClaySculpt, Gulgong. He titled this work *Markers,* which he saw as resting points in the landscape. Writing about this work McGrath said, 'Most early Australian explorers chose suitable natural sites as camps, forward posts and resting places in their quests to cross the uncharted land. Subsequent explorers, new settlers and travellers have also used several of these original sites as resting points. Some of the sites have become known to us as landmarks in the form of towns, settlements, crossroads and cairns, serving as points of foci for security, association with time, distance and place, and as historical references'.

McGrath's Gulgong site-specific work investigated the nature and meaning of resting and arrival points in much the same way as this would have been noted by the original European Australian site makers, the early explorers. The creation of a marker concentrates attention to a position on the land or a map identifying a point of reference along the way of a journey. The sight line between one marker and another produces a sense of direction, an imaginary line along which one cannot

factor in the Gulgong site work as being complete. These two guiding principles informed the project at the outset. All markers were to complement the special features of terrain, vegetation, outlook and land use of this often dry and delicate landscape setting. 'As well, the site work was planned to have a life of its own, where permanency was not a primary consideration. Important to the purpose of the work is the way it would be altered and used over time. Seasonal changes and continuous weathering through sunlight and water bring changes in appearance of the eight markers. And, best of all, the markers are located in the heart of sheep run country making them excellent rubbing posts.'

Gathering a group of artists and students to assist him, McGrath built the markers on a downhill slope, each one different and each staked in the ground. One highlight of his project was the firing at night when all markers were linked by a rope of flame that travelled uphill vitrifying the clay and making a permanent sculptural installation. Seen from a distance the hillside became a theatrical performance as well as environmental art.

Chuck Wissinger, **Dinosaur's Backbone***, 1995. Work in Progress.*
Gulgong NSW, Australia.

CHUCK WISSINGER, coming from Alberta, Canada, claimed that his first impression of the Gulgong site was of a 'picturesque vista of pastoral tranquillity and a bird lover's paradise – avian symphony ignited at the sun's first glimmer.' Wonder at the unfamiliar and splendour gradually tempered, however, as the ravages of a two-year drought came into focus. What should have been a wild unkempt forest appeared as more of a groomed public park. All undergrowth within reach of kangaroos and sheep had long since been browsed away. Parched pastures, near empty ponds and a litter of bones strewn about the landscape further testified to the devastation of drought.

These rural lands provided a perfect forum in which to express visually the concepts and sensibilities that have long been central to my work. An interest in the environment nearly led to my pursuit of a career in biology and ecology. Of particular interest is man's relationship to the broader ecosystem. I marvel at our inability to share our domain with the rest of creation, and our disrespect for other life forms. I believe this to be a direct result of our poor grasp of mankind's place in the broader time-space continuum. In cosmic terms we are the faintest of flickers. We push buttons and tamper with delicate balances that stabilise the closed systems on which we depend. Frequently our actions place us at odds with the natural order, ourselves and others. Over the long haul, we risk unravelling the fragile web of life on which we depend.

In regard to creating objects and images, Wissinger is quite eclectic, moving back and forth across a spectrum of conceptual, visual and technical perspectives. His work is produced in both high and low fire using a variety of firing processes, as well as clay in conjunction with other materials. Pieces range from small stoneware items to a 183cm (6ft) high wood, steel and stone installation, and from narrative to purely abstract. These include large installations initiated by Wissinger for The Works Festival in Edmonton, Canada, and murals undertaken with former students at a number of lakeside communities in Alberta. 'Increasingly, I find myself intrigued with clay used in combination with other materials, that is, welded steel, wood, stone and bone. The use of juxtaposed materials is often more responsive to creative impulse than clay used alone. This is particularly the case when trying to create a sense of dialectic or opposition as is central to my work.'

Clay continues, however, with its 'pleasures and pain', to be Wissinger's preferred medium. Frustration with its cumbersome nature and limitations is outweighed by clay's ability to capture raw tactile energy, he says.

I arrived at Gulgong's ClaySculpt with a fixed idea of what I would create and the materials from which it would be made. Given that the intent was to create a large-scale work in ten days, I saw mixed media as the most appropriate approach. Walking around the hills, I soon abandoned my preplanning and sought to create a monument to the site utilising clay with materials found in the immediate vicinity. Thus, the piece merges into the environment, acting as a focal point which distills the raw primal essence of its surroundings. The attempt was to integrate the piece physically, visually and spiritually.

A weathered tree stump firmly rooted to the ground on the crest of a gradual rise was chosen as the anchor point for the sculpture. 'The piece cantilevers off the stump which would have been standing prior to white settlement, anchored in the past. Two bowed trunks of a fallen tree were dragged to the site, turned top to top, shaped and joined, forming a shallow arch sloping from the ground to the stump. Symbolically, the arch implies a portion of a circle, the closed cycle of life, death and rebirth. The ancient stump and logs directly linked to Australia's past create a physical and metaphorical foundation on which to mount the installation's focal point. From a visual perspective, these natural elements are textured strong forms in their own right. Rising from the earth they form a linear half arch which blends into, yet contrasts with the physical nature of the site.'

Geometric hard-edged planes and facets were cut into the logs to create a counterpoint to natural form and surface, as well as a visual tie to elements which rest on the log arch. The milled wooden slab affixed to the log arch with found metal elements reflects the impact of white settlement. These metal components of discarded farm machinery, some crudely hand-forged, echo the toil required to eke a living out of this pioneer land. Crowning the piece are ceramic elements which loosely refer to the articulated vertebrae of dead animals and to the stone spine that crests the hill top which runs the length of the property. These, Wissinger believes, are the immutable structures on which life and land are supported. Metaphorically a dichotomy is created as the clay elements, which are as durable as stone, are supported by a structure which is far less lasting.

The skulls resting on rocks which encircle the piece came into being as a joke. But as I walked the surrounding countryside each day I discovered the remains of more and more dead animals. It seemed increasingly appropriate to incorporate something of them directly into the installation. At the risk of compromising the overall piece I explored numerous options. I concluded that placing 16 skulls on stones set at cardinal compass points would enhance the sense of monument and mystery, as well as pay homage. Choice of site and relative placement of the piece was considered with care. I sought to create an installation which stood as a stele or obelisk defining a site of significance.

As a monument to place, the installation is intended to evoke respectful contemplation. The piece is best viewed in the early morning or late evening from a north–south axis in silhouette with low light.

Moving light and shade are important elements in the work, further enhancing drama. The overall form surrounded by these 16 points can be interpreted as a sundial marking the passage of time. Hopefully this installation symbolically reflects the dynamic of opposites on which all of existence pivots. As all matter is bound together in this interwoven dialectic, so are individual and collective values and actions shaded by vagaries of this perpetual push and pull. As well, this site, imbued with primal beauty, stands in the face of unflinching harshness. I find this compelling – even seductive. Thus the intent was to reflect upon life's fragile perseverance in the web of opposing forces.

LEFT: *Irit Musen.* **The Lady of the Rain.**
Gulgong NSW, Australia.
*In the background, Tørbjon Kvasbo at work
on his project at ClaySculpt.*

OPPOSITE:
Richard Launder. **Ground Markers 1995,** *Earth Works.
ClaySculpt, Gulgong.*

humane and small, she awaits humbly, unlike a mighty goddess that makes the rain fall.

During Musen's excursions in the region in her search for a suitable location for her work, she encountered numerous skulls and skeletons. Dried out, clean white bones 'suggested and, indeed, determined porcelain as my choice of material. I decided to place my sculpture on the edge of an almost dried out reservoir. The woman, who is a symbol of life, fertility and continuity of the species, lies at the boundary of the water source. She is made of a thin and cracked white shell; she is incomplete and fragile, like those dried up bones that can be found on the land around her. She lies motionless, as if waiting for the water to fill the reservoir and thus revive her. Between the two parts of her fragmented body there is a piece of barren soil that also awaits fertilisation by the rain.'

Heaven (the rain), earth (the material) and the human being in between (the work itself) refer to one of the Chinese concepts of the world, one which Musen has subscribed to in the past few years.

> The woman lies calmly, filled with earth, awaiting the rain to invest her with life. I remember with wonder the heavy rain that started falling on the night of the firing of the sculpture, as if all the elements, wood, fire, earth, iron and water, joined forces toward the work's completion. I hope that my *Lady of the Rain* will stay on site, at the edge of the reservoir, that she will absorb the tranquillity of the land and blend into it until she is an integral part of the environment.

Some of the artists invited to Gulgong's ClaySculpt took the opportunity to extend their usual practice into more conceptual concerns. **RICHARD LAUNDER**, coming from Bergen in Norway, has always sought the intellectual aspects of ceramic art. He is known for his innovative forms on a domestic scale but for the Gulgong project he wanted to make a large-scale earth

IRIT MUSEN, a sculptor from Israel, takes inspiration from the land, adapting her ideas to suit the specific environment in which she places the female figure at the centre. She writes:

> I arrived at Gulgong with a specific project in mind but changed it completely after my encounter with the region. Longer acquaintance with the land further modified the new project and, instead of forcing my preconceptions and ideas on it, I let the land act upon myself and the forms. The open and extensive landscape ruled out my original idea of three vertical forms that cut across the sky line. Horizontal shapes seemed more in harmony with the land and the soft curves of the surrounding mountains. I felt that an undulating female form would respond to the landscape and echo its shape. The necessity to economise with water and use it sparingly is embedded in my consciousness and way of life from early childhood – the vital need for water forms an integral part of my education in Israel. Therefore my work, *The Lady of the Rain*, is

work that he felt was appropriate to the site. Paul Campbell-Allen, writing a review of the project for *Ceramics: Art and Perception 21*, found Launder's work 'powerful and thoughtful.' Richard Launder's earth works progressively drew him into their presence and their reason for being: 'The main components were a grave-sized pit with a horizontally fluted interior and a mound constructed from clay excavated from the pit. According to Launder, these acted as markers in the landscape indicating water (the near-dry dam in which they were placed) and, symbolically, its importance. These two features, with their positive/negative con-notations of dichotomy, made reference to Europeans in Australia cutting into and building on the landscape. In severe contrast, a swept area surrounded by stones held reference to an aboriginal hearth which, even when charred by fire, would soon fade back into the land.' Launder's work provided the site with a 'living

sculpture' as successions of rains and droughts have covered or exposed the work by turn, continually weathering and wearing it away, leaving only a scattering of turquoise-glazed porcelain tips on the side wall. It did indeed gradually 'fade back into the land'.

The artists mentioned in this introductory chapter serve as examples of ceramicists responding to a particular environment, in this case the open spaces of rural Australia. Throughout further chapters we can assess how ceramic materials and techniques have been used to advantage for the making of environmental sculptures. Many factors have to be considered; these include the physical site for the work, the accessibility of the site and its use by the public, the particular ceramic techniques involved, the permanency of the sculpture against weather and abuse, and the intention of both artist and client in placing the work in the environment – that is, its meaning and purpose.

CHAPTER TWO

Symbolism and Culture

NINA HOLE HAS BEEN INVITED to build sculptures in the environment in many countries, including Denmark, Australia, Canada, Taiwan, Portugal, the UK, Greece and the USA. Using a modular clay unit, and building and firing her sculptures on the site on which they will remain, her tools are minimal but the concept is full of symbolism. Her origins are Danish but her education in ceramics took place in the USA and she feels that she combines Danish practicality and American daring in her work; this, she says, has helped her develop a new concept, which she calls 'sculpture kilns'.

I have, for many years, had a vision of working in a large scale but there has always been the technical problem of kilns and their inevitable shortcomings. Building large objects and firing them on site is not a new idea but using my module system with different clays including paperclay, and firing them, is a concept which I have been developing. I first tried out these ideas in 1994 in Denmark with the help of students and my colleague, Jørgen Hansen. The main premise of this concept is that the sculpture and kiln are conceived as one and work together as a functional and visual whole.

Hole's technique is a simple building-block system. The blocks are made from U-shaped slabs, each about the size of a small firebrick with one of the sides of the U longer than the other. The blocks are then stacked, one on top of the other on their side, with the open ends alternating. The system is strong and can easily support a 4m (157in.) high structure, which becomes a natural

HOLE

ANDALUZ

CSEKOVSZKY

TAYLOR

MISHIMA

McMANUS

OPPOSITE: *Eduardo Andaluz, Stoneware form for School in Fuerteventura, Canary Islands,1985. Stoneware with matt blue enamel, electric kiln, fired to 1200°C (2192°F). Height: 3.5m (138in.).*

21

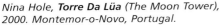
Nina Hole, **Torre Da Lüa** (The Moon Tower),
2000. Montemor-o-Novo, Portugal.

chimney in itself. The sculpture thus has all the necessary aspects of an up-draught kiln incorporated into it. 'I use one to two tonnes of clay for a sculpture kiln and since I often have to use scrap clay, I add 25–30% paper pulp to give strength at the green stage and to make the clay lighter and more plastic.' The building blocks create an open-weave wall system and this allows for fast drying and quick firing, often in the same time-frame as it is being built. Sometimes, depending on the weather and situation, a slow fire is started in the sculpture before the building is completed. The whole structure is covered with an insulating ceramic-fibre blanket tied together with wire before the firing which is fuelled by wood. When the sculpture kiln has reached about 1000°C (1832°F), the fibre blanket is removed to reveal the glowing and incandescent form.

Nina Hole believes that the sculpture kiln is a natural consequence of her work with raku that exploits the sequences of firing and unwrapping. 'After I unwrap the work I can play with a combination of sawdust, borax, copper carbonate and whatever else I have on hand. I throw this mixture on the glowing structure and the reaction gives a wonderful sparkling of fireworks. One can actually watch the changing process while the sculpture cools and then enjoy the magic when all the colours emerge.' Using a number of assistants when she builds a sculpture kiln, she encourages their input of imagination, feeling that this interaction of ideas, talk, strength and determination has enriched all concerned in her unique adventure. It is the process involved in these environmental works, she says, that is sometimes more exciting than the final product, with the next project always just another step along the road.

Symbolism and mythology attract Hole because of her surroundings in her native Danish countryside, with pagan elements such as runic stones, passage graves and burial

mounds. Nel Kooij, writing about Hole in *Ceramics: Art and Perception 13*, describes the influences of Hole's life:

> Fascinated by the humour of the intriguing chalk paintings in her village church, her urns slowly became houses and her houses changed into churches. The life of an individual in any society is a series of passages from one age to another. Many of the ceremonies of human passage take place in a church. Yet Hole's buildings also represent a contained emptiness released through windows or opening to the surface.

In Kolding, Denmark, at the Trapholt Museum, when Hole and Jørgen Hansen built the initial environmental work during a one-week workshop for graduate ceramic students from across Scandinavia, the students were asked to build three tall cylinders, each with a different ceramic building technique. The structures were built on top of bricks, which acted as fire boxes, and were dried and fired

in situ. The techniques were promising but the problem with unevenness in temperature had yet to be solved. The pieces weathered and were later removed. The second sculpture built in Gulgong, Australia, was entitled *House of the Rising Sun* and was unwrapped as dawn broke during ClaySculpt. Hole reports: 'I was asked to build a spirit house that would be part of the surrounding landscape and in doing so could involve a number of people. I had never been to Australia and it was difficult to imagine a spirit house placed in that foreign environment. I decided to leave an open space in the house form to take in the land and with it its spirit.'

View Finder in Edmonton, Alberta, Canada, provided a different situation. Hole was asked by the Works Festival to build the 1996 *Legacy Project* during the 14-day art festival in Edmonton. The piece was to be built to fit a 3 x 3m (10 x 10ft) wide window of the Telus building. The sculpture kiln was built outside on the plaza

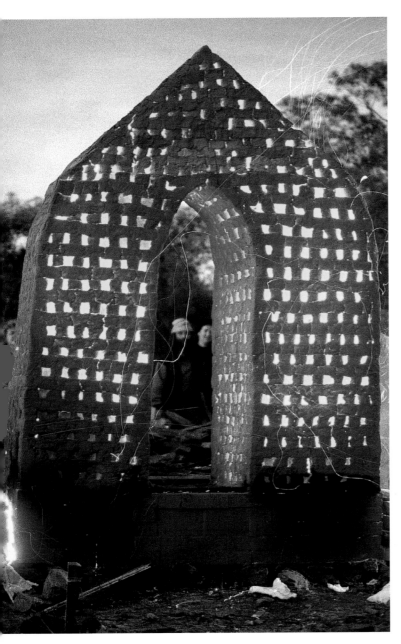

Nina Hole, **House of the Rising Sun**, 1995.
Gulgong NSW, Australia.

OPPOSITE:
Nina Hole, work in firing. Taiwan.

of the Telus building and later reassembled indoors to protect it from the harsh winters. Another project in Napa, California, USA, and titled *Napa Knobs* was built in 1996 to celebrate the Clay and Wine workshop in Napa Valley. Hole reports: 'We built a somewhat oversized fire box with an A-frame construction on top. Knobs were

made as part of the construction, placed along the outer sides of the piece.' This piece stands in the grounds of Napa Valley College.

Another workshop, in Kalmar, Sweden, was in remembrance of the signing of the 600-year-old Scandinavian Peace Treaty. The aim was to build a strong piece, an impressive battleship to celebrate the Danish Queen who, long ago, became leader and forced a peace treaty upon the Scandinavian countries. The *Battleship* was placed at the waterfront on one of the small islands in Kalmar.

The organisers of the International Potters Festival in Aberystwyth, Wales, asked Hole to build a sculpture kiln within a six-day building and firing period. Hole reports:

Because of the short time span, we decided to make a sculpture that was the inner house form of the spirit house that was made in Australia. Building on the university campus, it seemed appropriate to build an inner house core for that event that had almost no opening to the environment. It was a more solid form to capture the energy, a sense of spirit and kept within the woven structure, only revealing the smallest openings as possible on both sides. The pressure, expectations and the energy of being at the Festival, were overwhelming. Our dynamic group was strong enough to overcome rainstorms, lack of time, wet wood, small chimneys and other problems. When the sculpture was unveiled, sawdust was thrown immediately on the glowing piece. Each time the sawdust hit the piece it would flare – this also gave the clay a richer colour – and a new energy was sparked.

All the sculptures are, in reality, large raku pieces. The construction of the slabs allows the heat to move through the modules without too much cracking and also allows for fast firing and cooling of the sculpture. Nina Hole makes some comments on using this technique:

Approaching each new project, we are faced with many uncertainties. This includes the short time period, available materials such as the clay body, the weather and new assistants. These all challenge me but also make the project vulnerable for the organisation. One has to remember that each work is designed for a specific event and particular environment and is designed with consideration given to time frame, circumstance and location. Some pieces are designed to be dismantled and reassembled in a new location. One has to remember, too, that sculpture kilns

are not made in vast quantities. They are not built as an action piece, or to be the highlight of a festival, party or celebration but each piece is thoughtfully planned, pushing ideas each time to create a sculpture that is unique for the event. We always have to remember that one is not working in one's own studio where everything is conveniently placed and materials are known and tested. One must be willing to accept that the project may fail.

Writing about Hole's ceramic sculptural performance in *Artists Newsletter*, (January 1997), Paul Scott noted:

> Her work makes reference to homes and simple architectural dwellings, and she fires them *in situ* to dramatic effect . . . the performance element begins as, propelled by regular wood stoking and enhanced by nightfall, the wrapped structure begins to glow brightly at each kiln fibre join. Then, at the peak of the firing cycle, the kiln blanket is removed and the ceramic structure is displayed in its glowing glory. It is at this point that all the effort and time seems so worthwhile. As the structure cools, daylight reveals a form part-fossilised by fire, the natural colour of fired clay enhanced by the flashing from the flame.

John Graham, writing about Nina Hole's work for The Works 1996 *Legacy Project* in Edmonton, Canada, sums up their appeal: 'The works evoke a contemplative mood that can be found in ancient Mayan and Hindu temples and yet share a conceptual sensibility that is found in several postmodern buildings.'

A later sculpture kiln was built in Charlotten, Copenhagen, under heavy dark grey clouds, and assisted by a nine-man crew. Claus Dominie Hansen described the completed sculpture, saying: 'It stands there, speaking its own silent powerful Nordic language' (*Ceramics: Art and Perception 38)*. In Greece, as a way of commemorating the meeting of the International Academy of Ceramics, Nina Hole was invited, sponsored by the Danish Insititute, to build a sculpture in the grounds of the School of Art in Athens. Working with American Fred Olsen, the form, 4m (187in.) high, is the tallest Hole has built so far. Sara Hakkert, writing for *Ceramics Technical 16*, said, 'Hole always takes into account the specific location of each project.' Hakkert cited Greek art and mythology as well as current events that combine to inspire Hole to make a work of symbolic significance.

Symbolism and civilisation have always played a part in the work of **EDUARDO ANDALUZ** of the Canary Islands. He writes: 'In my works I try to state and develop my interest in that field in which philosophy and the spirit of different cultures and civilisations converge; where religious and sexual symbols join and come to a kind of cohabitation, creating a series of rituals that become sacred. The mythology of the world lies within this framework, and my work is imbued with these images.' Andaluz's stay in India and eastern countries where there are many different religious beliefs, diverse cultures and polytheistic religions, determined his interest in these related subjects. From this point he realised that art, in a general view, 'should always move around the sacred world and that aesthetic reflection needs rationalism'.

Within the development of this stylistic interest, Andaluz's works are shown in sets.

> I make series or small groups of three, five, seven . . . . They are sets with unit relations as, in language, words are united to form a sentence. To me, creation is a type of ritual. We take on a specific thesis, we act, we doubt, we contemplate, only to start all over again. The actual cultural field must keep away from totalitarianism and closed circles. It should act through gentle steps with constant changes. Cultural matter should create new thoughts. In this way spectators are able to keep moving from inside, so there is no need to feel tied to a place, nation or exclusive ideology which obstructs our personal freedom.

Andaluz believes that even with all our differences, we cannot deny that we are all one species. Through history, he says, our most important aim has been searching into the sense of being.

> My environmental works are created as an answer to architecture's need of completing a wall or a particular environment. Big panels and sculptures are made to fit in zones that have been designed to house them. On these occasions, my relationship and the opinion interchange with the architects is important. That helps me when choosing attributes that will prevail over the work. It is my aim that my pieces will fit with the architecture making a whole unit; so I have to consider the general ambience, the amount of natural light, the artificial lighting, the chromatic approach in the area, if it is an open or closed space, for example, as well as knowing if it is going to be an area with movement, people crossing and walking around. Sometimes a panel or sculpture is placed in a quiet space as a background or a curtain.

Eduardo Andaluz. Work in progress.

With these references in mind and using specialised working methods, he enters his studio to start work on a project. Andaluz says undertaking commissions of this kind is always a challenge, an adventure that makes him add new elements to the creative process, so different from when he works on a personal sculpture. Working on public projects allows the pieces to have access to a large number of different people whose eyes are not familiar with the art field or are not used to looking at art. Most of his commissions over the past 15 years have been made in collaboration with an architect. He says: 'We know each other's ways of working. When we start designing the whole project, we meet to exchange ideas. This means that my work and its surrounding space will fit and become a coherent whole'.

Andaluz uses a modification of the coil method, pounding out strips of clay with a mallet before attaching the coils to each other and building the forms. Always, he says, before building a sculpture, he makes numerous drawings and a model or maquette he uses for reference. Invited to the 1990 Ceramic Symposium in Tashkent, Uzbekistan, to make a work for the sculpture garden in that city, Andaluz's work was reviewed by the organiser of the event, Hakinov Akbar,

for *Ceramics: Art and Perception 5*. Akbar wrote of the resemblance of Andaluz's work to antique architecture in form and colour, and commented on the impressive dialogue and interaction between the works of Andaluz and other works in the group, saying: 'The compositions are full of light and harmony and united by a kind of invisible half-sphere; they give a complete focus to the whole composition.' Celestino Hernández, in *Ceramics: Art and Perception 21,* writes of Andaluz's works as being 'ruled by exactness' while 'working with the sacred world of idols and altars of adoration within which the artist searches for answers for everyday life.' Eduardo Andaluz was born and educated in Buenos Aires, Argentina, and later settled in Gran Canaria. His experiences influence his expression in ceramics. Symbols of the civilisations he has studied and the early cultures of Latin America that form his inheritance are translated into a contemporary language that give us insight into other cultures.

A use of architectural modelling and sculpture is a central feature in Hungarian public art. Symbolism and cultural mores dominate. House walls are decorated; roof tiles and finials are modelled in brightly-coloured glazed terracotta. Travelling through Hungary one has the sense of a specific and traditional culture full of symbolism. **ARPÁD CSEKOVSZKY** was born in the small village of Csikostottos, Hungary, in 1931, moving to live in Rakosliget in 1939. He attended the Secondary School of Fine Arts and continued his studies at the Ceramics Faculty of the Hungarian Academy of Applied Arts, graduating with a degree of merit in 1956. A year later he became the assistant of Miklos Borsos. He continues to teach at the Academy although he retired from full-time teaching in 1992.

When asked to comment on his work, he says:

I consider both my individual art work and teaching as a kind of service by respecting and serving eternal human qualities, first of all humanity. In my tutorial schedule I try to help my students broaden the possibilities of ceramics.

*Eduardo Andaluz, **Landscape for a village**, 1996. Malaga/Spain. Refractory clay, fired in a gas kiln, 1300°C (2372°F). Height: 2 m (6½ft).*

Besides traditional modelling and technology, I show them different ways towards architectural and figurative ceramics by drawing attention to the architectural artefacts remaining in our craft. To complement my teaching programme, I involve teachers of architecture. In return, I am given all kinds of help by the Faculty of Architecture.

Csekovszky's studio, where he can regularly be found, is situated in his garden. His works have been commissioned for buildings and public places in Budapest and many provincial towns. Other pieces have been placed in museums and collections such as the Hungarian Museum of Applied Arts, Budapest, the Janus Pannonius Museum, Pecs, the International Ceramics Studio, Kecskemét, and the International Collection of Ceramics at Vallauris, France, or are owned by collectors. He describes his methods:

The material I use for my ceramics is made for buildings and is unglazed fireclay, fired in an open-flame kiln. For firing I use wood to bring out the natural colour of the clay, and enjoy the power of the flame and fire. In this way, the surface of the forms become enriched and appropriate for the situation where the work is to be placed. I like this technique of firing and that is why I prefer terracotta. Wood-fired clay enhances the natural beauty of the primary modelling. Larger-scale works make an impression on me and, as a result of that, I made, as early as 1957, a 2m (79in.) high sculpture of an idol. Since then the method of modelling from clay strips and slabs of clay has been used to make many sculptures and figures. During my career I have worked on the spatial representation of some models such as the man and the horse, the man and the chariot and, finally, the charioteers.

For Csekovszky, these works appear as a formal manifestation represented as simple symbols without any compromise to detail. It is possible to see by their earthy structure, he is interested in works that feature the symbolic. They are cross-shaped, combined together, connected or placed next to each other.

The location – for example, in the city or country, with their different day-to-day values – can influence the subject matter and style of an artist's work. This is demonstrated in the work of Australian ceramicist, **SANDRA TAYLOR**. Between 1987 and 1989, Sandra

Taylor was commissioned to make two major ceramic works – large murals exploring the painted surface. These were the Bligh Park Shopping Centre mural, at Windsor in NSW, and the Harbourside Festival Marketplace, Darling Harbour mural, in Sydney. In exhibition works that followed, the painted surface (on simplified forms) evolved into a symbolic language of personal mythology.

Born in Sydney in 1942, Taylor graduated from the National Art School, East Sydney, in 1966. Her early professional experience included teaching positions in the ceramic departments of St George TAFE, the National Art School, Sydney College of the Arts, City Art Institute and Sydney Teachers' College. She has conducted workshops in numerous regional centres, and has presented lectures at various colleges, universities, conferences and seminars over a 30-year period. When she was living in Sydney the urban situation provided inspiration for the suburban satire series of the 1970s and when, in 1982, she relocated to a large and isolated cattle property in northern NSW, this major lifestyle change resulted in a change in the theme of her work as well. With buildings and studio complete in 1985 came works with a new found direction – a city-bred response to the land – depicting rural life and the hardships that came with it. In 1993, the property became a centre for creative exploration; Blackadder Creative Retreat enjoyed a reputation drawing people both nationally and internationally to its residential workshops. A Visual Arts Craft Fund Fellowship year in 1995 brought with it the opportunity for reflection and another shift in direction – suburban iconography re-emerged as metaphor for human frailty. A further move in 1997 had her establishing home and studio in Mullumbimby, NSW, a town offering an alternative lifestyle.

She describes the significance of the changes: 'Years ago I began drowning in the processes I had created for myself – so happy at first – so much to say, so much to do. Then something happened that took all the fun away. I needed something more direct and immediate. I decided painting was the answer so, without a clue how to go about it, I embarked on the process of almost frustrating myself out of existence in search of the illusion of 3D.' Believing that her need and ability to paint seemed to be her major strength, and the passion for what she was

*Sandra Taylor, **Darling Harbour Mural** (section view), 1987. Sydney, Australia.*

trying to make work about – the life around her – she began to imagine what it would be like to be the bird or cow or dog, and then tried to express the feeling of the animal life around her. 'Someone must have noticed these works because I received a large mural commission – 30m (98ft) of painting on tiles. I used imagery from where I lived – the day-to-day things that happened, the overflowing richness of life in rural Australia. The mural had to be delivered within 10 weeks. That commission gave me prestige; it was the right sort of building, had the right sort of exposure and times were good.'

Some smaller commissions were undertaken and then another large one 'popped into my lap'.

> When I saw the site I was bewildered – a forgettable brand of shopping centre in the middle of hundreds of curbed and guttered barren building blocks. "For first home owners," the developer enthused – "just do me birds" he urged. The idea of 60m² (646sq. ft) of flapping birds screeching across the top of the shopfronts froze me to the spot. I'd been warned that he would have preferred neon but had been convinced that a ceramic tile mural would be cheaper.

This was not the mural world Taylor had hoped for but then, 'it would be a challenge,' she thought, 'a way to get more painting practice. The developer received more than birds for his money. The shop owners looked up to their mural with pride and I couldn't believe I had done it. I see now that those murals were my apprenticeship.'

The imagery that Taylor employs has evolved into a personal symbolic language. Writing about Taylor's work for *CraftArts 27* in 1993, Robin Tudor found that Taylor's

go on unaware, tending to our lives, taking more on board while everything around us is falling foul and before we know it, we have turned into what we never wanted to be. I am thinking here about man's destructive nature and the need for power, of the destruction of war in the larger world and man's war against himself. I am trying to ask what is important in life? What are we striving for and what are our values? My move from animals as symbols to human figures is more revealing. There is no crutch for either the maker or the viewer and so the ideas are not filtered through satire. It is more direct and possibly more confronting.

In the same article, Stephens describes Taylor's expressive use of colour:

Black is the colour of grief or loss of humility; it can also represent strength and power. It is contrasted with lighter tones: white for purity and innocence; pale green, the colour of new growth and tenderness and hope; and blue for faithfulness and tenacity, a certain strength and, of course, the swirling waters. She has moved from landscape and narrative style to a greater ambiguity, simplicity and abstraction. There is a sense of the surreal and of the ridiculous.

Taylor agrees that she has always needed to break away from the expected, the things that please, but her use of symbolism and humour softens the blow of her satire.

KIMIYO MISHIMA is noted for her large-scale works, which grace a number of architectural sites throughout Japan. 'Anyone with an interest in contemporary ceramics is certainly familiar with the special characteristics of the Japanese artist, Mishima Kimiyo, whose works look like newspapers, magazines and other kinds of printed matter,' writes Suzuki Kenji in the book, *Contemporary Ceramics, Vol. 15* (Kodansha, Tokyo, 1985). An influential member of a number of art associations and regularly winning major prizes for her work, the physical scale of Mishima's work is much larger than she is. Full of vitality and strength, her works in three-dimensional form resemble stacks of newspapers and magazines yet are made from ceramics. Suzuki continues: 'She did not, however, apprentice herself to anyone in order to learn how to make ceramics; essentially she taught herself by reading books and visiting potters'

imagery portrayed a penetrating and introspective quality while having a dig at society: 'Throughout Taylor's professional career, her work has been characterised by satire. Targeting the soft underbelly of Australian society and culture, she exercises a potent brand of tongue-in-cheek sarcasm that rarely misses its mark. Her provocative exhibitions often leave people chuckling at her wit and discussing her choice of animal protagonists and her Australian-esque imagery.'

In an article by Helen Stephens in *Ceramics: Art and Perception 24* in 1996, reviewing the exhibition *Romantic Dividends*, Taylor is quoted as saying:

It touches me deeply, this human dilemma – this business of trying to find some meaning in life. The struggle for love, acceptance, security and for material gain. These things that we struggle for so often turn against us, but we

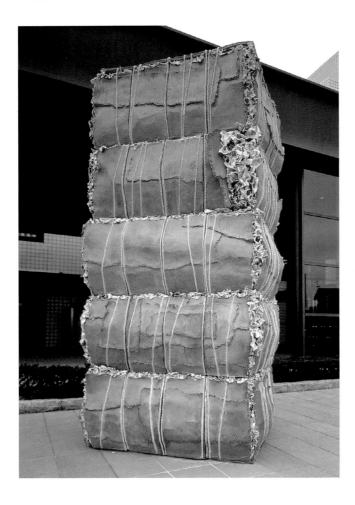

LEFT: *Kimiyo Mishima,* **Package***. Toki City. Dimensions: 300 x 147 x 125cm (118 x 57½ x 49in.).*

OPPOSITE:
TOP: *Kimiyo Mishima,* **Newspaper***. Silk-screened ceramic. Yamaguchi Prefectural Museum of Art. Dimensions: 113 x 138 x 90cm (44½ x 54 x 35½in.).*

BELOW: *Kimiyo Mishima,* **Outer Wall***. Silk-screened ceramic, stainless steel. Building Oriental Hotel Osaka. Dimensions: 5 x 15 x 15m (16 x 49 x 49ft).*

studios and attending ceramics classes. For Mishima, ceramics was not the end in itself. She needed something that could be shaped freely and would act as a support for printing.' In the catalogue of the exhibition, *Clay Work Now – 1*, shown at the Yamaguchi Prefectural Museum of Art, Mishima points out, 'My ceramic works of printed matter have been consistent from the beginning. The early works of newspaper packages still retain the distinct flavour of ceramics because of a lack of comfort technically with the materials. Since then, I have tried as much as possible to remove every trace of that.' The transfer of newspaper and magazine print and photographs on ceramics is accomplished through the use of transfer paper. Transfer paper had been used in industry early on in the mass production of ceramics. The process of copperplate print transfer was first used in Japan around 1887, following which lithography came into use. The use of a paper pattern to print directly can be considered a rudimentary form of silk-screen printing;

paper patterns were used in the ceramic centre of Arita from the 1850s. Transfer paper was available for purchase and it was technically possible to use the photographic silk-screen process in combination with ceramic decoration inks; however, it seems as though no one made use of these techniques in the fine arts. The use of industrial techniques in the arts is a modern idea, Mishima believes.

Mishima's works using these techniques attracted attention for the first time at the First Japan Ceramic Exhibition of 1971, sponsored by the Mainichi Shinbun Company. The works were titled *Packages*, and they looked like newspapers wrapped in bundles. They belonged to the lineage of Pop Art, which was flourishing throughout the international art world in the late 1960s, and proved the suitability of ceramics for that genre. Mishima continues to construct works in clay, many in large scale for environmental situations in parks, gardens and public spaces in buildings. In her words: 'The mass media such as television, newspapers and magazines is well developed and we are pushed along by the information which bombards us. The fear and unease that is caused by the information that reaches us may pass, but the fear and anxiety caused by the enormous amounts of information that do not reach us is even greater.' (*Clay Work Now – 1*).

To quote Suzuki again:

In Mishima's work, a feeling of uncertainty is created by the mystery of that which is hidden. There are also works which look as though they are wrapped bottles, as well as works that look like crumpled up pieces of waste paper, and the psychological effect is the same. Impelled by the scale, I feel that Mishima's aim is to create a psychological atmosphere changing the quantitative to the qualitative. She was, it seems, captivated by the idea of making large-

ABOVE: *Pip McManus,* **Swingers Café**. *Alice Springs. N.T., Australia.*

OPPOSITE
Pip McManus, **Fern Mosaic**, *(detail), 1996. Darwin Botanic Gardens. Dimensions: 1.5 x 2m (58 x 79in.).*

scale work; to do this type of work in ceramics, though, one must contend with many technical difficulties. In her most recent work, Mishima has succeeded in overcoming these barriers.

In the Toh series of ceramic books, Akihiko Inoue, Professor of Art at Okayama University, wrote in an essay on Mishima's work: 'In her work, Kimiko Mishima tries to give form to the fears and pleasures of civilisation caught up in the inevitable entropy.' The three-dimensional clay forms and the fragility of the material attracted Mishima to the medium. Her work has been described as playful and mysterious, and she acknowledges her fascination with printed material. Yet she recognises that the mass of printed material that bombards us daily is turned into garbage that overwhelms our surroundings. Mishima's own work has expanded into environmental installations but she has retained her sense of self and her world. Her expression, although focused on the surface printing, is by no means limited to it, and she is expressing her reaction to her culture by symbolic means.

In recent years the work of Australian artist **PIP McMANUS** has increasingly focused on tile design and production, both for floors and walls and this has led to commissions with an environmental and/or architectural context. Some commissions, such as those in the Darwin Botanic Gardens and the Uluru Kata-Tjuta Cultural Centre, have necessitated collaboration with other artists, architects, designers and landscape architects. It is this need to consider varying requirements and to keep in mind at all times the larger picture that is most demanding, McManus believes; at the same time, it is often the most stimulating. 'My impulses towards esoteric imagery and references must sometimes be tempered by the specific demands of the brief. The final artwork has to be sympathetic to the materials and final vision of the surrounding environment. Nevertheless finding an integral place in any brief is always a challenge and for this reason I continue to seek out projects which frequently take me away from the isolated world of the studio artist.'

Some of the commissions undertaken by McManus include tile panels for the Swingers Café, Alice Springs, signage at the Alice Springs airport, Uluru Cultural Centre (coordinating the decoration of murals and paths), the fern mosaic at the children's playground, Darwin Botanic Gardens, in 1996, and in 1997, a ground mosaic and signage for the Alice Springs Desert Park. In her work with Aboriginal women, McManus has taken on the role of coordinator, liaising between the designers and Aboriginal artists and taking responsibility for technical requirements such as glazing, firing and installation. She believes that positive comments from the public about these collaborative works have shown willingness by everyone concerned to understand cross-cultural complexities and that this leads to mutual respect.

Pip McManus has always been interested in interpreting the country around her. Reviewing an exhibition of McManus' work at the Residency, Alice Springs, in 1989 for *Ceramics: Art and Perception* 7, Faye Alexander wrote: 'Living in Central Australia, one is acutely aware of the surrounding natural environment. Symbols of the landscape and its culture abound in the work of Pip McManus and show her ability to interpret her feelings and reactions to the landscape and turn them into attractive, emblematic and sought-after images.' In a later work, *Poisoned Well*, Pip McManus uses the hand and the leaves of trees to symbolise problems of humanity and genocide, an ongoing challenge faced in world politics. Cath Bowdler, writing on the installation in *Ceramics: Art and Perception 41*, described the mass grouping of 100 green-glazed hand forms as 'representing the diversity and complexity of human nature and its fragility and beauty ... of fertility, growth and continuity.' Here the message was darker and the viewer was confronted with a conscience-stirring message relevant for our culture. The symbolism was subtle but, at the same time, acquainted us with the artist's intention.

C H A P T E R   T H R E E

In Harmony with Space

AN ARTIST COMMISSIONED to enhance a particular environment strives to make work that is true to his or her artistic integrity, has relevance to the intention of the client and, at the same time, harmonises with the allocated space. This poses a challenge to the artist who, in turn, challenges the people who are to view these works. **SATORU HOSHINO**, a respected Japanese artist who has undertaken many large-scale works in the environment, was commissioned to make a ceramic relief at the Mitsuke Civic Concert Hall for a project called *Arcadia*. Describing the project, he says: 'Nestled between the Japan Sea and the three mountains of Echigo lie the abundant rice fields of the Echigo plains and the city of Mitsuke. Mitsuke and its outlying areas are known for weaving but, in keeping with the times, has become a centre of the fashion industry. I was honoured to have the opportunity to take part in the planning stages of the Mitsuke civic auditorium, the first of its kind to be constructed in Niigata Prefecture.' This building is considered strategically important in the city's recent cultural upgrading. Arcadia is a unique facility planned specifically to enhance musical performances. This three-storey reinforced concrete building is composed of a main concert hall, a more intimate concert hall, practice rooms and a foyer to the west of the entrance of the main concert hall. 'In designing a work appropriate to the site, I took into consideration the audience's inspired state of mind as they emerge from the hall into this foyer during intermission and after the final notes of the evening fade to echoes in their minds. I chose, therefore, to create my works,

HOSHINO

BASARIR

NAGASAWA

WINOKUR

CARUSO

ZAMORSKA

JERNEGAN

OPPOSITE: *Nino Caruso, **Sculptures for a Roundabout**, 2002. Terracotta. Coimbra, Portugal. In collaboration with Mario Ferreira da Silva.*

Satoru Hoshino, *Mitsuke cultural city hall Arcadia.*
From Birth of Bubbles, Ancient Woodland and **Peat Deposits**, *1993. Clay, smoke fired. Dimensions: 2.7m x 13.7m (8.8 x 45ft).*

naming them; *Birth of Bubbles, Ancient Woodland* and *Peat Deposits,* and adapt them to this wall space.'

The area available for Hoshino's work was the west wall of the foyer in front of the main auditorium which, like all the interior walls, was covered with a light grey paint. Architecturally, the combination of the convex curved wall with thick pillars at either end produced a visual tension. The centre of the foyer is open to the second floor. The high ceiling lends a vertical awareness to the surrounding area, forming a dynamic space. 'The area for my work was 2.7m (8.8ft) high. The gradually curving wall is 13.7m (45ft) in width. The major challenge involved making the best use of this long curve. The subsequent challenge was incorporating the large pillars that broke into the space.'

This wall and its convex curve force the viewer to move in order to take in the whole work. What might appear an insurmountable challenge became, for Hoshino, a contemporary place and inspired him to confront the viewers.

> I chose to employ a method which would show my forms as if they were floating up from the void, composed, not of a single band, but of bits and pieces gathered together

to accommodate the characteristics of this wall. As viewers would be forced by the curve to move along the wall to view the work, I took advantage of that by making the work like an installation and by including the pillars in the work to add depth. Secondly, I placed the three works along the wall based on my observations that people are drawn around a curve such as in an illustrated Oriental scroll or story.

The wall between the black ceramic pieces of Hoshino's work is not there to produce a reduced version of the world through the medium of clay but to create a new cosmos; a new order.

> My fingers and hands leave their mark on the clay, giving it the imprint of primitive physical actions. It is as if humanity and clay, life forms in their first stages of creation, and the pieces of random ceramic on the wall are induced memories floating up into the conscious mind. Pieces of imagery appear to each viewer in a different way and produce free associations and connect with stories. Without the addition of the viewers' creativity this work is not complete.

As both a viewer and the artist behind this work Hoshino spins and interconnects the metaphorical title,

*Bingül Basarir, **Sculptural Wall**, 1992.
Presidential Administration Building.*

remembering the story of life's creation. In an article for *Ceramics: Art and Perception 15*, Tani Arata writes of the contrast between chaos and order found in Hoshino's works, and how clay is an important element used to make works of art. He believes that Hoshino is working as an artist 'on the frontier of post-object ceramics' with three aspects of style: a purely visual objectification of clay; installations; and the creation of forms with physical traces related directly to the material. The 'emergence of memories' is implicated, he believes, in various ways in both material and subject matter, giving the viewer a sign into an unknown field which is beyond a simplistic view of art.

Satoru Hoshino, writing on his own work, is emphatic that it is the clay itself which beneath his fingers appeals to his senses, the material awaiting the artist to reveal its secrets. Hoshino says that each time he touches the clay he is on a journey not only to discover the promises of the world but also to find himself. He does not seek the superficial but the possibility to make order from chaos by means of the tactile quality of the clay. 'Only the tangible can be a tactile object,' he knows from his experience.

BINGÜL BASARIR, Turkish ceramic artist, believes that the art of ceramics is a way of expressing oneself as well as a comment on the whole of life. She says: 'I usually derive my inspiration from nature and man-made forms: human beings and the happenings of nature in contact with man are my materials. Generally I make independent forms but when working with a concept for murals, I consider primarily their harmony with space and architecture.'

Basarir began her study of ceramics in Istanbul in 1960. Since 1962 she has participated in various national and international exhibitions, as well as having private shows. She has exhibited her works in France, Italy, Czechoslovakia, Hungary, Spain, Germany, Yugoslavia, Australia and Scotland. She has made wall panels for public and private buildings. Her works are in private and public collections such as the Faenza International Ceramics Museum in Italy and the Everson Museum of Arts Syracuse, NY. She has received awards such as the Gold Medal at the Prague International Ceramics Exhibition in 1962, as well as two gold medals from Faenza International Ceramics Competition in 1975 and 1979, and first prize at the Turkish State Painting and Sculpture Competition in 1992. A member of the

International Academy of Ceramics, her works have been featured in many publications. Using traditional Turkish glazes, often based on blue and turquoise, her tiled walls and freestanding sculptures are site specific. Working with natural shapes and stone-like forms, Basarir analyses them for their physical properties, trying, as she says, to discover the secrets of their origins.

Bingül Basarir has worked through a series of periods in which she concentrated on various themes and phenomena concerning mankind in all aspects. Oder Unsal, writing for *Ceramics: Art and Perception 42*, noted that Basarir's ceramics made before her thematic works were mainly decorative and functional.

> She was then concentrating on textures and reliefs. The reflections of these themes can be traced today in her murals and wall pieces. In the lectures that she gave all over the world, her huge murals and walls attracted as much interest as her reflective works. These works belong to the period when she concentrated on themes such as evolution, transformation, metamorphosis, nature and environment. She incorporated different media in her works by using waste products such as burnt lignite coal and recycled glass. In her most recent works, she has been using a new technique which provides her with a lighter ceramic material: clay mixed with sawdust.

Many of Basarir's works are based on stories of the various civilisations in Turkish history as well as her own

ABOVE: *Bingül Basarir,* **Aqua Sculpture***, 1997. In the garden of the Cultural Centre at Bozoyuk City in Northwest Anatolia. Dimensions: 300 x 200 x 30cm (118 x 79 x 11¾ in.).*

OPPOSITE: *Setsuko Nagasawa working in her workshop in Paris on a ceramic wall for a cemetary in Geneva, Switzerland, 1989.*

experience of life. Unsal concludes: 'In the work of Bingül Basarir we experience the past and the present at the same time.'

'**SETSUKO NAGASAWA'S** approach seems to me to be specifically contemporary in that it continually calls into question the materials and techniques she uses and also by virtue of an international dimension to which today's artists aspire and have access,' wrote Maria Thérèse Coullery in the introduction to a catalogue on Nagasawa's work. 'And yet Setsuko Nagasawa, born in Kyoto, Japan, has her roots in a specific and peculiarly rich soil where working in clay has, in the course of history, produced exemplary works and technologies.'

Nagasawa's training in ceramics took place in Japan and at Scripps College, USA, with Paul Soldner, and later in the south of France where she at one time established a studio. A further period of study was undertaken in Geneva at the Fine Arts School and the School of Decorative Arts, where she has remained to teach for the past 20 years. With a freedom of expression, Nagasawa works with both objects and larger installations, undertaking commissions and holding major exhibitions. For an important exhibition at the Musée Ariana in 1996 a catalogue was produced with texts by Phillipe Lambercy, ceramicist and teacher, and Roland Blätller, curator of the Musée. Both draw attention to the striving for pure materiality in Nagasawa's ceramics. 'Installation art,' writes Blätller, 'appreciated by Nagasawa for its ephemeral qualities, led her quite naturally to work with architecture – with its own demands for solidity and permanence that justify the use of ceramic materials. Apart from the fact that they interact with the surrounding spaces, her architectural works are charged with a symbolic message.'

Through the interplay of materials, forms and techniques, Nagasawa has developed a sense of space which she expresses in the clay installations she makes. Besides teaching, she organises exhibitions, fulfilling the role of a critic, and works as an adviser to museums and curators. Maria Thérèse Coullery has written:

> The way she looks at the work of others is based on a culture maintained by curiosity. The whole itinerary of her life enriches her work. It is as if by moving further away from her origins, she comes more authentically close

to them. Tradition and invention, past and present, form and decoration, object and space, fired and raw: an ever-renewed dialogue of opposites finds in the plastic language of Setsuko Nagasawa an expressive power on the enlarged scale of an encounter in which East and West are reconciled.

Maria Thérèse Coullery believes that is why the work of Setsuko Nagasawa is both a challenge and a source of questions in the contemporary field of art today.

Commissioned to design and make a water fountain for the College Rousseau in Switzerland, Nagasawa visualised a page of paper, yet to be written on, coming to rest in the college grounds. She wrote for *Ceramics: Art and Perception 3*, 'There is a white page. I imagined this white page flying in the sky. It came down slowly to lie in the middle of the walkway. The nature of this piece of paper is to be free, just like the air, like thoughts and like culture. I would like to suggest that this white porcelain page is both the symbol of the surface and the inscript of knowledge. Just like water, knowledge runs indefinitely up and down – resource and rebirth at every moment and every point of the flood tide of learning.' Frank Nievergelt, in *Ceramics: Art and Perception 11*, reviewing Nagasawa's work as part of the Nyon's Third Porcelain Triennial in Switzerland, commented that Nagasawa works in a conceptual sense when undertaking ceramics related to architecture. Her work for the Triennial was both an installation and an architectural object – her three white square elements, each consisting of nine porcelain tiles displayed on the castle's terrace, became a plan for the garden.

Philippe Lambercy has written, also for an exhibition catalogue, that the work of Setsuko Nagasawa is 'eminently ceramic. No reference provides us with an introduction to it: neither an historical or functional reference, nor an anecdotal one. No purely technological demonstration is capable of explaining this type of approach, even if the various responses of the material appear to provide us with the key.' He believes the work is 'responsive to the fundamental properties of the chosen medium and it reveals these either by restraint or by excess: breaking plasticity, fusing the refractory. These properties present, among other things, the curve or the vertical, the horizontality of the liquid surface, all of which are qualities developed through fire.'

In 2003, Setsuko Nagasawa was the subject of a catalogue on her collaboration with architects and designers on large-scale projects. These projects date from 1983 – a fountain, *Concours de Martigues* – to the project at the Ecole Superieure de Commerce, André Chavanne, in Geneva, entitled *Mirror of the Sky*, in 2000. This work, of 3000m² (32,291sq. ft) set on a horizontal plane, is a ceramic triangle that captures the reflection of the sky and the geometry of the nearby buildings. A further commission, won by competition, is set in the garden of an 18th-century castle, the Chateau de la Grange à Manom, on the border of France, Luxembourg and Germany – the financial sponsors of the competition. This project consists of two paths of 325m² (3498sq. ft) of porcelain elements. Other projects include walls, fountains and garden elements set into the ground.

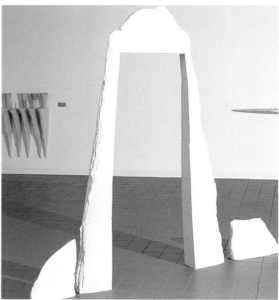

TOP: *Paula Winokur. Applying grouting during installation.*

ABOVE LEFT: *Paula Winokur,* **Fireplace Site XXI.**
Dimensions: 155 x 240 x 40cm (42 x 94 x 16in.).

ABOVE RIGHT: *Paula Winokur,* **Architectural Entryway, Ozymandias,** *1992.*
Porcelain. Dimensions: 2.4 x 2m (7.9 x 6.6ft).

Françoise de l'Epine, writing in *Ceramics: Art and Perception 22,* suggests that Setsuko Nagasawa achieves a dialogue between simple forms and an economy of movement. She writes: 'The elements play with light which hovers slowly over the roughness of the clay. Gestures are in accord with a rigorous conceptual ideology. She combines her thoughts on space with that of the material.' Commenting on Nagasawa's notions of space, these writers all concur that with an awareness of the possibilities in ceramics for making installations, either with multiple objects or as part of architecture, Setsuko Nagasawa expresses a profoundness that transforms scale.

Involved in scale and harmonising with interior space, **PAULA WINOKUR** of the USA, has undertaken many private commissions for fireplace surrounds as well as installations and architectural pieces. These latter, as described by Marion Wolberg Weiss in a review of Winokur's exhibition at Parrish Museum, Southhampton College, USA, in 1995, made a powerful statement of 'diverse sizes and shapes; the objects created an arresting aesthetic environment that became an art work itself.' Weiss was reminded of 'the ruins of an ancient temple, mysterious and disorientating like the surface of some distant planet.'

In Paula Winokur's words:

My work in the past 15 years has moved between a modest scale to a rather larger or physical scale. I had for a long while wanted to be able to make work which was at least as big as a person ... so that it could be confronted in a different way, that is, physically touched. When a friend invited me to make a fireplace surround for her newly renovated home, it gave me the opportunity to explore some of the ideas that had been percolating in my head over this time; this opened up a new path. Making the work became the easy part, learning how to satisfy various clients and going through all the preparation work to finally closing the deal was another area entirely. Working large scale and having to consider the site became another part of the problem solving that making art is about. I enjoy it. I like the fact that a piece will have a permanent home. Working on commission is not right for everything that I do but producing the fireplace surrounds is satisfying.

Art critic John Dorsey, reviewing Paula Winokur's landscape sculptures at the National Museum of Ceramic Art, for *American Ceramics 8*, 1991, described the work as 'dreamlike and surrealist'. He called attention to their haunting quality saying: 'They consist of horizontal planes from which rise verticals asymmetrically placed to create the tension of space, and their different sizes create the illusion of a vastness of scale.'

Scale is a subject that Paula Winokur graphically describes:

The landscape and, particularly, mountains, rocks, ledges, precipices and rifts have influenced me in the past few years and this information is used in the large-scale pieces as well as in the smaller works which I make. I started using a dense white porcelain some time ago and find that it works well even if I push the scale well beyond what is normal for porcelain. Translating, in odd ways, the dark brooding landscape into shimmering white forms intrigues me still.

Edward J. Sozanski, of the *Philadelphia Inquirer*, reviewing Winokur's exhibition at the Helen Drutt Gallery where Winokur regularly exhibits, also finds scale, architecture and space in her work to be monumental and poetic. 'It combines art and artisanry with grace and intelligence,' he writes, 'the structures invoke the spirit of the earth.'

A union of materials and ideas, almost as an act of nature, is the way Robin Rice explains the work of Paula Winokur in an article in *American Crafts* in 2000.

'Winokur represents nature – specifically geology – with seemingly effortless simplicity, these are sensitive, powerful forms. In Winokur's hands clay never abandons its character as an essential element of the earth's crust and, in a felicitous overlapping of material and subject, the artist frequently exploits its inherent tendency to mimic geological processes. By manipulating textural contrasts in a series of wall-mounted works, Winokur records varying rates of flow as if within a glacier.' There is a sense in Paula Winokur's work, says Rice, that everything, no matter how permanent it appears, is engaged in an ongoing process.

Harmonising modern sculpture within an ancient setting is a prime focus of the work of **NINO CARUSO**. From his workshops in Rome and at Todi in the Italian countryside, Caruso works in large scale, undertaking commissions for walls, fountains and freestanding sculptures as well as site-specific works that may involve a whole community. Enzo Bilardello, critic and curator from Rome, writing on Caruso's work for *Ceramics: Art and Perception 21*, finds analogies between Caruso's work and that of ancient artists.

Modern artists can be as accomplished in the arts of those who worked in ancient times. The artists of the pre-classical and classical epochs thought in terms of immediacy without considering the problems of reconstructing the past or of anticipating the future. In their poetry and their rigorous attention to art, what we see in their work is more a result of our own sensibility than of their intentions. Their terracottas and marbles were vividly coloured, giving the effect of an intentional expressionist form of art; the softness of the shapes and facial expressions are due to the erosive action of time which has removed their peremptory nature, leaving them open to more diverse and polysonic readings . . .. Nino Caruso is a sculptor who has chosen clay – terracotta and porcelain – to express himself, using the most ancient techniques that man knows after the use of splintered flint. Inevitably, he causes us to think again about the objects that have been handed down for thousands of years. Caruso has an ability to inspire anew. He gives us a timeless dimension where ancient and modern join together again to represent each other.

In addition to his knowledge of the past, Caruso brings to his work a control of the materials and the freshness of inspiration.

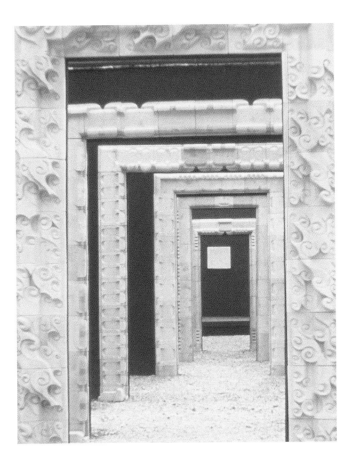

LEFT: *Nino Caruso,* **Etruscan Doorway,** *1987. Castellamonte, Italy.*

OPPOSITE:
Nino Caruso, **The Dyonisos Door,** *2002. Terracotta. Brufa, Perugia.*

There are elements of an ancient language that come through his terracottas: the flutes, the waves, the columns. With Caruso, the object that results is a pure form, endowed with a commemorative function rather than a practical purpose of architectural structure. His work has a significance which gives it life. The formal qualities that we read into it relate to the craftsman's technical ability and not to our perception of the work. It is on a razor's edge: modern, full of inventions, yet makes use of an ancient vocabulary and technique.

Sited in the most disparate places, from stock exchanges to hospitals, from offices to the depths of the subways, Caruso's works seem the result of knowing thoroughly an urban society that questions and continually renews itself about the questions of the community and memory. His work changes the way we think when we consider urban sculpture. Without an evident practical use, rather for contemplation, we are forced to consider balance, beauty, the importance of history and monumentality. 'In principle, Caruso is not intrinsically drawn to figuration,' believes the art critic, Billardello: 'The human body has a limited appeal for him so that

evokes an ancient figurative work, he tends to stylise what the ancients represented naturalistically. Angular and slightly theatrical, his figures transmit the idea of a ritual.'

Gillo Dorfles, writing on the modular structures and the reference to architecture in the work of Nino Caruso in *Ceramics: Art and Perception 2,* also draws attention to the long-standing history of ceramics in architecture. Referring to the relief claddings on buildings and the walls and screens, he believes in the technical and creative ability that Caruso has to adapt his sculpture to harmonise with the environment, at the same time as the works are being effective as sculptures. 'The variety of textures, the play of light in the cavities, the patina of the ceramic – all these qualities generate effectiveness,' he writes. Caruso's method of construction is an innovative one. Taking large blocks of polystyrene, he cuts and shapes the blocks with a hot wire to the exact shape and size he requires. The shapes he cuts are sometimes geometrical, sometimes based on undulating free-form curves. The pieces are then cast in ceramic, fired and sometimes glazed. The assembly of the pieces, either in single or multiple modules, depends on the artist's concept and the intended site. With their own reason for being, Caruso's sculptures and wall works, while providing a focus for the eye, always remain in harmony with their surrounding space.

Describing Caruso's work as 'monumental' in a text written for Caruso's exhibition *Oneiric Memories 1998–2002,* Claudia Terenzi wrote: 'The ongoing feature of Caruso's production, from the open-air portals to the colonnades, ornamental panels and friezes, is that they are designed to be supported by a pre-existing architecture or to impose a form on open space in one of his many installations.' Nino Caruso has written books on ceramics and his work has appeared in journals and books internationally. A major book was published in 1997 by Hoepli, Italy, on his life and work. He is active in giving workshops, being a juror and artistic director for international seminars. He is currently director of

the Academy of Art in Perugia. His work has toured in exhibitions throughout the world and he is sought after to undertake commissions in many countries. One of these commissions resulted in a monumental work atop the summit at the Shigaraki Ceramic Park in Japan; another is a rotunda, 60m (197ft) in diameter in the town of Coimbra, Portugal. In this work Caruso used four modular elements that could be combined in different ways to make a series of 20 columns. He describes the project in *Ceramics Technical 16*, outlining the methods used, the collaboration of his fellow artists and the time element needed to complete the installation.

When Polish ceramic artist, **ANNA MALICKA ZAMORSKA**, was invited to create a piece of work in conjunction with the Vratislavia Cantans International Music Festival in Wroclaw, she needed to find a way in which her work would harmonise on several levels with the site and for the occasion. The idea was that the music and visual art should complement each other.

The music selected for the event was to be played on the glass harmonica, an instrument for symbolic and mystical music. Zamorska chose a huge Gothic church for her installation. The concert was given by Sasha Riekert, the church was the Kosciol Sw. Wintcentego. Arts writer, Zofia Gebhard wrote on the project for the concert catalogue, calling the work a three-dimensional vision. Gebhard believes that Zamorska 'dressed the space, adorned, embellished and disguised it. It was a play with form and space.'

Anna Zamorska is known for her work with multiple elements which, when hung together, form a significant work of presence. Using porcelain, fired to vitrified density, its gleaming nature reflects on many points; when moved it tinkles with delicate sounds. Many descriptions could be applied to these works: romantic and mysterious; cold and hard; glamorous and provocative; sensual or sensitive; all in contrast and all imaginable. Later forms have taken on more aggressive attitudes, her stoneware wolves and similar animal forms with sharp porcelain teeth, are placed in the

ABOVE: *Anna Malicka Zamorska,* **Wolves**. *Grogged clay and porcelain, fired to 1380°C (2516°F). Garden of Dr. Maciej Zagiewski, Wroctaw Municipal Museum. Dimensions: 0.8 x 20m (2½ x 65½ ft).*

OPPOSITE:
ABOVE: *Jeremy Jernegan and Steve Kline,* **Current Watermark**, *1999. Glazed ceramic and painted steel.*

BELOW: *Jeremy Jernegan laying tiles.*

landscape and may represent a playful nature or they may not, but they seem at home in the natural environment that surrounds them.

Organiser of major symposia in Poland, Zamorska has achieved a worldwide reputation for her work in porcelain and for her ability to draw artists together for the benefit of their own work and the larger realm of ceramic art. Jacek Kotlica, writing in a catalogue of Zamorska's work, published in 1998 on the occasion of her exhibition at Keramik Galerie Bürkner, Keramion, Germany, acknowledges her influence on Polish ceramics, not only in terms of the prizes she has received but for her innate talent and diligence. 'Her sculptures,' he writes, 'exploit a whole arsenal of artistic expression – she transgresses and multiplies. She believes in the power of her own imagination and in our ability to associate and confront far-away traditions, cultures, myths, rites and emotions – she believes in the universal basis of art that has always been appealing to people who are curious to find out more about the world and themselves. Taking themes from music, fairy tales, figures from *comedia dell'arte*, she displays her fantasies, her erudition and her humour. Zamorska invites us into the sacred circle of culture symbols and proves that ceramics is an art of noble and refined form.' Iwona Strzleewicz-Ziemianska, writing for the catalogue, finds positive energy in Zamorska's personality and her art which 'manages to escape from precise rules. She is, first of all, a sculptor,' she writes. 'You need to see the work, touch it, feel the power.'

JEREMY JERNEGAN is a ceramic sculptor living in New Orleans, USA, with a home and studio on the waterway of Chef Mentur Pass. He has been head of the ceramics area of the Newcomb Art Department of Tulane University since 1990. He writes:

46

Like many artists, my work develops from formal visual and conceptual stimuli. I am intrigued by the juxta-position of object next to object, and particularly by the tension between order and chaos. Since 1988, my work has been focused on sculptures composed of multiple elements, often appearing loosely stacked. I find the complex visual interaction occurring in such works both challenging and surprising. Many of the problems posed and solved arise from the specific forms making up a piece, their physical relationships and the gestalt of the completed work.

Jernegan is conscious of utilising a life-scale format in his large pieces specifically to establish a physical relationship equivalent to that with an individual. The seemingly precarious balance in many of his totemic forms creates an uncertainty and in some cases this can be related to the metaphorical allusion to the un-certainties within an individual and the outcome of his endeavours. Jernegan says both the colour and tactile qualities of surface carry associations relating to age, growth and decay.

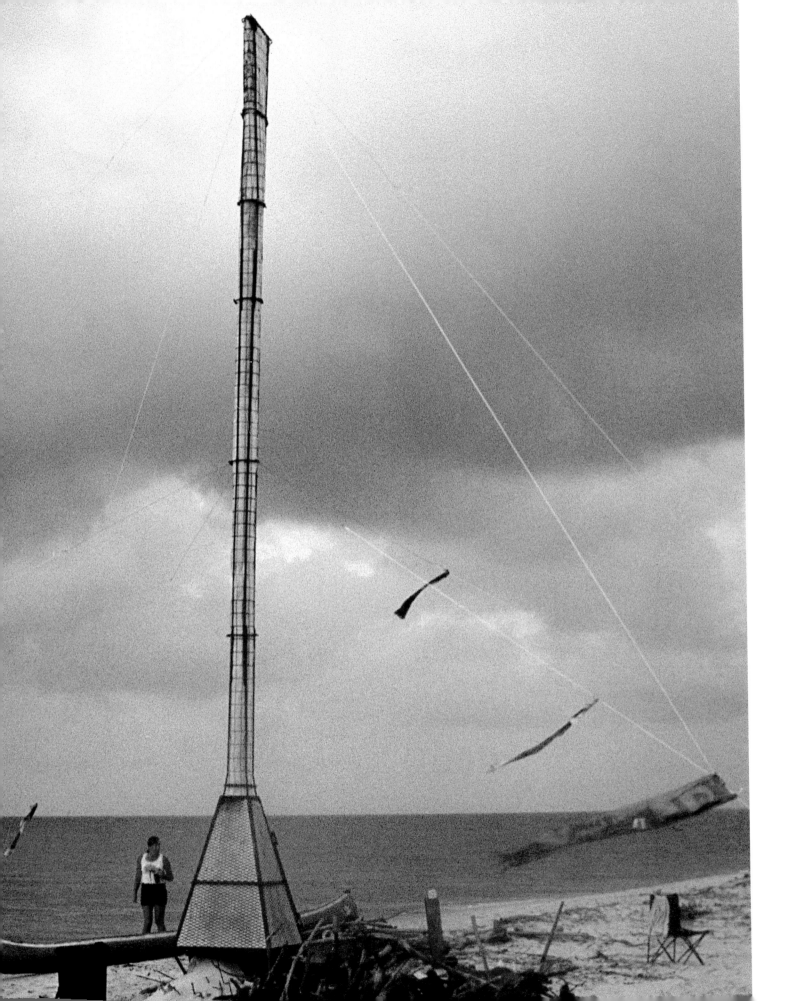

For several years I have been working with images associated with maritime navigation and locomotion. Part of that is a formal interest in the particular objects, shapes and colours, and their potential for modification and variation. However these images also carry allusions to movement, travel and progress through uncertain and changing environments. The parallel between navigating through space and through the course of one's life is not a new concept but one which has interested me for some time. Continuing an earlier series of pieces that involved highway travel as a point of metaphoric departure, my current work makes use of images derived from buoys, fixed markers, as well as steering oars, chains and anchors.

Jernegan's 1998 exhibition, *Medusa's Raft*, continued themes of travel and questions the need to establish oneself, to achieve stability or contentment. Steel and ceramic mono-printed wall pieces explore the formal relationships between image and objects, as well as alluding conceptually to stasis and movement.

My interest lies in interpreting the formal structure in a vocabulary of familiar forms and alluding to the uncertain mixture of individual determination and chance that guides the outcome of all our rafts. The nature of the ceramic material itself adds a paradoxical quality to these. Its mass, weight and fragility divorces these pieces from their sources, and emphasises that things are not as they seem. A viewer's recognition of the consequences of severe imbalance and collapse of a standing piece adds a psychic tension, appropriate for an image of uncertain outcome.

A 2004 project built by Jeremy Jernegan is a sculptural kiln, built on Horn Island (a small barrier island off the Mississippi coast) as a navigational marker and kiln. Writing for *Ceramics Monthly* (January 2004), Jernegan described the project: 'When Brian Nettles, instructor and ceramics coordinator at the George Ohr Museum, Biloxi, Mississippi, invited me to participate, I was interested in developing a piece that would have a broader reference than a performative kiln.' Jernegan took into account the artists traditionally associated with the area and because navigational references have been a primary theme in his sculpture for more than a decade, developed a piece that functioned as a fleeting marker, a sign of a journey in progress. What resulted was a 8.5m (28ft) high 'oar' pulled upright and secured by anchors, lit by fire and incandescent in the night as

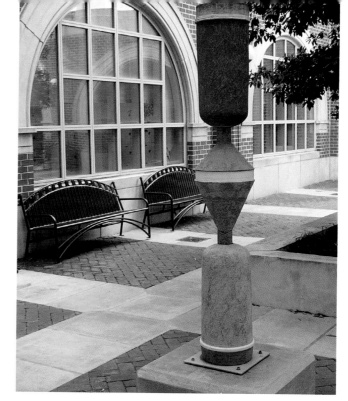

Jeremy Jernegan, **Marker #4**, 1994. Tulane Law School. Dimensions: 225 x 40 x 40cm (88¾ x 15¾ x 15¾ in.).

OPPOSITE:
Jeremy Jernegan, **Georges Oar Kiln**, 2003. Horn Island, Missisippi. Dimensions: 8.5 x 0.9 x 0.9m (28 x 3 x 3 ft).

the flames ran upwards, fanning out at the top.

One of Jeremy Jernegan's important public art works, undertaken for the city of New Orleans, is sited at the front of the United Passenger Terminal. Working with sculptor Steve Kline, and reported on in *Ceramics Technical 9*, the sculpture forms a marker in the competitive urban environment. The concept focused on the Mississippi river as the central and defining characteristic of the city. The sources of imagery were derived primarily from historic and contemporary river travel and commerce. This major project, involving standing steel sculptures in a river of sculptural ceramic tile, took many months to complete but a coherent public art work was the result, Jernegan believes. He writes: 'The project made me conscious that public art requires a broader, more inclusive vision than studio work, and therein lies its challenge, satisfaction and compromise. The artwork's dialogue is with the city as well as the individual viewer, and that is an open-ended conversation.'

C H A P T E R   F O U R

Of Spirit, Energy and Meaning

Invited to take part in ClaySculpt Gulgong because of her ability as a sculptor in clay and because of our collaboration at the Muju experimental sculpture symposium in Korea where we each held workshops, **Tova Beck-Friedman** was able to build a figure in the Australian landscape, which she considers one of her best works. She explains: 'The event in Gulgong brought me to the Australian bush – a captivating place of wide open vistas, dramatic light and an expansive horizon.' As Jill Ker Conway describes in her book *The Road From Coorain*, 'Worn and gnarled by wind and lack of moisture . . . trees rise up on the horizon so dramatically they appear like an assemblage of local deities.' Beck-Friedman continues: 'Looking for a site that would receive my sculpture, I came upon a circle of trees on a gently sloping hill. It was only natural for this enclosure to have a 'deity' in its centre, and establishing one there became my project for the symposium. As with all my forms, this one is also abstracted, only hinting at parts of the body – abdomen, buttocks and legs; nevertheless, she is fecund and heaving with life-giving force. I titled the piece *Drawing Down the Moon* because the time spent at Gulgong was magical – during the ten days of the symposium the moon grew and reached its fullest on the night of the firing.'

At another symposium, this time in her native Israel, in 1997, Beck-Friedman was invited to create an environmental work, *Triple Stelae*, which was realised within the setting of the Third International Ceramic Biennale in Be'er Sheva. The theme for this biennale was adobe sculpture. Fifteen invited artists

BECK-FRIEDMAN

ROBERTS

GOLLEY

NICKEL

WILLIAMS

SERAK

BOBROWSKI

OPPOSITE: *Tova Beck-Friedman, **Triple Stelae**. Be'er Sheva, Israel.*

(from Europe, the USA, Israel and Thailand) created permanent sculptures at the Remez Park, located in the centre of Be'er Sheva, a city in the Negev desert. At the end of the symposium, when all 15 works were unveiled, the city had gained a new sculpture park. Situated at the edge of the park, *Triple Stelae* is a continuation of her work inspired by archaeological ruins. It is reminiscent of ancient architecture and is composed of three columns (each 3m/10ft high) in cement-added adobe with a figure, either carved or in relief, in each. Beck-Friedman's earlier works had a more horizontal theme. *Stepping Stones* was designed to create a meditative, tranquil environment. It is an outdoor sculpture, and was installed at Riker Hill Art Park, Livingstone, New Jersey, in 1986. The 'stones' are made of high-fired clay, and grouped in three islands of white gravel. In an article on Beck-Friedman's work by Jude Schwendenwien, published in *Sculpture 11/5,* an installation in the Quietude Sculpture Garden, East Brunswick, was reviewed: 'Israeli-born sculptor Tova Beck-Friedman's assertive and evocative sculptures remind us that primitive symbols and a solid connection to nature are absent in contemporary society.

The work stands in an isolated outdoor area. Titled *Goddesses* (1988), five figures (the tallest is 1.5m/5ft) refer to familiar goddess forms without falling into stereotypical interpretations that often marginalise such work. They are completely evolved creations made from stoneware, earth and wood.'

Two of Beck-Friedman's exhibitions in New Jersey – at Schering-Plough Corporation and the Newark Museum – took place at major sites. Reviewers of these works found them 'full of a life force'. In an article entitled 'Primeval World of the Sculptress', Rachel Mullen of *The Bernardsville News*, in 1992, describes the sculptures at the Schering-Plough Corporation as 'rich primitive images which rise from the ground like ancient weathered statues'. saying that 'they are testimony to female archetypal images as expressed in ancient myths. If one looks long enough at this group, the figures seem to come alive. One can distinguish an elbow, shoulder, a turning head, trying to break away from the forms which enclose them.' The weathering of the outdoor pieces is part of the artist's design.

Beck-Friedman wants the elements of nature to create the final texture and surface of the work, showing nature's power over man: 'In my recent sculpture, I draw on the many traditions and myths that point to humankind's long-established custom of worshipping unusual stones. I synthesised the human figure with stone-like forms to create primordial images.'

In her *Adam/Adama* series, she draws attention to the linguistic relationship between humanity and earth. The surface of this series of columnar wall reliefs evokes the feeling of charred dry earth.

With many sculptures placed outdoors in public environments and many solo exhibitions to her credit, Tova Beck-Friedman continues to undertake residencies and exhibit installations of her work. Terry Litchfield wrote on Beck-Friedman's early work for *Women Artists Slide Library Journal 24*, after an exhibition at the Amos Eno Gallery in New Jersey, USA:

> Her work, *Goddesses*, marks the culmination of research into the myth of the goddess, worshiped for a creative and magical role in society. The goddess of the prehistoric myth is far removed from modern-day concepts based largely on woman as sex object or virgin, both roles patronising to women. Her themes echo her sympathy

with nature, and she is sensitive to the message running through life from its inception in pre-history. Her sculptures make a visual statement about the life force inherent in all things.

With attention drawn to the 'simplicity of form and economy of line', Beck-Friedman, however, wishes to convey a more essential meaning: 'The body is rounded, earthy, the shape intentionally redolent of nurturing and procreating. Her fecundity is displayed and emphasised, a oneness with nature.' In giving form to the mythical goddess, the artist says she is reasserting ancient female values.

Two Canadian women artists, **ANN ROBERTS** and Trudy Ellen Golley, arrived at ClaySculpt in Gulgong with energy and ideas. Roberts engaged a group of artists to build a female goddess-form overseeing the orchard to entice life-giving rain; Golley's group made paperclay fruit to lie at the feet of the goddess. The choice of the site, on a rocky promontory where the rising sun would shine daily on the ample hips of the figure and be visible at dawn from the farmhouse across the valley, was important because it gave a postmodern context to placing a heroic sculpture in an Australian landscape. Roberts writes: 'The dry drought-twisted eucalyptus trees were so impressive to this Canadian that they became echoed in the tangled hair of the sculpture allowing the hollow figure to become a kiln, with the firebox between her feet. The spontaneous ritual dance lasted for 18 hours after people brought twigs and leaves to encircle the goddess with a warming and drying ring of open fire. The group dynamic continued the following night when the cage-and-blanket kiln reached yellow-white heat and was climaxed by a downpour of much needed rain – a truly mythic encounter after years of drought.' These works were fired *in situ*, the clay vitrifying sufficiently so the forms became permanent sculptures. Both artists continue to bring spirit and meaning to their lives and work.

Ann Roberts is a ceramic sculptor, teacher and art activist living in Ontario. For the competition for a sculpture for Wilfred Laurier University, Roberts was chosen to undertake the work. Here she details how the competition was run:

> The sculpture was commissioned by the university

through a two-part open competition in 1991. The first part required artists to send slides of their work and a curriculum vitae to a panel of jurors who selected three finalists. These three artists were paid $1000 each and asked to produce a maquette, a series of drawings to show the siting of the sculpture in a campus courtyard, and a budget for the $30,000 project. My entry, *River Riders*, was the final choice. The concept grew out of previous work which used, as its theme, the ancient dilemma of the overloaded boat. Instead of fleeing migrants and desperate escapees, this boat, a Canadian canoe, would typify the skillful balance needed to navigate through university life. The two humans are gender-equal, both hold a paddle in the steering position. The parrot in the centre represents the exotic – those who come to our universities from other lands to help us understand ourselves through understanding others. Birds are also a mythical link between earth and heaven. The canoe and its occupants are flattened as a reference to the pictographs left on the walls of rock along the waterways used by Canada's indigenous peoples. Three-dimensional modelled hands were used to draw attention to the need to grasp and steer a path on the lifelong search for enlightenment, while the concrete rocks are delicately balanced – a reference to the dangers of the journey.

Roberts's *Goddess Tables* were made in 1996 and 1998 and are a continuing theme that began in 1994. They are hollow-built, white clay, with white matt and shiny glazes fired in oxidation.

They represent the large, spring-time ice floes that carry with them the next generation of roots or sprouting seeds. As signifiers of regeneration and hope,

ABOVE: *Ann Roberts, **River Riders**, 1991. Bronze and concrete.*

BELOW: *Ann Roberts, **Goddess Tables**, 1996 (left), 1998 (right). Oxidised stoneware.*

OPPOSITE:
*Ann Roberts, **Orchard Goddess**, 1995. Gulgong NSW, Australia.*

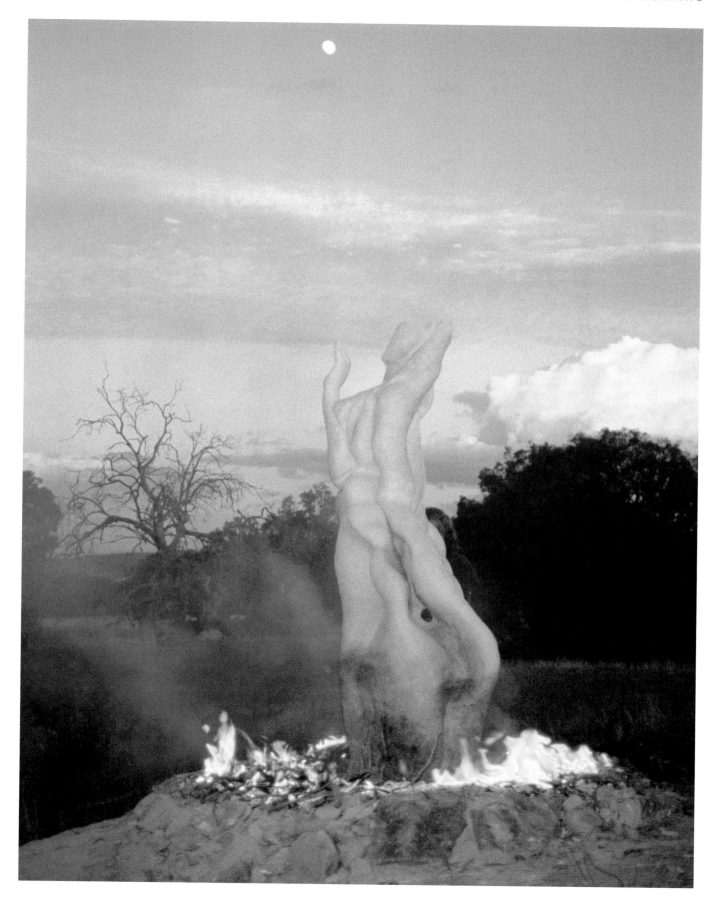

they drift and scour their way down Canadian rivers to lodge in new ground where some of their cargo takes root and continues the cycle of life. As the floods subside, they remain on the river banks, reminiscent of prehistoric recumbent stones awaiting a ritual libation.

Since leaving South Africa in 1960, Roberts has been an undeniable presence in Canadian ceramics. First as a functional potter and later as a sculptor, her output has been prolific. She has now retired from the position of Professor of Art at the University of Waterloo, Ontario, and chair of the Canadian Clay and Glass Gallery board of directors. Gloria Hickey provides an appreciation of the artist and her work: 'Largely because the sculpture, like the woman, is articulate and characterised by literary allusions, viewers frequently describe it as intellectual. However, Roberts produces sculpture that is noteworthy for its emotional and aesthetic truthfulness. Over the past 30 years that Roberts has been making sculptures, she has consistently tackled the universal themes of life, death and sexuality – the big issues with which we all live, day by day.' Writing in *Ceramics: Art and Perception 56*, the collector Fred Holtz noted: 'She infuses vital new life into the old forms of animal figurine sculpture, and has found a way to express her robust view of life in vigorous, complexly evocative and emotionally resonant pieces.'

Ann Roberts says she makes sculpture because the physical presence of the third dimension awes her with its reality. Through the action of sculpting, ideas become concrete images, pieces of her life become enmeshed in the fabric of each sculpture. Using women to portray the interaction of life forces, she believes that contemporary women wish to be in control of their lives and destiny yet are tied to the forces of nature of which they are a pivotal part. 'I would like them to be perceived as sensuous and active participants in the game of life,' she says. In 1997 Roberts was elected to the Royal Canadian Academy of Arts, where she remains actively involved. Her work has been portrayed in a number of journals and is in important collections including the Royal Ontario Museum, the Museum of Civilisation, the Canadian Clay and Glass Gallery, and museums in Switzerland, Turkey, the Czech Republic and Hungary.

LEFT: *Trudy Ellen Golley,* **Embodied reCollections***, 1999. Installation. Photograph by Paul W. Leathers.*

ABOVE: *Trudy Ellen Golley,* **Embodied reCollections***, 1999. Installation. Photograph by Paul W. Leathers.*

TRUDY GOLLEY expresses her philosophy of ceramics when she says: 'No technique should be merely an end in itself but rather it should be a means to an end; which is to say any technique or tool should be exploited to fulfil the artist's vision.' Golley believes a comprehensive technical training is critical because one must develop a vocabulary and know the language before one can say anything profound. She works with a white stoneware paperclay for about half her work and porcelain for the remainder. The thin sheets of clay that make up her 'stack' pieces are made from porcelain that has been stretched thinly by throwing the clay in a stretching motion on a canvas-covered table until a paper-like thickness is achieved. The sheets of clay are then torn to create a deckle edge. Layers are stacked up, hollowed out as required, to make the stacked effect of old documents. 'Most of my work is fired to cone 6 for the first firing to harden the body yet this still leaves it porous enough to

accept glaze readily. Subsequent firings range from cone 2 to cone 010 or lower depending on the piece. Most pieces are fired a minimum of four times.'

Golley's works represent her personal history.

I find that I attempt to explain the world to myself through the physical manifestation of an object directly related to my experiences. I question the constructs that have formed me and continue to influence me by observing gender stereotypes and the various ways in which they are promoted. Recently, I have turned to the investigation of fairy tales. I have been looking at these seemingly harmless stories to see how they can mould our actions as we grow up and, in the case of women, may contribute to producing inhibited and passive behaviour. I am, however, most familiar with the 20th-century edited versions of most fairy tales that leave out depictions of female strength, bravery and sexuality, giving an un-balanced point of view that fails to generate the positive impact such stories were originally meant to have. Given this, I am now looking at some of the original versions of common fairy tales and ancient mythology, looking to them for the background material for use in the continuing story of myself.

Golley has undertaken a number of commissions for domestic interiors. 'Working with art consultants and interior designers has led me into this exciting area. I have had the pleasure of working with clients who are sensitive to my work and give me latitude in creating pieces which are about my own work, interests and sensibilities.' Golley is given free rein to create within the limitations of size, colour and budget as set out by the client. To stay true to her own spirit and meaning while pleasing the client has given her room to produce work that is unique to the particular space in which it is to be placed.

The first step in the commission process for me is to fully familiarise the client with my work and philosophy so that there will be no surprises down the road. Because I work so much with the notion of being female, my work generally revolves around an implicit sexuality. The clients need to know the symbolic content of the work to ensure their comfort and understanding of the works they are commissioning.

Working on commissions also gives Golley the opportunity to produce large works that she would otherwise not be able to make. For example, most of the commissions have been large wall installations in ceramics and glass, which, combined with light, create shadows and which use the entire space. To this end, she says, it is satisfying to work in an environment with controlled light sources; the work can be designed to make optimum use of the changing light conditions during the days and seasons to enhance the work and set it off. Richard White, writing about the exhibition *Changing Attitudes* at the Muttart Art Gallery, noted: 'In 1993 I became re-acquainted with Golley's work as a result of curating an exhibition for Suncor Inc. entitled Ceramics: Past/Present which included her work. It intrigued me because of its power, mystery and tension. While the work has evolved significantly over the years, the artist still creates her sculptures by stacking or connecting distinct elements together. Golley has created wall pieces and has introduced a new element to her vocabulary of visual symbols

– a stack of sheet-like layers. For the artist, this is a metaphor for the layers of meanings or pages of histories connected with understanding art, self or a specific issue. In most cases the layers are pierced by a vessel further emphasising the internal/external duality of sculpture and life. Allegorically, this could be interpreted as an individual searching through the layers of personal history to arrive at a new understanding of life. On another level, it could refer to the current examination of the role of women past and present. Golley's work contains architectural, anthropomorphic and autobiographical elements that address and challenge the active/passive roles of gender stereotypes,' wrote Shirley Madill for *Winnipeg Art Gallery Tableau*. 'Light as symbolic of one's inner spirit is also symbolic of the suppressed aspect of female sexuality.' Golley herself, writing in *Contact Magazine 4*, says she wishes to make connection with the people who view her work. 'To my mind there can only be life in a work as a result of the cycle of destruction, purification and rebirth.' This, she believes, is similar to the transformation of ceramic materials by fire. An exhibition project mounted by Mentoring Artists for Women's Art (MAWA), titled Ground/Connection, featured Golley's work, among others. In the catalogue essay, Amy Gogarty wrote: 'The architecture of the powerful and empowered female body has been the subject of Golley's work for years. Images of containment – physical, physiological and spiritual – link the body of architecture and symbolic vessels in a continuous metaphor.'

Also featured in the Ground/Connection exhibition was **GRACE NICKEL**. Recognised for her large-scale installations using paper clay, wood, wax, canvas and found materials, Nickel, who lives in Winnipeg, Manitoba, has been a prominent Canadian ceramic artist for some years. In the catalogue essay for the exhibition Ground/Connection, held in 1995 at venues in Canada and the USA, Amy Gogarty believed that what was important to Nickel was 'the sense of touch and memory she imparts to her lustrous surfaces'. Decoration and ornament continue to receive new life, says Gogarty, with Nickel investing her installations with 'frank and sensuous decoration'. This exhibition, which also included the work of Trudy Golley, Sally Barbier, Joan McNeil, Thérèse

TOP LEFT: *Trudy Golley,* **Uterus is a Pear Shaped Form**, *1995, wall piece. Length: 75cm (29½in.).*

TOP RIGHT: *Grace Nickel,* **Light Sconces**. *Ceramic, glass, wood, silk, light. Private installation, Ontario. Height: (tallest) 246cm (97in.).*

ABOVE: *Grace Nickel,* **A Quiet Passage**. *Gallery installation. Photograph courtesy of Winnipeg Art Gallery.*

Grace Nickel, private installation. Ontario.

Chabot and Katrina Rozman, celebrated mentoring in feminist art practice as an active and energetic activity of participation and example. Nickel, already interested in the natural cycle of birth, decay and regeneration, chose Chabot as her mentor for this project. Amy Gogarty continues, 'Grace Nickel addresses spirituality and ritual with her finely worked surfaces, symbolic elements and visceral imagery. Nickel relates her attraction to austerity and detail to her Mennonite heritage with its ethos of simplicity and spirit. She plays with dualities – rigid versus compliant, sturdy versus fragile and protective versus vulnerable – to suggest the polyvalent nature of spirituality and experience.'

Grace Nickel's exhibition, A Quiet Passage, was reviewed by Helen Delacretaz for *Ceramics: Art and Perception 52*. She wrote:

> Since 1992, Grace Nickel has approached her ceramic art by concentrating upon site-specific installations. The meanings of 'A Quiet Passage' are both personal and universal, representing a journey for the artist as well as for all those who encounter it. Nickel finds harmony between architectural references and natural symbols. Architectural motifs developed in Nickel's work after she moved her studio to Winnipeg's Exchange District in 1996. The repeated references to nature in the ornamentation of its neo-classical buildings influenced the artist to juxtapose the ornamental elements with the organic abstraction already present in her work. The duality of architecture and nature echoes the dualities of our existence: the dichotomy between the artificial and intellectual, born of reason, and that which is natural and organic, born of evolution.

GARRY WILLIAMS, a Canadian ceramicist from Calgary, has been working with installations and environmental sculpture since the 1980s. His work has featured in cultural, environmental and ceramic magazines and he has won a number of awards and scholarships. For an exhibition, Clay Between my Fingers, presented both in Vancouver and Banff in 1993, and curated by Sylvie Gilbert, Williams was one of the four artists invited using ceramics as a major material. Gilbert, writing in her introduction to the catalogue, noted the use of clay for broader cultural and social meaning. 'Clay can be thought of symbolically as flesh or dough,' she writes. 'It bruises like flesh, it memorises fingerprints and retains marks such as those made by a ring on a finger. Clay is earth. However, in addition to its material properties explored specifically throughout the Western aesthetic history of ceramics, clay objects have a wider commercial and cultural existence.' Amy Gogarty, writing specifically on Williams's work in the exhibition was struck by 'its corporate propriety – its crisp and chilly elegance'. Gogarty draws our attention to two orientations of containment, one of commerce, exemplified by the use of Wedgwood-like vases, the other by 60 traditional earthenware oil jars, in this case planted with Alberta rye. Gogarty believes Williams locates his work in the midst of ethics, aesthetics, material culture and labour, finding in it both economic and political reality. 'Williams points to the fundamental role craft has played in mediating the global flow of communication. By engaging tradition and memory, contemporary craft confronts us with where we have come from and how we are shaped by transhistorical forces. Drawing upon the essentially symbolic as opposed to the essential nature of contemporary craft, Williams opens up new discursive spaces and imaginative possibilities.'

For an exhibition titled Cathedrals, Williams presented a grid-like arrangement, which comprised squares, pots and growing trees. In the catalogue essay called 'The

OPPOSITE
TOP: *Garry Williams, **Same Song, Different Chorus**, 1991. Terracotta, sound, mixed media.*

BELOW: *Garry Williams, **Cathedrals**. Terracotta pots, plants, gravel.*

Garry Williams, **In the Same Breath**.
Terracotta, mixed media.

Wilderness and the Grid', John Stockman believed Williams was presenting us with an artistic truth, which he labelled 'objective correlative'. By this he meant that Williams, instead of using an idea to get attention for himself, reversed the situation; a syndrome of ideas, situations and beliefs that realises itself on another level of existence. Stockman talks about his 'detachment, artistic transparency and non-egoic devotion to the concept within his mind . . . which induce social conscience within the awareness of the viewer without romanticising, without narcissistic alienation, without being nasty and without presumptuous didacticism.'

In a similar manner, Les Manning, curator of the installations titled *Inside Out*, held at the George R. Gardiner Museum of Ceramics Art, Toronto, Canada, in 1998, found that Williams created an evocative environment of contemporary social issues that provocatively showed the changing role of men at the end of the 20th century. Williams wrote at the same time that he was interested in combining historical sculpture with personal and contemporary issues. While his figures in the

installation were deliberately ironic, he hoped to show how cultural and environmental factors have shaped our perception of masculinity and its reality. These comments echoed his own words at the time of his environmental work *Same Song, Different Chorus,* shown in 1991, when he wrote: 'I am questioning society's current ideological position in regard to our environment. My work seeks a special function in art; one that addresses the state of living in an age of instability and crisis. In focusing on the disorder in the world, I wish to emphasise the need for awareness, involvement and change.'

A definitive essay on installations and their meaning in art was written by Mitchell Merback for the catalogue of Cooled Matter, an exhibition shown in conjunction with NCECA (the National Council on Education for the Ceramic Arts) conference, Ohio, in 1999. This essay was later expanded for *Ceramics Art and Perception 39.* The exhibition featured the work of six North American artists – Charles M. Brown, Sadashi Inuzuka, Walter McConnell, Jennifer Lapman, Garry Williams and Katherine Ross – and showed how installations could

*Vaclav Serak, **The Rainbow Fairy**, 1998. Ceramic, steel, lights. Fountain at the entrance of the town, Bystrice pod Hostynem, Czech Republic.*

transform an environment. Writing about the work of Williams, Merback said,

> Williams is an artist whose environmental consciousness prompted him to use unfired clay and organic matter in the art gallery with the intention of working through the traditional language of nature's aestheticisation. Williams knows that the *locus classicus* for this language is the garden, the perennial refuge from urban-industrial society. In most of his installations from the early 1990s, he transfigured the gallery into a kind of garden, and this brought into play two rival constructs: the garden as an interior space ornament-alised by natural elements, and the garden as an exterior space, a landscape, restructured and "tamed" by architecture.'

In his artist's statement for the installation, Williams wrote, 'Through the format of sculpture and installation work, situations are created that question ideological, cultural, philosophical and physical relationships to objects, materials and environments. By focusing on the theme of disorder in the world, I wish to emphasise the need for awareness, challenge, involvement, empowerment and change.'

One of the Czech Republic's most noted ceramic artists is **VACLAV SERAK**. In addition to his teaching and exhibition work he has been commissioned to make a number of fountains for public spaces. One of these fountains was reviewed in *Domov* (The Home) magazine, which described his 1999 work thus: 'It vaults over an imaginary entrance to the town, Bystrice pod Hostynem, acting as a stop on the way, an open gate, the place of meetings and plays; it reminds one of eternity as well as fleeting moments. Stone, ceramics, steel, water and beams of light shape the variability of the atmosphere.' The fountain is situated in the popular pilgrims' place in the region of Morava under the mountain Hostyn, with its famous basilica and monast-ery at the top. The pilgrims from the Czech Republic, as well as from neighbouring countries, visit it during the whole year, and especially on holidays such as the feast of St Mary when an immense number of people and processions come to see and honour the miracle. The fountain celebrates the specific spiritual atmo-sphere of the town. The municipal leaders wanted to

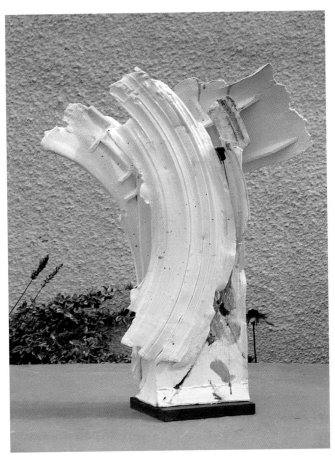

*Vaclav Serak, **The Breeze of Hope**, 2000. Porcelain. National Museum of History, Taipei, Taiwan. Height: 70cm (27in.).*

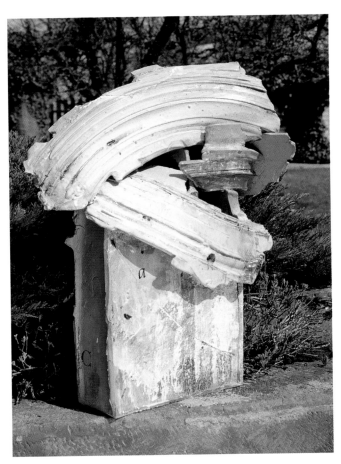

*Vaclav Serak, **Garden Ceramic Sculpture**, 1999. Stoneware. Height: 80cm (31½in.).*

emphasise the atmosphere of the town, and Serak's work, entitled *The Rainbow Fairy*, is the third decorative fountain to be sited there. The mayor of the town, searching for a new and contemporary project, contacted the Academy of Art, Architecture and Design in Prague. Wanting the best material for the purpose, not necessarily a traditional one, but one with the possibility of colour, expression and with the necessary conditions for weather resistance, he chose ceramics. The project needed to consider the architectonic conception of the whole area as well as the separate design of the fountain. Wanting an experienced team who had made similar works in the past, the architect, Bohumil Chalupnicek, contacted the academy and Vaclav Serak, the head of ceramic studio. Serak writes: 'The first project, including sketches and models of alternative designs, was presented in 1997. After much discussion, the *Rainbow Fairy* project was chosen.'

The work on the ceramic components of the fountain were made in the working studio of the academy.

I chose a special refractory material, originally used for glass kiln lining. It has high resistance against weather and is able to withstand acid damage as well. The body of the arches was divided into sections about 40 x 60cm (15¾ x 23½ in.) each and these were hand-pressed in moulds. When fully dry the panels were decorated with underglaze colours and covered by a smooth, thin layer of feldspathic glaze, and then slowly fired to 1280°C (2336°F) in electric kilns. The montage of ceramic parts was built on a concrete construction and assembled in place.

The water aspect of the fountain's installation is concentrated in the middle arch in an area made from glossy stainless steel. In the interior, on the whole of its length, a narrow opening conceals hidden water jets,

*Gina Bobrowski, **Drawn by Nature**. Bill Briggs and his team took a week to install it.*

which make a fine, misty screen. In the base of the fountain a set of coloured electrical lights project coloured rays into the water giving a rainbow effect at night. Runway lights illuminate the lines in the pavement. Serak says: 'The installation of this fountain is probably one of the best of our team's architectural works. The fountain is fully functional and works for the joy and satisfaction of all citizens and visitors and has become a popular attraction.'

GINA BOBROWSKI's ceramic sculpture records observations derived from life wherein she hopes to find a larger meaning. Her recurrent themes are language, tolerance, transformation, and the relationships of nature and wild spaces to civilised tame ones and intuitive processes to rational ones. She writes: 'Improvisation facilitates creating or composing, without rehearsal or premeditation. These approaches draw on an assimilation of process, form and background experiences and combine with curiosity and the ability to live spontaneously, completely and honestly. This kind of intelligence is similar to what we see in animals, children and visionaries, in cross-cultural folkways and in non-westernised cultures and systems which support more animistic community-based attitudes.'

Bobrowski's sculptural work questions traditional ideas of beauty. It is physical, generous and narrative.

I work in several formats as dictated by aesthetic need – figurative sculpture, interior and outdoor sculptural installations and functional pottery. All rely on specific geographies as the source of their surface and imagery. Whatever the format, a certain playfulness is retained through the celebration of the material. I am concerned that many adults have either lost or forgotten their ability to play because of the need to keep a distance between themselves and direct experience.

Raised by a creative family, Bobrowski's personal relationship with the environment runs deep.

I was raised in a semi-tropical environment where nature dictated everything. The air was so wet and so thick one felt as if one could swim through it. I began working with horses when I was ten years old, among ancient live oak trees and lagoons. The urban environment inspired me too, the mix of New Orleans' cultural and political influences and the odd pervasiveness of nature. The influence of the specific place: first in the surface of my work and my approach to form, then in wetness or dryness of palette and imagery used. Found objects and mixed media also speak of specific place. After receiving my MFA from the University of Georgia in Athens, GA, I spent several years living in the northernmost tip of the Atchafalaya basin in rural Louisiana. I remember my childhood experiences of living in close proximity to natural forces and animal manners. I welcomed a later move to my current home in a semi-rural village in north central New Mexico because of the singularity of its

geography and culture. Here the landscape seems monumental and invulnerable but is actually quite fragile. Within a year of the move west I recognised my need to work more directly with the space itself and some of my works use surfaces derived from the native clays and oxides found throughout New Mexico.

In 1996, the director of the Laumeier Sculpture Park and Museum invited Bobrowski to present a one-person exhibition in four of their galleries in 1997 and an outdoor sculptural work a year later.

I made several site visits in different seasons and provided proposal drawings for both installations, which are now in the Laumeier's permanent collection. I built all of the major sculptural work, the large figurative elements without assistance. To delegate any of the figurative components would have compromised the overall aesthetic of the work. Form and surface are simultaneously and intuitively approached during the building process. Layers of raw clay washes, slips, stains, raw glaze

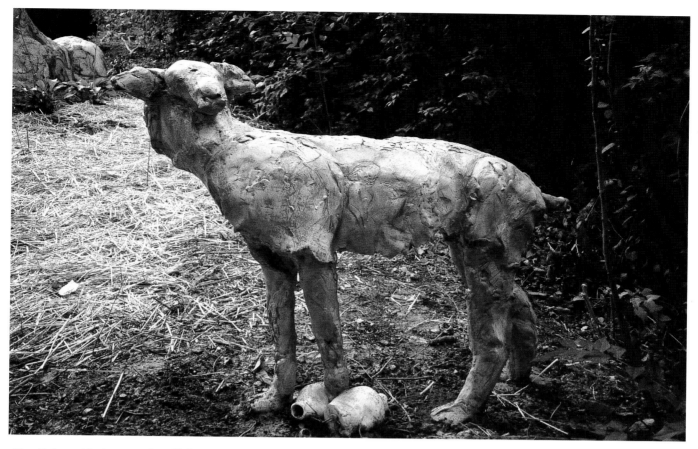

*Gina Bobrowski, close-up of **Wolf**, from **Clearing, Drawn by Nature.***

OPPOSITE
*Gina Bobrowski, **Clearing, Drawn by Nature**, (detail), 1997. Dimensions: 25 x 8 x 5m (82 x 26 ½ x 16 ½ft).*

and non-ceramics materials were used. Throwing the simple forms (the vases and the birdhouses) was shared by project assistant Triesch Voelker. Voelker and I took turns throwing my vase forms over a period of five days. We alternated shifts, which usually lasted a couple of hours each. I kept the vases leather-hard until all were thrown, and then I assembled and inscribed them.

Some of the pieces for the installation were built in sections by a coil, scrape and slab approach without any internal structure, others were built over foam and paper forms. The pieces were then removed, fired and re-assembled in a slab mosaic process. Multi-weather epoxy was used to assemble all the clay-to-clay sections after firing. Silicone caulk was also used and the works were anchored into the ground with steel bars. I used a terracotta body and slipped surfaces with vitreous engobes. Seams where sections had been joined were hidden with oil paint and coated with varnish. Once on site, I drew the sculptural placements on the ground. Some plants were added for a sense of immediate growth and eaten within a week by the park's appreciative rabbits. Site assistants

were Triesch Voelker and Laumeier grounds manager Bill Briggs and his crew of four. It took us a week to install the work.

Writing about Gina Bobrowski's sculptural installation in *Ceramics: Art and Perception 41*, Daniel Duford found meaning and spirit in the work: 'Gina Bobrowski's sculpture is connected to the spirit world of dreams, beings of the ether who whisper in your ear; close inspection reveals a microcosm of meaning.' He went on: 'Another of Bobrowski's strengths is that for all the profundity and layered communication, there is a sense of play that keeps the work fluid.' Duford reminds us that for centuries sculptors have been incorporating work into manicured landscapes, introducing ruins and follies into formal gardens. Gina Bobrowski, he feels, has turned a path into a pilgrimage, the clearing into a shrine, while activating the space with objects.

C H A P T E R   F I V E

Fragmented Patterns, Geometry, Rhythm and Methodology

PUBLIC ART HAS BEEN CLAIMED as showing the aesthetic value of a community, expressing its ideals and history as well as its aspirations for the future. Ornamentation of buildings, once the usual expectation as part of an architect's designs, has, with financial tightening and the popularity of an austere international style of urban building, been limited. However, there is now a revival in decorative elements added to or included as an integral part of buildings. Many of these ornamentations take the form of patterned wall claddings and free-standing walls of architectural merit.

Writing about the works of **JACQUES KAUFMANN** in *Ceramics: Art and Perception 20*, A. Lewy Gazeau, an art historian from Geneva, points out that fragmented large-scale works are related to myth and the remnants of history: 'Walls are simple examples. They are surfaces, they are also façades relative to an epoch, to climate. The ancient ones are an epic. Walls are a contrast, not only because they materialise the section without from the section within but they also become a contrast between rigour and hazard. After the measuring ruler, the vertical level and the plumb-line, there is erosion. Walls have the simplicity of an ordinary reality and if they screen anything, it is our projections. Their opacity reflects hazardous things, whereas their structure defines logic and reason.'

Jacques Kaufmann, from Frangy, in France, has been a ceramic artist for more than 25 years, receiving distinctions for his work and being represented in international public collections. Now making permanent and temporary

KAUFMANN

BRANDT-HANSEN

KUIPERS

ROBISON

TEUTEBERG

DOWLING

FARRI & DOWNIE

BUNNELL

MARSHALL

OPPOSITE: *Justin Marshall. Geometric detail of tiles.*

ABOVE: *Jacques Kaufmann,* **Homage to the Little Spoon**, *2003. Carouge Museum, Switzerland.*

LEFT: *Jacques Kaufmann,* **Penetrable sculpture**, *1997. Rotonda Anotnelli, Castellamonte, Italy. Bricks and blue pigment.*

structures in bricks, he says that the important factors in his art are space, the materials, time and energy. It is a question of dimension, he believes, using bricks to make a work. This means that the finished sculpture can be large scale and made in a relatively short period of time. Bricks are modular units capable of being built into stable and complex forms and the bricks themselves dictate the form and, as he says, give it shape. 'Depending on the space to be filled – in the city, in nature, in a museum – it is necessary for Kaufmann to respond to the character of the site. There is a permanency about bricks, made for building lasting monuments, and they will remain as a measure of time.' In the essay on Kaufmann cited above, Gazeau writes:

Jacques Kaufmann has invented a work to overcome the reality of walls, to show that works of art do not represent art, they demonstrate it. He makes walls like variations – walls that arch, thin walls that double up, walls one walks around. Avoiding the game – that is, the trap of the maze – one is tempted to see simple things. The prolongation that continues between right and left, the side of the outside that touches the one of inside, the bottom that ends at the top and bricks as a measure of earth.

Spanning ancient times until now, walls of bricks show the origin of the clay from which they were made. In this way Kaufmann believes his works are linked to the ground, to abstraction, a unity of time and space.

ELINA BRANDT-HANSEN sees patterns everywhere: 'Even our sky is filled with patterns,' she writes. 'To our eyes, the star constellations do not make any detailed composition but I often think that this is because we are too close, if we could see the sky from far out in space, the stars will be part of a pattern-covered fractal, perhaps reflecting even more units on the other side of the universe.'

In the mid-1990s, Brandt-Hansen was introduced to the word 'fractal'. Although she had been working in the area of repeating parts of the main composition within a piece, the concept of fractals alerted her to the idea that every little detail is a reflection of the whole unit. Some fractals one is able to see by eye – the fern or bracken plant, or a bird's feather – but today one can also discover the wonders of nature through microscope lenses and explore microscopic universes. 'People have often asked me if I am particularly interested in mathematics. To be honest, I had great problems with that subject at school but my fascination with geometrical rhythms, fractals and structural patterns is, after all, perhaps not so far away from the Pythagorean thought that the underlying universal principle is numbers. When you have been working as an artist for some years, you start to recognise patterns and rhythms in your development as an artist.'

After working for some years with textiles Elina Brandt-Hansen realised that clay was her medium. However, because fabric and clay had been 'walking hand-in-hand', it was natural to combine these two materials at art school, where she was persuaded to transfer the fabric qualities into clay.

When experimenting with ornaments cut into cardboard, Brandt-Hansen found that compositions, constructions and shapes were occurring almost by themselves. 'On purpose I always make too many ornaments for what is needed but I play around with them and new ideas show in the next piece. The solution or the idea of a piece is already hidden within the ornaments and the challenge for me is to have an open mind to the possibilities of transferring these discoveries into clay.'

Brandt-Hansen starts with full-size sketches, which are usually quite detailed. To be able to work with large pieces that also are quite thick, and, at the same time, being able to keep the range of colours that porcelain gives, she had to find a way to combine porcelain and stoneware.

> Either I roll thin layers of porcelain on the stoneware, or I wrap thin layers of porcelain around stoneware coils. Then the coils are cut and assembled into ornaments or shapes. I then build the piece bit by bit, usually on top of a sketch. When a piece consists of many thousand separate bits, and sometimes as many as 26 different colour shades, it becomes almost like tapestry weaving. Building the piece in small units, I need to impart a wholeness to form and decoration. The form becomes the result of the ornaments and, vice versa, the ornaments are dependent on the form

The aesthetic qualities of an object are essential to her, both regarding the actual expression and in craftsmanship. She wants her pieces to be not only decorative but visually challenging. By the use of optical illusion and also by using a transparent glaze, she creates new patterns and rhythms on top of the ornaments. She says she wants to give the spectator something to discover and often her pieces will reveal the same composition or patterns through all kinds of varieties in size, shapes and colours. For her, equally or even more important than aesthetics and optical illusion, is the recognition of the fact that both natural and cultural phenomena have rhythms, patterns and repetitions that we all are a part of. It is necessary for people to touch the work, she says, to discover the hidden patterns. 'By this intimacy with the objects, the spectator can more easily take part in the process. Recognition of the technical skills is also a field where I feel I can communicate.'

Elina Brandt-Hansen describes her methods of detailed pattern making in *Ceramics Technical 19*, saying: 'All my pieces include the use of a detailed patterned porcelain block. First, I make a coloured sketch of how I want the patterns to become. Then stripes of coloured porcelain are laid upon each other, with black slip in between, in lengths of 50cm (19½ in.).'

Invited to undertake a number of major public

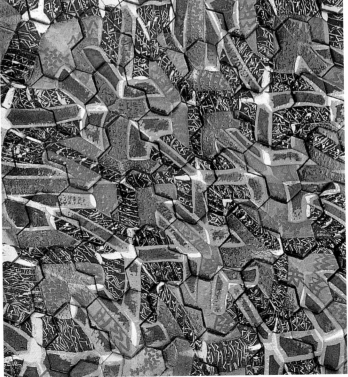

OPPOSITE PAGE
TOP: *Elina Brandt-Hansen.* **Platter,** *(detail).*
BELOW LEFT: *Elina Brandt-Hansen.* **Fractal Fragment,** *(detail).*
BELOW RIGHT: *Elina Brandt-Hansen.* **Platter.** *1994. 80 x 80cm (31½ in.).*

THIS PAGE
TOP: *Elina Brandt-Hansen places hundreds of tiles [ornaments] on top of a sketch before moulding them together from the back. Since the finished piece will have some tiles that tilt away from the surface, bits of cardboard are placed between the tiles.*
MIDDLE: *Thin sheets of different coloured stoneware are layed on top of each other on the outer part of the tiles. The sheets are modelled together before lumps of clay are added in order to build a solid base that has the same level as the edges.*
BELOW: *Because most of the process has been done from the back of the work it is an exciting moment to turn the piece around. The cardboard parts are removed and clay tiles that tilt from the surface will fill in the spaces.*

commissions, Brandt-Hansen found that working in granite and other paving materials would be more appropriate. However, her pattern-making has been similar to her work in clay. These commissions included the design, in 1993, of the pavement of Olav Kyrres Street (1000m/3280ft) in Bergen; in 1994, the design of the entrance hall floor at the Granvin Cultural Centre, Seljord, Telemark; and, in 1994, a design for the market place at Elverum.

In an article in *Ceramics: Art and Perception 16*, Les Blakebrough, describing Elina Brandt-Hansen's ceramics, cites the influence of the artist's environment on the island of Sotra near Bergen, Norway, calling her studio a world of rainbow and northern light, of scholarship and alchemy.

A graduate of the Bergen School of Art and Design, she is making her mark on that city and others in Norway, and beyond. The large assembled forms she produces have rich surfaces, either in texture or the array of colours and metal lustres; they are objects to contemplate for their own sake. They have an obvious monumentality; surface becomes the intrigue, emerging as a detailed tapestry of colour only to disappear under layers of volcanic lava-like material. This interplay of surface against surface is a fine balancing act and it demonstrates an amazing control of the medium. Her vocabulary is not metaphorical or allusive but exists in the demonstration of skill. Skill is a conceptual, moral and imaginative matter; its presence gives ceramic art its moral heart. Brandt-Hansen regards ornamentation as an important artistic means of expression and she is fascinated by the many variations and opportunities to produce different combinations.

Michel Kuipers. **The Watchdog**, *1990.*
Installation in progress.

Rhythm can also be expressed in a continuity of approach, the regularity found in working to commission, one project leading to the next. For Dutch artist, **MICHEL KUIPERS**, design aspects of the site are just one of the aspects that have to be taken into consideration. In his design for *The Watchdog* (1990) at the entrance of the residential area of De Kuil, Udenhout, Kuipers looked for an image that was between figuration and abstraction. He assimilated both natural and refined forms to relate the work to both the natural and the developed environment. The final design consists of two sculptural elements, one behind the other; the first has a natural profile, and the second is architectural and mathematical. By putting 'handles' on both sides he gave meaning to the seemingly arbitrary outline of the curved site. The disproportion of the two elements accentuates this: the larger animal profile expresses protection of the residential area symbolised by the small sentry-box.

A mural installed at the entrance to the International Ceramics Centre in Kecskemét, Hungary, *Looking for a*

New Order (1991), highlights the changed political situation in that country. A classical pillar was used as a symbol for the power, now broken, and the fragments rearranged. In doing so he sought to stress tradition in a culture that had lain dormant since the beginning of the 20th century. He wished to involve ceramicists in this process as well as the ceramic industry. Kuipers outlines his aims for this work:

In the mural I wanted to deal with the characteristics of relief: the three-dimensional in relation to the suggestive. On the corner of the wall I fixed fragments of a column to catch the attention of people coming around the corner. On both sides of the entrance the fragments of the column are almost flat. By the fluting on their surface I created the impression of a round column, especially when the sunlight passes over the surface to make the slightly curved surface seem round. The bases of these pillars are flattened on the wall; an oval of blue links up with the form of the pillar. Next to the entrance elements I mounted a third relief in which I tried to create a sense of space without making the three-dimensional projection too literal. I am intrigued by

*Michel Kuipers, **Still Life**, 1994. Schijndel.*

the friction one gets between realistic projection and the conceptual. The elements around the entrance are spread outwards to suggest a gesture of invitation; the handles of the jug-like profiles on top of the wall make a similar gesture. I have chosen to use images that suggest bowls and jugs to symbolise the Kecskemét Centre in a timeless way.

A major sculpture, *The Connection* (1993), was built by Kuipers at the roundabout between the village of Oeffelt and Boxmeer in the Netherlands. Kuipers designed the sculpture in which the identity and character of the village, as well as its joint future with Boxmeer, were expressed. The almost symmetrical form of the square is in sympathy with the layout of the roundabout so siting was important in order that the work could be seen from all the various angles. In the proportions he had to take into consideration the different eye levels of pedestrians and passengers in trucks and buses. The large scale of the location demanded a relatively big gesture. In this sculpture he deliberately chose recognisable elements to create a challenging junction between figuration and abstraction

with the elements leading to an interpretation of the content of the work.

Still Life (1994) was designed for the public garden in Boschweg Noordoost, Schijndel. Between the clusters of buildings along the main road, a piece of land remained that was destined for a public garden and had been planted with bushes and trees. The arts committee decided to give the garden a facelift and commissioned a work of environmental design. Kuipers was asked to develop a design that related to the environment that also indicated the connection between the public garden and the surrounding residential area. Kuipers writes:

> I did not try to create an organic connection between the garden and the rest of the area but chose to strengthen the character of the garden. My intention was to design a still-life using vases without flowers for the garden of this flower-filled neighbourhood. Behind a freestanding stainless picture frame I arranged four terracotta vase forms. The sculptural elements are positioned in the centre of the garden and are outlined by a path.

Writing for a catalogue on the work of Kuipers, Mieke Spruit-Ledeboer, gallery owner and collector, says that his work is noted for the sculptural character of the forms and their philosophical content. 'His work is closely linked with present developments in modern art,' she writes, 'and, in particular, the fundamentalism where the emphasis is on the process as well as on the properties of the material.' Relating the works concerned with breaking and the tearing of clay and the reconstruction of the developed fragments to his interest in archaeology, Spruit-Ledeboer believes these works express a contrast between nature and cultivation.

> During the past few years his work has consisted of monumental sculptures, partly on commission, along with a series on a smaller scale that sometimes serves as a sketch for the larger work.
>
> Since 1983 Michel Kuipers has taken an interest in the pot form as a theme for sculpture. He reduced the form to elementary concepts of geometry using modules. Because he confines himself in the work to what he

believes is elementary and essential, he stimulates the fantasy of the beholder and invites him to complete the sculpture in his mind.

Michel Kuipers studied at West Surrey College of Art and Design, Farnham, UK, and took an apprenticeship in England with Tony Benham, where he gained an insight into the aesthetics of porcelain or stoneware. He realised, however, that it was a different direction in ceramics he wanted to practise. However, clay has remained his basic material because he finds he can combine his interests in natural processes and archaeology with the production of sculptures. 'Kuipers links sculpture with the earth by means of lines that, from the first vertical disc, are drawn on the surface by which he suggests an organic connection,' writes Ad Kraan for the catalogue *Beelden in Noord Brabant*, (1990).

> He expresses the notion of culture and time by applying slightly different colours to linking parts of the sculpture. This way it seems as if the parts have been exposed to different influences in the course of history and date from earlier times before they were fitted together again. In some works Kuipers attaches a handle to a flat and rugged piece of clay: a contemporary sculpture that refers to an archaeological find.

During 2003, Michel Kuipers was commissioned to design a school wall with ceramic ornaments that related to tiles in the pavement. It was to be based on the idea of elementary symbols, related to the subjects taught at the school. Another project was an area in the central hall of a secondary school in Gemert. One of the steel pillars that support the roof between three buildings was replaced by a tree trunk made in ceramics. The tree is glazed in two colours, referring to the different sections of the school, and all three pillars show shadows of trees on the floor.

Another project that has involved Kuipers lately is 'grave sculptures'. He writes: 'I combine abstract and recognisable elements. I work with strict forms contrasting them with the earthy structure of clay in which colour plays an important role. I find it rewarding to be allowed to use my ideas for a memorial for the deceased. It is important to relate the design to the person and in this way the sculpture becomes a true memorial.'

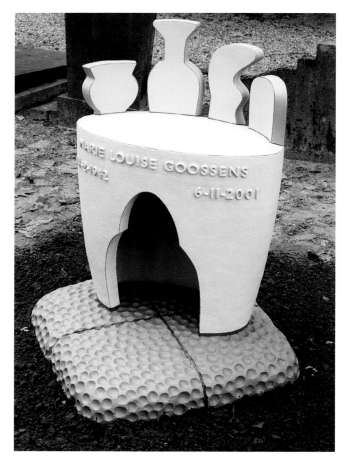

Michel Kuipers, **Grave Sculpture**, *2002.*

Jim Robison and helper, with work in progress.

JIM ROBISON, American-born and now resident in Yorkshire in the UK for many years, is known for his commissioned wall sculptures, which are based on geometrical patterns in high relief. He has written on the aesthetic and technical aspects of these ceramics for a number of journals and also for his book, *Large-Scale Ceramics*. His article 'A Sense of Place' was published in *Ceramics Technical 6*.

Commissioned work gives scope for flights of imagination that an artist dreams of, but it also brings with it a great sense of responsibility. Nowhere is there a greater thrill of anticipation than when being offered the challenge of a substantial work of art. Yet there is a certain trepidation at the core of this excitement because you feel the weight of expectation and the pressures of obligation that come with this offer.

Robison takes into account several key factors when working on a commission: location; clients' requests; time-frame; budgets; and the commitment needed by both artist and customer. 'The location,' he says, 'includes the shape of the area, the textures and colours present, the direction of natural light and what artificial light will

be available later.' For Robison, however, location includes the historical and natural environment in which the work is to be placed. A visual awareness of this environment and interest in the history of a place provide a rich source of inspiration. 'My own interests in texture and shape can be stimulated by historic buildings, cultivated fields and meandering streams. In fact, I believe an element of history about a place is often an essential ingredient of public art work.'

Jim Robison likes to involve his clients throughout a project, and not only in the initial design, inviting them to see the work at various stages during the making. This builds rapport and shows the client the extent of his commitment to the commission. 'On occasion, I have gone so far as to ask the architect for whom I was working to invite the brick masons to come to the studio. They will be involved in the installation and I want them to see the work in advance, and create some enthusiasm for it. Their handprints were added to the soft clay during the work on one commission and later the installation went without a hitch.'

Robison, now with several commissions behind him, says he divides a project into time slots, estimating the time he should take to complete each section. These sections include: wet clay; leatherhard construction and refinement; careful drying; raw glazing (no bisque firing); once firing (to stoneware temperatures in a gas-fired reduction kiln); and installation of the completed work.

> The budget should, of course, be among the first items discussed, along with how and when payments are to be made. Usually the client is receptive to a design fee although, in small works, this may be part of the whole project. If extended time and effort are required, it is good to break the total bill into segments including a start-up fee for materials and initial expenses; a midway point when work is well under way and as such can be seen by the client; delivery of the finished work; and installation. It is often wise to keep installation as a separate item because it may involve building work and outside contractors. On one occasion, at a Cambridge shopping centre, installation requirements included the erection of scaffolding and the use of an electric hoist to lift heavy segments of a free-standing relief sculpture to a ledge above a shop front. This required specialised help, arranged through the contractors, and the entire installation had to be completed at night so that shopping was not interrupted. Above all, get a commitment in writing. Verbal agreements may be all right among friends, but you won't get paid if the project falls through.

Each of Robison's commissions has had its own requirements, problems and rewards.

> I tend to look at the design and content requirements first: the dimensions of the rooms, the size of the walls, the likely viewing distance of any audience that will influence the scale of shapes created, and the boldness of pattern and texture. Where there is a specific content, such as historical events, significant architecture or specific landscape, then

ABOVE: *Jim Robison,* **Park Sculpture**. *West Yorkshire, UK. Stoneware tiles and cut stone.*

OPPOSITE PAGE
Jim Robison, the installation of the **Holmfith Victoria Square feature**. *Ceramic and stone. Artwork includes landscape images and a tourist map. The surround of local stone provides seating for visitors.*

research must be undertaken, libraries visited, photographs taken and drawings done. I make lists of possible inclusions and sketch potential solutions, attempting to assess the importance of each along with its visual potential. Public commissions require a detailed drawing of each proposal. I do not trust my own drawing to communicate the full flavour of three-dimensional relief, colour and texture so I often create a scale model as well. This helps to clarify ideas, visualise scale and often solves problems of construction before they arise. The model will be glaze-fired and displayed along with larger samples of colour and texture.

Using his favoured working methods, which have evolved over the years, Robison builds up relief sculptures

(often hollow to reduce weight) by constructing geometric shapes on a slab base. These shapes are receptive to applied textures and slips.

> Working from drawings and models, the overall shape of the mural is marked out on sheets of plywood or chipboard supported by strong tables. The wood is covered with builders' paper, which is strong and waterproof. This prevents the clay from sticking to the wood or drying out too quickly. From sketches, an outline drawing of the overall work must be made, which details the shapes of individual tiles. I try to imagine the finished product with the divisions as part of the overall design. Where possible, the edge of a shape is used as a dividing line.

The importance of a plan becomes apparent as divisions are made. Two vertical ribs are necessary at any join between two tiles. Robison cuts inverted keyhole slots in the background clay at this point to provide the eventual mounting points for each tile.

> And finally, of course, the kiln shelves determine the maximum size and to some extent the shape of the individual pieces to be fired. Contrasting areas of light and dark are created with porcelain slip. This has been painted and combed on flat slabs before being bent into shape, creating organic river shapes. Cling film is used to keep painted areas clean while other modelling and construction work is done.

Installation is facilitated by the use of the shanks of substantial screws and large washers through the keyhole slots, which have been made in the back of each tile. To accurately locate these screws on the wall, a paper rubbing is made of the back of each tile. These patterns are then arranged and taped together on a piece of board. A centre punch is used to locate the position of each screw and the whole hardboard template is fastened to the wall and used as a guide for drilling.

Writing about Jim Robison in *Ash Glazes*, the author and potter Phil Rogers recognised Robison's ability to work in large scale, and his expression of ideas to be paramount. 'In understanding Robison's work one has to appreciate the love he has for the Yorkshire landscape and all that it contains – its rocks and crags, its dry stone walls and lichen-covered gateposts, the patterns – all these have their part in his interpretation of his surroundings.' Rogers describes the character of

the work as 'complicated constructions, usually geometric in nature, reminiscent of the crystal structures found in geology or the stratification of rocks'. Using a mixture of ash and clay, Robison sprays his forms to highlight areas, some of which have already been treated with slips or colouring oxides. Copper and cobalt washes, porcelain slips and textured areas are also used. In the words of Mary Sara, writing for *Ceramics Art and Perception 18*, Robison's techniques give his work 'a sense of fiery molten rocks being extruded, compressed, cooled and eroded'. Describing a number of commissioned projects undertaken by Robison, Sara acknowledges the influences of the Pennine landscape where the artist lives and has his workshop and gallery, describing it as 'gritty where it is impossible to be unaware of angles. This diagonal stratification of the natural world is the strongest design element in all Robison's sculptural ceramic forms.'

Jim Robison combines his commissioned projects with making abstract sculptural works and large garden and wall pieces. Formerly head teacher in ceramics at Bretton College, University of Leeds, UK, he continues to support young and established potters through teaching sessions and exhibitions at his Booth House Gallery in Holmfirth, West Yorkshire. Writing about his work for *Artists Newsletter* (January 1997), he describes how he prepares himself mentally and physically for specific works and the thrill of his discovery of the relationship between himself and past generations of potters as he looks at ancient works. He writes: 'To work in clay, in whatever capacity, is to recognise the continuity of human endeavour.'

Since 1986, **SABINA TEUTEBERG** has been undertaking public art works and private commissions for buildings and gardens in the UK and Switzerland. Born in Switzerland and resident in the UK, Teuteberg specialises in colour: for tiles, large garden urns, as well as for her commissioned tableware. Enjoying working with industrial methods, she outlined her ideas to Peter Gerdes in an interview for *Ceramics Technical 1*: 'I realised that it was possible to use a clay surface like a canvas. For me, this involves placing thin layers of coloured clay on a base slab which is rolled or pressed to fuse the surfaces. In a sense it is collage in clay. At this stage I began to look at industry, hoping to find a way to make these slabs useful. My interest was not in mass production but the process offered a solution that could be adapted for my requirements.'

In this way, Teuteberg found a freedom of expression as well as a controlled finish for the piece; the process created a contrast, a certain tension.

> When decorating I take into account the function of the work. I have in mind the user and the pleasure which should go with any such piece. The decoration should allow the user to rediscover the object continuously, to interact with it. The opportunity arose when I was asked to create the floor surface for a foyer to an exhibition space. I looked towards industry for a solution. The result was a combination of plain vitrified industrial floor tiles and multi-layered handmade tiles using the traditional Victorian floor design as a starting point but taking a contemporary approach by breaking up the symmetry. These irregularities force the viewer to look twice, to rediscover.

Out of this first project grew others such as a facelift for an entrance lobby to a block of council flats in London and various floors in private homes.

> The brief for the lobby provided me with a particular challenge: up to 200 people, among them many children, use the space daily. This means that everything had to conform to official health and safety regulations. Moreover, the space had to include a resting facility. This meant I had to design and construct a vandal-proof seat using industrially available and handmade materials. All cultures know some form of welcoming mat, so I translated this concept and created a modern kelim rug in ceramic material for the floor.

In addition to the surface treatment on tiles and flat planes, Teuteberg wanted to explore form. She says: 'One of the triggers was my first visit to Malaysia under the auspices of the British Council. On this occasion I became acquainted with the work of traditional local Chinese potters. I was particularly fascinated by their technique of assembling large storage jars. But first I had to find a new infrastructure. My kiln is not large enough to allow grand experiments. I tried transporting the big jars on a trailer to factory kilns.' As a consequence of the problems encountered with this, she decided to work where the clay and the kilns (and the sympathy of the

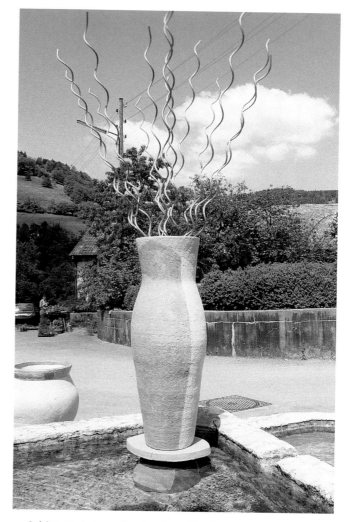

*Sabina Teuteberg, **Garden Pots**. Hand pressed in sections and assembled. Coated with coloured slip and glazes. Fired at 1260°C (2300°F). Installed in a private garden.*

people in the industry) are situated – in her case in Lausen, Switzerland.

> In the course of my stays there, which became a regular feature in my life, I discovered that this exchange of expertise between industry and artist is welcome on both sides. The Lausen factory produces high-fired claddings for industrial purposes. These people have considerable knowledge about shock-resistant clays, precision moulding and large-scale extrusion. A huge factory hall became my studio and my perception of space and materials changed. Suddenly tonnes of material were forklifted around for me and technical expertise was available in overwhelming abundance. The challenge was massive. No experimenting discreetly behind my own four walls – here people watched and waited. Making the large Chinese-inspired

vessels was not so much the problem, decorating them was. I was building traditional forms but took them into the 20th century by way of decoration.

The symbolic representation of the figure captured in vessel form has always attracted Teuteberg and because she was already working with large objects, she felt the time had come to explore the human figure on a scale of one to one.

I now also felt confident enough to experiment in this industrial environment. Technically, I became almost fearless. The industrial surroundings allowed me to do just about anything on a technical level. But what did impress me, however, was to stand in front of an alter ego, in front of one of these figures which took on a life of its own. They became expressive, as did their moulds. The solid form, the hollow form, and an empty form – all representing the one figure and all of equal importance even though in the end only the hollow form survives. A metaphysical experience, indeed. The figures were fired in the factory tunnel kiln, laid on a bed of sand and fired to 1300°C (2372°F). They found a resting place in a private park overlooking the surrounds of Basel.

As a result of this work, she received an order to build a site-specific fireplace in a private home. This involved building a curved clay slab of approximately 6m² (64½ sq. ft). This opened up for her a completely new understanding of the possibilities of moulding. 'Speed was of the essence: the form had to be filled with clay in one day. Once filled, the slab was cut up into elements of different shapes which were fired, transported on site and cemented together by an expert stove builder.'

Objective observation, rationalisation and problem-solving methods are important aspects of the work of **IAN DOWLING** of Margaret River, Western Australia. These disciplines continue to play a role in representing abstract images or emotions in physical form. With his interest in rhythmic pattern based on repetition of particular elements, a modular system can generate ceramics of a larger scale where the viewer becomes part of the space of the work.

With an early preoccupation with science and mathematics – he has worked as a teacher in regional Western Australia – his individual pieces are textured tiles to be fixed to walls or blocks to be built into

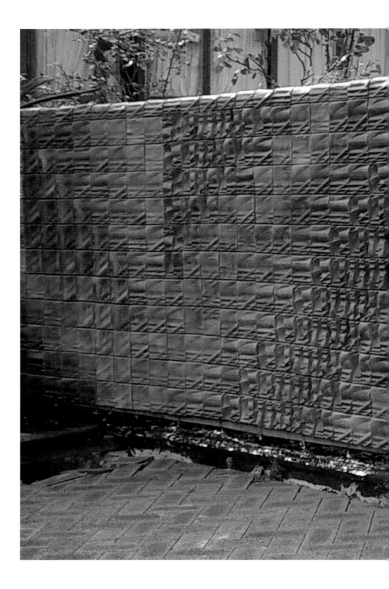

freestanding structures. Starting with the design of these, repeated production gives him elements to play with. Arrangements are laid out, put together, pulled apart and changed, over and over again. He writes:

The tools I use include directional lines common to each element; shapes within the elements; number of repeated elements; variations in the depth of texture; and light and shade. Positive and negative space within the structure, surface and colour variations, form of the overall structure, alignment of the structure and the space around the structure. Unity and harmony are achieved by using the relationship between each of the elements. For example, the 'saddle' is one of the primary shapes used. It can be connected in groups of two to eight to make various blocks. It is a geometric object similar to that made by stretching

Ian Dowling, **Courtyard Wall***. Margaret River, Western Australia.*

an elastic film between four points in space. By definition it is both under tension and in equilibrium. When saddles are joined and built into a structure, these characteristics carry through to the whole form. Since this is more than just an exercise in stacking geometric blocks, decisions made by the artist at every stage of the process influence the depth of the experience of the viewer.

Several wall and freestanding sculptures have been completed by Ian Dowling, made at his Margaret River pottery. Major works have been commissioned by the Margaret River Education Campus (MREC); one 2004 work is a 7m (23ft) high water wall constructed from slip-cast textured ceramic tiles. Earlier public works include an 11 x 4m (36 x 13ft) concrete panel textured using clay as the imprinting medium, also for the MREC. Within the

repetition of elements a visual rhythm was created and this search for rhythm comes from his interest in the patterns of activity at all levels of life, from the single cell alignments of peat moss to the way humans form communities. Dowling believes there are many influences on how a particular individual responds within an environment. When the influences and the responses have some regularity, out of the chaotic activity a rhythm may develop. Layers of rhythm can develop within a structure or patterned surface.

Ian Dowling continues to work as a potter between his commissioned works, responding to requests for exhibition pieces throughout Australia. He says: 'The pulse of activity can be erratic, both in the life of the artist and the rest of existence. Just as the work is leading to producing regularity of form, my mind is turning to

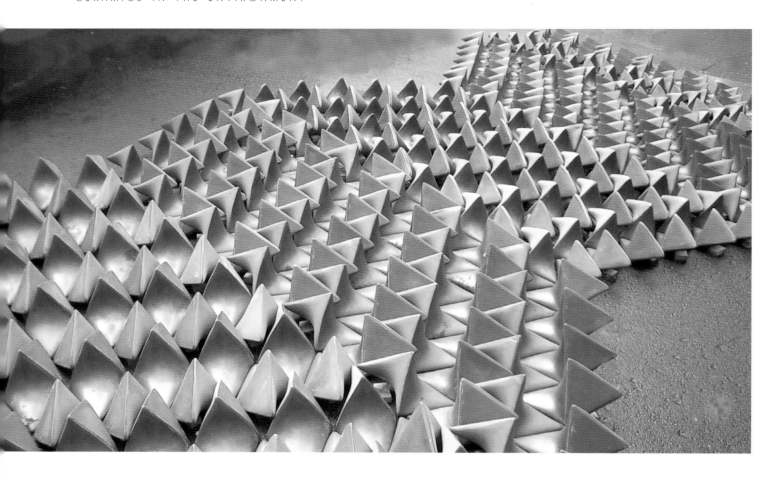

ways of interrupting that easy rhythm, punctuating it with agitation or fading it to quiet.' He cites the influence of the Italian artist Nino Caruso, with whom he studied briefly, saying:

> Many contemporary artists use repeated forms to influence our perception of an object. Caruso's architectural modular ceramic walls and objects are rooted in the archaeology of his own Italian environment. I like to alter the size of tile elements in my work and break out of the grid created by the basic shape and allow for modular textured applications over a three-dimensional form or on a surface that is anything but flat and rectangular. Different elements can alter the effects experienced.

Ian Dowling cuts wheel-thrown clay sections and reconnects them to form the basis of a new set of repeated elements. 'This is just one example,' he says. 'Cast forms can be broken down and rejoined to explore alternatives for repeating irregular shapes. Each time a new element is picked up, the possibility for a new rhythm arrives.'

DIOGENES FARRI, in association with SUSIE DOWNIE, was commissioned by Great Lakes Council in NSW, Australia, to work with Russell Saunders (a Manning district artist) and Tobwabba Art to make a ceramic pavement and mural as a centrepiece for an entry court structure in a park. This project was completed in 1998. The design is divided into five sections, illustrating the 'Dreamtime' of the original inhabitants of the area through to the Worimi tribe's first contact with white settlers (escaped convicts from the Second Fleet), the arrival of cedar-tree cutters and timber transport in the early 1800s, and contact with other Aboriginal tribes. It includes a tribute to the marine assets of the area and a reconciliation theme.

ABOVE: *Ian Dowling,* **Saddle forms**. *An arrangement of individual pieces.*

OPPOSITE
ABOVE (BOTH): *Diogenes Farri and Susie Downie, work in progress.*

BELOW: *Diogenes Farri and Susie Downie.*
Ceramic Pavement and Mural, *1998.*

Facing a project for a public site is different to developing work in one's own studio for an individual show. In contemplating the large selection of materials and possibilities that are part of the requirements of a large-scale project, the artist/craftsperson is forced to break the boundaries that have been framed by individual studio production. When you prepare an exhibition you do your best to produce a certain amount of work. A selection is made and exhibited to the public in a gallery or shop. In public work, you have only one chance and the selection and appraisal is constant from the concept design, through the making, to completion. Making a work for a public space brings art out of the gallery setting, presenting it to a community as part of their daily lives. The art gallery can sometimes be seen as an exclusive, almost private place with many people feeling inhibited about stepping inside. Bringing artwork outside into an open space allows people to interact with art in a relaxed way.

It is important to reflect how we see ourselves involved in the art of ceramics. The mythology of 'artist' makes us dream we are exceptional creative autonomous beings. This collaborative project offered me the experience of taking the simple role of artisan; the humble position of interpreting another's painting in the ceramic medium in which I am skilled. I attempted to feel what the artist felt in the painting. The experience gave satisfaction without pretension, the satisfaction of contributing the best of one's skills. Each individual contributing to a project plays an equal role in accomplishing the final outcomes and determining the degree of success.

To transpose the small painting and enlarge it into more than 24m² (258sq. ft) of pavement called for some decisions to be made. The original brief called for the entire work in mosaic; however, the decision to make the background in larger pieces of terracotta tile helped maintain the integrity of the original artwork.

Terracotta tile mix was spread over a board to a thickness of 2.5cm (1in.). The design was drawn on the leatherhard slab and the motifs that were to be interpreted in mosaic were cut and removed. The background was sectioned into manageable tiles of an irregular pattern following the mosaic motifs. Careful numbering was needed. Variations in atmosphere when firing the background tiles (1120°C/2048°F) provided a range of terracotta colours that gave life to the large-scale work. A vitrified coloured clay body was developed to cast the tiles needed for the mosaic to a thickness of 1.5cm (⅝ in.). The mosaic was fired to 1140°C (2084°F)

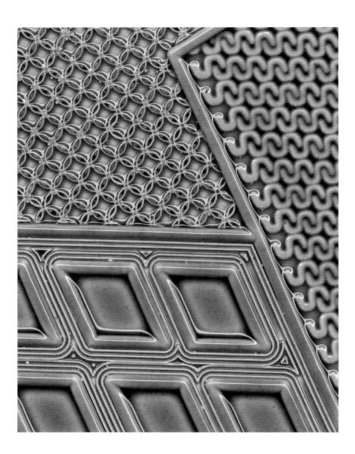

and set into concrete in manageable sections. The tiles were set individually by two professional tilers on a reinforced concrete slab laid to council specifications. Grouting followed the colours of the mosaic design.

KATIE BUNNELL and **JUSTIN MARSHALL** have created low relief tessellating tiles with an illusion of depth for cladding on wall and other architectural applications. They write:

> This project developed out of our combined interest and experience in the creative use of computer technologies in the production of ceramic forms. As practising makers we both believe that the successful integration of computer technology in designing and making ceramics requires practised craft skills, and that access to hands-on, in-depth knowledge of established materials and processes is necessary for the development of high-quality products.

Bunnell's earlier research outlined the potential that computer technologies have for the development of more economically sustainable craft-based production

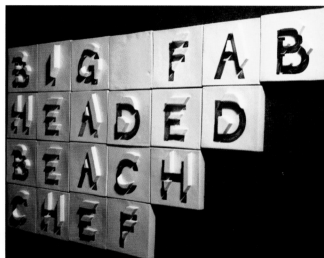

OPPOSITE PAGE: *Katie Bunnell and Justin Marshall,* **House Tile Project**, *(detail of house).*

LEFT: *Katie Bunnell and Justin Marshall,* **House Tile Project**.

BELOW: *Justin Marshall,* **Shadow Letter tiles**, *1998.*

of high-quality ceramic design. She found the main advantage of using computer technology was the ability to develop, reproduce and transfer designs to CAM machines that would exactly reproduce the qualities of line and form created using CAD alongside the development of these new and unique aesthetic qualities that could not have been achieved using other technologies. CAD/CAM enables a 2D drawing to be converted into 3D on computer and then onto a model, before investing in large projects.

Marshall's research and artwork has explored the integration of CAD/CAM in the creation of relief tiles and tessellations, and the use of shadow to create illusions of form. Writing for *Ceramics Technical 15*, they discuss the project's three key elements: the development of a tessellating design that gives an illusion of three-dimensional depth and that allows the users to make their own decisions about the final arrangement of tiles in their chosen location; the development of a relatively straightforward technical method of producing low relief using CAD/CAM; and the development of a production process for low relief tiles using technologies that would facilitate small-scale batch production by a regionally based ceramic manufacturing company.

The technologies used allowed a 'family' of designs to be developed, reviewed and adapted and, through this process, unique characteristics to be created. The use of CAD and CAM technologies facilitated the production of detailed designs otherwise impossible or impracticable to produce, and the simple variation of tooling and depth of cut allowed a range of effects to be created.

> The processes we used facilitate the exact reproduction of size and shape, making the technical challenge of producing detailed tessellating hexagonal tiles more approachable. We believe this project shows that there is potential for further investigation into employing 2D drawing packages in combination with 'low end' tool path software and CNC milling in the creative production of a range of low relief ceramic surfaces. Through this project and future projects we hope to achieve some dynamic and creative links between research in education and business.

The project was funded by the Arts and Humanities Research Board (AHRB), UK, and supported by Falmouth College of Arts, and was carried out in 2001.

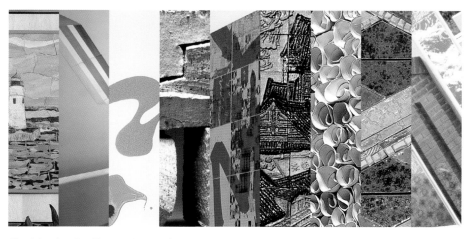

C H A P T E R   S I X

In Service to the Architect and the Material

CERAMICS – THAT IS, FIRED VITRIFIED CLAY – is an ideal material for art in public places. It can be used for load-bearing structures, it is strong and protective, withstanding hot and cold temperatures, and has sound-insulating properties, it is fireproof and can be used as a covering that is damp-resistant. Its aesthetic values can be compared to paintings. Ceramics can form an integrated component with architecture and it can strengthen the architectural expression where quality of material has importance. Ceramic materials can be used in conjunction with mixed media to give wider technological possibilities and offer further challenges to an artist.

ELLE TERRY LEONARD specialises in site-specific commissions in clay for corporate and residential clients. These include relief murals, fireplaces, and wall and floor treatments. Her complete studio services range from concept and consultation through production, shipping and installation. She writes: 'It is important to me that my work fits as a lasting personal complement to the architecture or environment for which it was created. I want the touch of the hand to show. More important than ever in our technical world is our connection to the rest of humanity.'

Leonard's work process is a complicated one. Using clay loaded with grog, she rolls out large slabs, which are cut into various sizes and patterns before attaching sculptural elements to them. The work is then dried, fired, glazed and fired again. 'Tile art is demanding physical work,' she says of her countertops,

LEONARD

DE CROUSAZ

STEHR

KECSKEMÉTI

LISLERUD

ZHANG

ZHU

TUNICK

SMITH

OPPOSITE: *Sandor Kecskeméti, Monument, 2002. Fired at 1380°C (2516°F). Photograph by Tihanyi-Bakos.*

Elle Terry Leonard, **Baltimore Harbour** *(wall murals). Cafeteria at the Johns Hopkins Bayview campus.*

fireplaces, tables, floors and back splashes for bathrooms and kitchens. 'The look of Leonard's work is distinct,' wrote a journalist for the *Bradenton Herald* in 1985. 'A mural for the Barnett Center in Sarasota shows curvilinear motifs, coin shapes that connote currency, as in the Greek issue struck in Syracuse of old. A 6m (20ft) long cut-out mural of bromeliads on an outside wall of a St Petersburg beach house in Florida ties to another history – that of Nile temples with their decorative motifs of lotus, papyrus and palm.'

Leonard, whose first ambition was to be an archaeologist, enjoys clay because it is permanent and becomes a part of history. She also likes the idea that her work is incorporated into spaces where people work or play. 'The time-line of ceramics fascinates me – to think that someone thousands of years from now could pick up a piece of fired earth and take the time and interest to research its age and origins. The more handmade objects there are around the better to soften the commercial world.' Leonard has completed six 2.4 x 2.7m (8 x 9ft) murals for Arvida's Fairway Bay Condominium on Longboat Key and a mural for the lobby of Barnett Bank in Sarasota, USA. She says she likes getting her hands dirty. 'I like hands-on,' she says. 'I don't like sitting at a desk. The best way to learn is by doing.'

In 1972, Leonard apprenticed with several potters

Elle Terry Leonard has been featured in *The Guild: The Architects Source*. She writes: 'From the first Guild edition, I received a commission from a Missouri restaurant called Trotters. The client wanted art thematically linked to their name so my mural depicted a horse race with a crowd from the 1890s standing in an old stadium. I collected photographs so that I would have actual faces to work with. I put several people I knew in the mural.' Later, another commission used recognisable landmarks. This time the site was a cafeteria at Johns Hopkins' Bayview campus and the subject was a view of Baltimore Harbour. The project's art consultant sent her 22 photographs, all taped together. She had taken a boat ride and snapped her camera every few minutes. 'I had a huge photographic spread. When it was finally completed, people came up to the mural and recognised areas where they lived. I thought if people can relate to the mural that well, then I've done my job.'

Other commissions undertaken by Elle Terry Leonard include murals in Florida for Arvida Corporation, Longboat; Chamber of Commerce, Sarasota; City of Venice, Venice; Worldgate Marriott Hotels and the Worldgate Athletic Club, Reston, Virginia; Kaiser Permanente, Silver Springs, and at Johns Hopkins Hospital, Baltimore, Maryland. Her latest commissions include works at Tampa International Airport, Tampa, Florida, and the Esalen Institute, Big Sur, California.

but decided to specialise in architectural ceramics. In addition to her family and work commitments, Leonard also teaches. Working in conjunction with architects, Leonard believes it is important to please people, and she doesn't think giving people what they want compromises her position as an artist. If one works in large scale, then there has to be a place for it to go, she says. And she finds that her ideas are given credence when she offers clients designs on such diverse themes as floral motifs to banking. 'Most people prefer me to decide,' she says. Leonard's art often takes the form of textured multi-coloured murals but can also take the form of table bases, jacuzzis, flower pots, fountains and single tiles.

Happy when working within the guidelines of the design of an architect, ceramic artist **JEAN-CLAUDE DE CROUSAZ** has undertaken a number of commissions. Born in Paris in 1931 and studying ceramics in Geneva, de Crousaz has maintained his workshop in Bernex (Geneva) since 1955. He was a teacher of ceramic art from 1980 to 1996 in the schools of decorative art in Geneva and Vevey. His work has been shown in personal and group exhibitions in Europe and Asia. He writes: 'The ceramic media is the best material for decoration in architecture because it has the same permanency as stone. But the architect is the head of the project and his ideas are the most important.'

On the completion of an architectural commission for the insurance company, Provinzalversicherung, located in the Kölner Landstrasse in Düsseldorf,

Germany, Fons de Vogelaire reviewed the ceramic commissions which included the work of Carmen Dionyse, Barbara Stehr (coordinator of the project) and Jean-Claude de Crousaz. Describing the work of de Crousaz, he had this to say:

> Calligraphy, though of a figurative quality, was the stylistic device employed by Jean-Claude de Crousaz, the Geneva potter, in the bird motifs he drew on his pots. These were executed with virtuosity. Some years ago, however, he began to work in a different style: the loose strokes were replaced by a geometrical procedure in shapes and colours which allowed for movement and imagination. Barbara Stehr came to appreciate his work when, as a guest professor at her art school, de Crousaz demonstrated a variety of skills and capabilities. At her suggestion, the Provinzial asked him to decorate 24m (79ft) of the side wall of its restaurant on the right side of the entrance. This is not a single, uninterrupted surface, but a dynamic sequence of angles, short planes and long curved surfaces.

Jean-Claude de Crousaz does not improvise. His style exemplifies precise scale drawings and colour schemes, and his adaptation to the architectural reality is based on study and professional skill. In this project, the collaboration of his son, Hughes de Crousaz, proved to be of importance. De Vogelaere cites the classic work *Gödel, Escher, Bach: An Eternal Golden Braid* as having an influence on de Crousaz. In this book, Douglas R.

Hofstadter, the computer philosopher, deals with a number of characteristics that are common to Gödel's mathematics, Escher's graphics and Bach's music. These three disciplines play a role in de Crousaz's work. Not one, but three braids are involved in this wall piece. Because of the corners and the curve of the wall it is not possible to have an overall view so the work looks infinite, inviting a moving perception, an experience in time rather than in space. The braids or ribbons on the curved surface resemble the single, double or triple strokes linking the groups of rising or digital notes in a music score.

The ceramics are equally striped: white and three shades of blue form the principal motif; white, blue and red a second, and pale blue fading into white for the quiet accompaniment of the third. De Vogelaere has said:

> That a musical description is not just my interpretation, should be clear from the title of the work: Musique d'Avenir. Less obvious, though not far-fetched, is the link with Maurits Escher. The broken stripes take a form of optical illusion. The breaks or folds one perceives are actually the result of cutting the ceramic panels for technical reasons. When not at right angles but triangular, these cuts produce the effect of a slanting fold which is, in turn, reinforced by colour shifts creating the impression of light and shadow. In contrast with Stehr's spontaneous, emotional approach, de Crousaz's creation illustrates the signification of contemplation and reason in art.

Working on the Provinzalversicherung project with Jean-Claude de Crousaz, both as consultant, curator and artist, was **BARBARA STEHR**, then professor in charge at the Institute für Künstlerische Keramik, Höhr-Grenzhausen. Stehr has regularly sought architectural commissions, not only for herself but on behalf of the students at the Institute. As a ceramicist she has achieved recognition principally for her large high-fired stoneware plates on which the poured glazes achieve a pure and painterly quality. For her own ceramics at the Provinzalversicherung Insurance Company, the restaurant wall, left of the entrance, was put at her disposal. For this she coordinated a row of nine panels, each 125cm² (19¼ sq.in.) and fired to 1280°C (2336°F). Fons de Vogelaere, writing for *Neue Keramik 10/95*, describes the project:

Barbara Stehr used special Keramion-stoneware panels

Barbara Stehr, **Tile***. Provinzalversicherung, Düsseldorf, Germany.*

OPPOSITE:
Jean-Claude de Crousaz, **Musique d' Avenir***.
Wall panel. Provinzalversicherung Düsseldorf. Germany.*

from Buchtal, well known in the world of architectural ceramics. It was at this factory in Schwarzenfeld, Oberpfalz, that Stehr made her plant- and fruit-inspired work. Here her familiar glaze-pouring technique, partly due to the influence of working on a much larger format, developed into a seductive painterliness in which she discovered a new freedom in terms of both colour and gesture – a simple clarity which went far beyond the usual restrained and muted stoneware tonal range.

Exploiting the principles of watercolour painting, Stehr laid an almost white ground on the pale stoneware surface, enlivening it and the colours, especially red and yellow, which were then painted or poured on it. 'The result is a dancing language of signs, an optimistic calligraphy similar to modern Japanese although entirely Occidental in the use of colour.'

For an article on the Institute for *Ceramics: Art and Perception 3*, Joachim Kruse asked Stehr about her architectural ceramics. He reports:

In 1991, Barbara Stehr made the Bingen Column, a 4.5m (14.7ft) column with a cylindrical base, a shaft, rosette and a head, executed in the United Stoneware Works of the firm Cremer and Breuer in Frechen. The column stands in front of the youth centre on Rhine Street in the historic city centre of Bingen, a town on the Rhine about 37 miles (60 km) south of Koblenz. In 1988, she made 70 ceramic reliefs, each 50 x 50cm (19.5 x 19.5in.), variations on the theme of a circle which were mounted at prominent points on the exterior of the State Employment Office in Kiel. Designs for these reliefs were shown in the 2nd Quadriennale Internazionale, Faenza, 1987, under the general title *La Ceramica nell'arbedo urbana*. In 1990, Stehr was a participant in an international ceramics symposium in Siklós near Pecs in Hungary, where she worked with specialists from Canada, Japan, Britain, Greece and Hungary. During this period she made large ceramic sculptures – upright, compact bodies.

Kruse believes that Barbara Stehr's previous independent work in ceramics prepared her for her teaching and mentoring responsibilities. He senses that new horizons have opened up for her, enabling her to take advantage of the possibilities offered by architectural ceramics.

The Hungarian sculptor, **SANDOR KECSKEMÉTI**, now resident in Germany, is working increasingly on architectural commissions using ceramics as his chosen material. Making stacked forms and linking them together to build horizontal and vertical structures, the large-scale works appear to have been formed by nature. Gert Meijerink, a Dutch art critic, has written in *Ceramics: Art and Perception 10* about the power he finds in Kecskeméti's work. Discussing one particular work, he says:

The enormous tension has reformed the keystone to the extreme. Nevertheless, the surface makes a tawny weather-beaten impression. In some places, the surface has been perforated with tiny holes. As with the smaller objects, which usually do not exceed 30cm (12in.) each, I cannot but think of associations with man or animal shapes, but when I look at it from another angle it could also be an ancient monument as in Stonehenge, or a prehistoric temple gate.

Kecskeméti uses ceramic materials in the traditional way, glazing and firing the works until they give him the effect he seeks. These techniques are as important as the modelling itself. He loves the fire and the challenge of the alchemist's play of temperature and colour, which, despite his experience of many years, still fascinates him.

'In their peace and naturalness,' writes Meijerink,

Kecskeméti's sculptures keep aloof from the present-day Western art in which the super-nervous game of stimulating and appropriating controls the field on works of art that often have to rely on technical capability. Kecskeméti's sculptures are silent witnesses of the search for unity – unity in total shape, unity in tension. That, to me, seems the heart of his work: finding the one point in which all tensions and forces come together. You don't achieve that by working hard at it but by staying alert until the right solution comes along.

Kecskeméti continuously searches for universal solutions; he does not shy away from experiment and embraces new ideas as he finds them. The result is a tension between recognisable classical forms and the new forms of his own imagination. Realising forms in porcelain, Kecskeméti was a successful entrant for the Nyon Triennial Award in 1989. Arnold Zahner, writing about Kecskeméti's work on that occasion recognised that this artist has no fear of working with the preciousness of porcelain. 'His work is easily

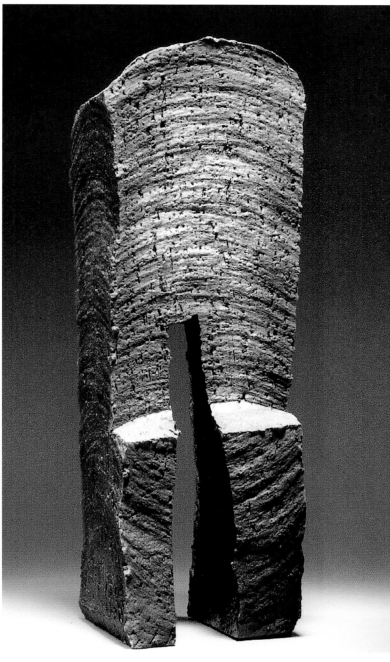

*Sandor Kecskeméti, **Broken cube**, 2003. Porcelain fired at 1380°C (2516°F). Dimensions: 28 x 10 x 10cm (11 x 4 x 4in.). Photograph by Dávid Kecskeméti.*

*Sandor Kecskeméti, **Gate**, 2001. Clay fired to 1100°C (2012°F). Dimensions: 20 x 6 x 5cm (8 x 2½ x 2in.). Photograph by Tihanyi-Bakos.*

transposed into imposing stone sculptures,' he wrote, 'but in spite of the audacity in his rough modelling of the material, he respects the delicacy of porcelain, endowing his works with nobility and grandeur.'

In her book *The Human Form in Clay*, author Jane Waller praised Keckeméti's work saying that it is filled 'with humanity and love. Each piece acts like a magnet drawing into itself qualities that come from its maker's own magnetic field: maturity of vision, wisdom and humour.' And as Kecskeméti' says: 'Different thoughts require different materials. An important rule about art is that everything is allowed.'

'Walls, like other objects, consist of surface and core,' writes Åsmund Thorkilsen, art critic and director of the Kunsterines Hus, Oslo, in a discussion about the ceramic murals of **OLE LISLERUD**.

The surface is traditionally hand-in-glove with the appearance while the core is partner to reality. The core carries the weight of the wall. The weight of the wall is carried by the bonding of the stones and bricks, by timber placed edgewise in a framework and by logs laid horizontally to form a cog. Bricks used as facing, mosaic or ceramic tiles provide no support. They are placed on the surface and their function is to articulate and decorate the wall. Lislerud's commission at the Oslo Courthouse is a unique example of an integrated and purposeful artwork. The large porcelain tiles do not appear as just a form of surface treatment. They are built into the wall so that they express the solidity that one demands of such a large building.

Lislerud has previously worked with freestanding portals and clay sculptures, and respects the construction

ABOVE: *Ole Lislerud with* **Huaxia Arch**. *Huaxia International Culture Square, Foshan, China.*

OPPOSITE
Ole Lislerud, **Lex Portalis**. *Supreme Courthouse, Oslo.*

methods inherent in building high supporting walls. 'Lislerud's architectural commission work has given ceramics a new application as a monumental contribution to art in architecture,' writes Thorkilsen. *Lex Portalis* is 33m (108ft) high, and covers the supporting column of the main room.

The construction is emphasised by the fact that the composition is black and aesthetically heaviest at the bottom, and brighter and lighter at the top. 'The symbolism is obvious. Every tile is like an appropriation of the pages in old law books. Small, rectangular openings have been created where the wall no longer needs to provide support. In these openings Lislerud has placed small sculptures. As a monumental work of art in contemporary Norwegian art history, Lislerud's architectural commission, *Lex Portalis,* shows characteristics typical of its time.' The inscription on the black porcelain is based on the Norwegian Constitution. The columns are convex at the entrance and concave on the other side. The tiles are placed in a grid, 11 tiles to the width, and cut to dimension to follow the curved walls. The staircase continues to the ninth floor.

The calligraphy at the fifth-floor level is based on the Viking Laws of Magnus Lagaboters Landslov. The design composition follows the architectural elements of the building and the shape of a portal, a theme that is varied in numerous ways.

Lislerud has completed a series of ambitious large-scale works that have been commissioned in Norway, the USA, Ireland, Germany, Japan, Mali and Turkey. He has completed a 100m² (1076sq. ft) commission for a church and feels that one of the most important recent ceramic murals he has made in the past two or three years is *Graffiti Wall – God is Woman*, at the Faculty of Divinity, University of Oslo. The art critic Janet Koplos, has written a review of Ole Lislerud's work and finds his architectural ceramics spectacular and successful. Referring to the work for the University of Oslo, she describes it as 'jarring. Here is not threat but uncertainty. On this wall, Lislerud floats various iconic images, one of them the famous outline portrait of Marilyn Monroe silkscreened by Andy Warhol … the Marilyn image is a bundle of contradictions, leading one to speculate on values, ideals and meanings.' Koplos notes that Lislerud, through his 40 public art works, is leaving his mark. One notable feature,

ABOVE AND RIGHT:: *Ole Lislerud,* **Huaxia Arch**, *2003. Stoneware. Huaxia International Culture Square, Foshan, China. Dimensions: 4 x 3.2 x 3.2m (13 x 10 ½ x 10 ½ ft).*

OPPOSITE
TOP LEFT: *Panels positioned in the kiln for firing.*
TOP RIGHT: *Transporting work in China.*
BELOW: *Working on silkscreen prints for the panels.*

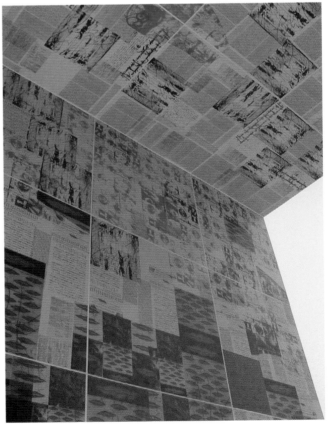

she writes, is 'Lislerud's constant provocation, through text and subtext, through imagery and iconography … integrate into architecture the contemporary expressions of photography and language.'

The art critic, Matthew Kangas, writing for *American Ceramics 12/4*, noted that Ole Lislerud, working with both sign and site, has moved his work 'a long way from the traditional Scandinavian concerns with form and surface, usefulness and perfection.' Kangas writes about Lislerud's command of space, and the opportunities for commissions from Norway's burgeoning art-in-public-places pro-gramme, citing Lislerud's *Lex Portalis* at the Oslo court-house as one of the most important and successful public

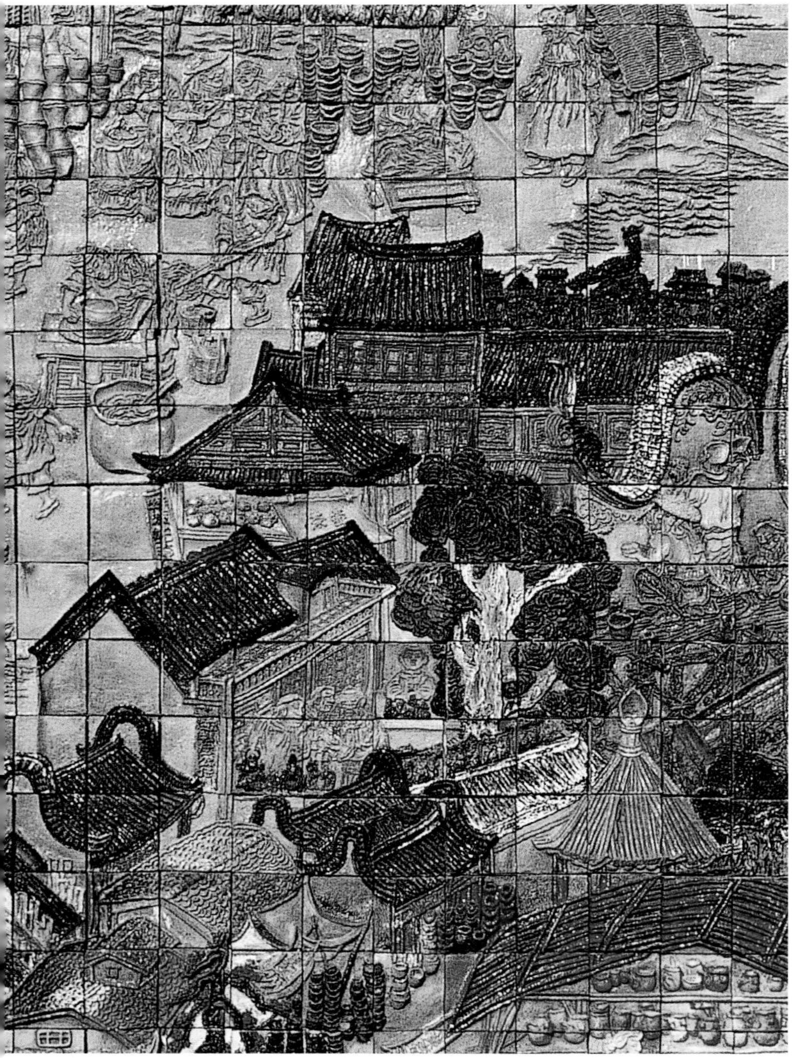

*Wenzhi Zhang, **The Historical Events of the Old Ceramic Town**, (detail of ceramic panel), 2000.*

art commissions in northern Europe to date. Lislerud acknowledges his cooperation with the selection committee, the architects and legal representatives, all necessary attitudes, he says, when realising a commission.

I-Chi Hsu, a ceramicist from Beijing and editor/publisher of the *Chinese Potters Newsletter*, writes that there are many contemporary examples of ceramics in the environment being made and installed in China. One particular work, made by **WENZI ZHANG** was unveiled in 2000. A large wood-fired ceramic panel titled *The Historical Events of the Old Ceramic Town* was installed in Shiwan, China (about 18 miles/30 km south of Guangzhou city). The panel is 17.1m (56ft) high and 6.5m (21ft) wide. It is composed of 390 (30 x 13) different ceramic pieces (57 x 50cm /22 x 19½in./ each). It was designed and made to celebrate the 500-year-old wood-firing dragon kiln, the Nanfeng Ancient Kiln, by ceramic artist Wenzi Zhang. It took Zhang three months, helped by six workers, to complete the panel. All the tiles were fired in the Nanfeng wood kiln in five groups and each firing took 24 hours. Only 12 pieces of the 390 were not fired successfully. The panel describes the ups and downs of the old ceramic town Shiwan at the end of the Ming dynasty about 500 years ago. The panel was installed in May 2000, just before the opening of the International Wood Firing Conference in Shiwan, of which Zhang was one of the organisers.

ZHU LE GENG was born in Jingdezhen, China, which the art critic, the Reverend Jung Kil Hong from the Southern Seoul Mercy Church, believes to be the world centre of ceramic art and the birthplace of porcelain. Zhu spent his sensitive teens in the chaos of the Cultural Revolution, watching his father, a famous potter, go through a time of cruel suffering and finally pass away like other artists in China at that time. Jung declares:

> In spite of this painful observation, the inherent enthusiasm toward ceramics encouraged Zhu to work with clay and to study ceramics at the Beijing Craft College. This experience enabled him to become a great ceramic artist, Zhu has won numerous awards from prestigious ceramic competitions throughout the world. This recognition also encouraged him to generate better work. He is an artist who has developed Chinese ceramics to become part of fine art. I believe that he began a new trend of ceramics.

As an artist, Zhu Le Geng is productive, and not only concerned about quality but also quantity. His work reflects the sense of metaphysical expression found in Chinese ink paintings and decorative glazed ceramics so that we are aware that his work is based on traditional Chinese art. 'Whoever appreciates his ceramics would feel that the work is truly Chinese,' says Jung.

> Yet his work is also regarded as contemporary art. Zhu believes that we often see many artists simply follow the conventional way or believe that Western pottery is the modern ceramic art even though European and American artists have denied their traditions to develop contemporary

Zhu Le Geng, **Wandering Between Time and Space** *(detail). Ceramic side panels. Wheat Auditorium.*
Dimensions: 2 x 4m (6 ½ x 13ft).

ceramics. However, Zhu Le Geng is able to create the most contemporary art yet it is still traditional. He continues to create prolific, unique and different work.

Although Zhu has built his career in a traditional and sound way, he finds a new direction each time. 'There are many architectural works complemented by oil paintings and sculptures, some of which are regarded as the mainstream of Western art. However the core of Oriental art – ink paintings and ceramics – has not been part of contemporary life so far. Zhu Le Geng decided to try something new in architecture, 'although we are not used to applying ceramics on buildings in the East – [we have] only the experience to adapt the decorative patterns of *Danchung* into architecture'. In his *The Light for Life* work, Zhu Le Geng achieved a high level in architectural art. He accepts ceramics as itself to make harmony with the interior of the building.'

Zhu's work, *The Light for Life* is 8m (26ft) high and 17m (55 ¾ ft) wide.

It reveals the image of life and leads the viewer to be moved by its mysterious atmosphere. Zhu understands what is the most effective way to work with clay and fully fills the wall. In another most impressive work he adorned a great music hall using ceramics. Although ceramics is theoretically known as an ideal material for acoustic multi-reflection, Zhu created a beautiful sound from the material. The character of clay is intimate, quiet and comfortable.

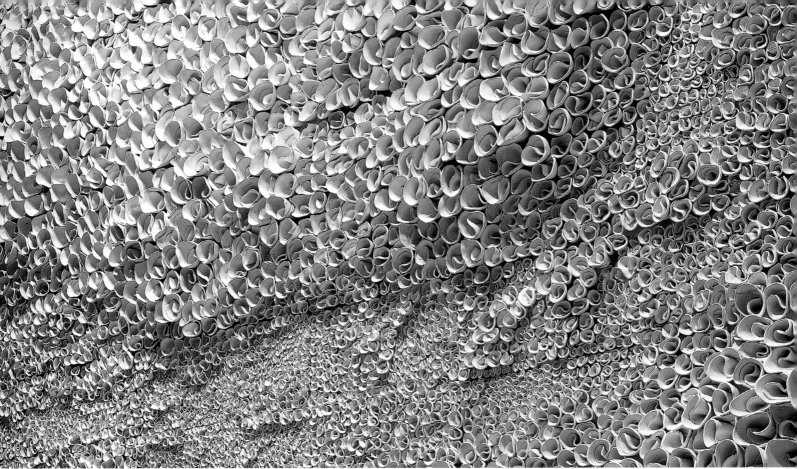

Jung writes that Zhu is able to make a peaceful aura in a stone building or in a brick church but is also able to enhance the sounds and the echo effect from his ceramic walls. 'I believe that Zhu's walls are masterpieces in the history of ceramic art. His *Wandering between Time and Space* mural in the theatre was completed in the scale of 54 tonnes of clay; it is like a ceramic palace. He tries to show the whole beauty of ceramics such as the aesthetics of pictorial art, crafts and structure and even of function. This project contains all these.'

The Reverend Jung writes that many new buildings will be constructed now in the East and he hopes that ceramic artists will be able to take part in environmental art such as Zhu Le Geng undertook for these projects. Jung believes that Zhu was able to make ceramics a part of architecture. 'There is no doubt that *Wandering Between Time and Space* proves that ceramics can be utilised as a material for acoustic reflection yet, at the same time, be visually beautiful – a masterpiece also celebrating the opening of the Milal Art Museum.'

SUSAN TUNICK, an artist living in New York City, has undertaken many commissions for murals and freestanding works that incorporate the use of her mosaic tiles. One such work was *Weeping Rock*, commissioned to create a site-specific piece for an estate in Westchester County, NY. The challenge was to make a richly coloured sculpture that was visible from the entrance but that did not overpower the landscape. As homage to the site, this two-part sculpture has ceramic mosaic sides and a cedar top. Most of the ceramic pieces are in the shape of moulded leaves. In some cases individual leaves from the gardens were impressed directly into clay to create unique forms. Additional ceramic elements include the initials of the owners and tiny porcelain chopstick holders depicting vegetables such as eggplants, beets and snowpea pods. The colour scheme on the front of the piece is a bold combination of pinks, reds, greens, blues and purples, while the back, with earthy glazes, mimics the colour and texture of the rocks, lichen and foliage.

The NY Metropolitan Transportation Authority in its Arts for Transit programme commissioned Susan Tunick to create works for the Prospect Park and Parkside Avenue stations on the Brighton line, also for

ABOVE: *Zhu Le Geng, working on a large wall piece, forming the individual pieces on tiles, and applying colour.*

OPPOSITE: *Zhu Le Geng, **The Light for Life**.*

turnstile areas located in the above-ground head houses that were built in 1919. The wall tiles and decorative borders were influenced by the Arts and Crafts Movement, popular at the time. For the walls in redesigned areas of these renovated stations, Tunick has created intricate, multicoloured ceramic mosaic murals and borders. Her art celebrates the old ceramic ornamentation in the station and is inspired by her fascination with terracotta and her childhood memories of nearby Prospect Park and the Brooklyn Botanic Garden. Tunick says her works for the sites, collectively titled *Brighton Clay Re-Leaf 1-3*, balance her respect for the stations' ceramic history, her recollections of the colours and shapes of the foliage in the park and garden, and her desire to add eye-catching modern design. Her designs on the walls of the Parkside station and the two entrances to the Prospect Park station are textured blankets of ceramic leaves, buds and berries, modelled on the willow, oak, sycamore and maple trees growing nearby. 'To maintain links with the stations' artistic past, I cast the leaves in colours that correspond to the original glazes of the tiles,' Tunick says. Her palette includes 40 shades of blues and greens at Prospect Park and 40 mustard and burnt orange hues at Parkside. The leafy murals are set on a background of ivory tiles, some vintage or restored and some made by modern tile-maker Lisa Portnoff. 'Although *Brighton Clay Re-Leaf* is a contemporary work,' says Tunick, 'it is a tribute to the artistic vocabulary that has served these stations well. For the passenger, it should strike an unconscious chord of unity, the happy marriage of old and new.' Tunick also worked with the architectural firm William Nicholas Bodouva to design exterior fencing for Parkside station.

Susan Tunick holds BA and MFA degrees from Bennington College. Widely known for her creations in architectural terracotta, she is also a lecturer, author and president of the Friends of Terra Cotta. She has received numerous awards, including a special citation from the American Institute of Architects and five grants from the New York State Council on the Arts. Her ceramic sculpture has been exhibited at Hebrew Union College, the Municipal Arts Society and Snug Harbor Cultural Center.

In an interview with Lenore Newman, decorative arts historian, reported in *Ceramics: Art and Perception 42*,

Susan Tunick spoke of her interest in colour, surface texture and pattern, and also space – both real and perceived.

> The wall reliefs, made up of hexagonal elements, range from small works with only two or three hexagons to larger ones with more than 20. The repetition of these forms relates to traditional uses of tile but the activity on the surface of each piece varies considerably. Within each relief, the design moves from hexagon to hexagon so that overall patterns are created. These patterns allow for different spatial readings and an interplay of figure and ground. In addition, the physicality of the hexagons, their thickness and their edges, and the carving within these forms play important roles in the evolution of each wall relief.

Tunick starts with a general sense of the entire piece – the number of units and their placement – making many drawings before she begins. This is important because after each hexagon is made it needs to be carved or incised with shapes in a specific way so that it will fit into the pattern.

> The colour relationships are not explored until I form, carve and bisque fire the hexagons for a particular work. Then I assemble the pieces on the floor and start to explore the glaze possibilities. This includes thinking about the value and texture of the glaze, as well as the glossiness of its surface. For the first glaze firing, I often leave sections of the bisque unglazed, coating some areas of each hexagon. In subsequent firings, these areas will be glazed, or they might not require it because I have decided to cover them with inset tiles or clay bands.

The kiln is an integral part of the working process.

> I respond to the result of each firing and decide what new colours or inset elements might lead the piece in the direction in which I want to see the work move. The colour builds up over a series of firings. The insetting of materials – which is really a variation on collage – has always been part of the creative process. When I started using ceramic mosaic shards on wooden sculptural forms I found it necessary to expand the colour range of my shards which came mostly from smashed commercial tableware. This was when I began making my own 'shards' or shapes to be incorporated into the mosaic surfaces. Clay's properties seem so special to me – how it starts out malleable and is ultimately so hard, and how varied the colour opportunities can be through either the exposed

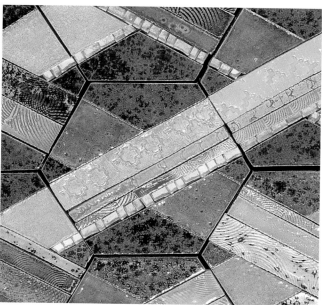

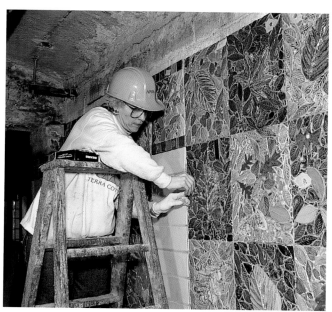

TOP: *Susan Tunick,* **Three Times Three,** *2002. Public School 222, Queens, NY.*
ABOVE LEFT: *Susan Tunick,* **24 Golden Hexagons** *(detail).*
ABOVE RIGHT: *Susan Tunick, work in progress. Prospect Park Subway. Photographs by Peter Mauss/Esto.*

*Susan Tunick, **Weeping Rock**. Westchester, NY. Two 2.4m (7¾ft) long sections.
Photograph by Peter Mauss/Esto.*

clay body or the use of glaze. Clay allows one to address two- and three-dimensional issues. When I became interested in clay surfaces in architecture during the early 1980s, I was mostly painting. Eventually I moved back into ceramics. I think that looking at architecture has been an important source for me both directly and indirectly. Looking at buildings from the street, on scaffolding, with binoculars or through a camera lens has forced me to be aware of scale and surface articulation. In a moment, as the sun goes behind a cloud, the change in shadows which results can completely alter the look of a façade. The edges, varied depth of the architectural components, the wealth of ornamentation and how these relate to the building's design, are of interest to me.

Tunick finds that looking at architecture helps her understand the spatial problems of site-specific commissions. 'For a successful outcome, it is necessary to study all aspects of an environment into which an installation will be integrated. This is true for indoor work, such as the project I executed for a New York City public school in Queens, and the outdoor commissions, some of which have been in wooded landscapes.' Tunick says that she doesn't operate with specific goals.

Usually I feel that I am following behind my work, being

led by it rather than leading it. However, I am interested in seeing ceramics reintegrated into our environment. I mean this in the broadest sense – into the landscape, into our interiors and into the façades of new buildings. I would love to see ceramicists collaborate with professionals in other disciplines – architects, engineers and manufacturers of tile, brick and terracotta. If this occurred frequently, I think it would definitely elevate the level of what is created.

Working with clay within an urban setting over a number of years through a series of public art projects in Tasmania has involved **PENNY SMITH** in a collaboration with the Tasmanian Art for Public Buildings Scheme (APBS), established 25 years ago. The first of its kind in Australia, the APBS demonstrated a visionary understanding of the way in which art works can enrich both public buildings and spaces in the public arena, and enhance the general public's access to, and understanding of, contemporary art in all its diversity. The APBS is based on the agreed principle that 2% of the pre-tender estimate for all new state government buildings and renovations is allocated for the purchase and commissioning of art works. The upper limit on art works for each project is $40,000 and only Tasmanian resident artists can be employed under the programme.

Smith believes clay is particularly suited as a versatile and permanent medium for translation and interpretation into the public arena. In the projects she has been involved with, not only has fired clay been used as an integral element within the art work itself, but many of the making techniques associated with ceramics have also been applied to other mediums. She writes:

In my own case, the use of moulds and the multiple dominate both technical and aesthetic approaches. The brief for the Woodbridge High School, Silverwater, in 1992, was based on the requirement for a decorative outside wall feature that would enhance the new wing of the school that was attached to the original entrance way. It also had to disguise the join between the extension and the original building and allow for any possible settling of the new.

The theme for this project was drawn from the local environment – that of the nearby Silverwater Bay, which

Penny Smith, **Morphology,** *2002. Howrah Primary School.*

during the ebb and flow of its tidal cycle, left behind a series of ribbed sand impressions. These patterns were used as the textural theme in making a simple three-dimensional 'L' shaped form from which to make slipcast moulds. These stoneware forms provided a basic unit that could be repeated in a number of different configurations against the painted backdrop of an ordinary brick wall. The units interlocked to create a solid mass, and provided a corner feature to conceal some ugly downpipes, or they could be used individually to create a sense of animation and to highlight the corner of a window.

Penny Smith. **Wapping History Wall,** *1996–98. Hobart, Tasmania.*

Penny Smith comments:

The Wapping History Wall for the Hobart City Council, 1996–1998, started as a public competition that John Smith, Milan Milojevic and I worked on. Unlike another project that involved the architect and the school, this had to be passed before the Hobart City Council's Lord Mayor and Aldermen: architects, engineers, plumbers, electricians, building contractors and local businesses. The project was secured by presenting a series of scale models, computer drawings, engineers' specifications, artist's renderings, costings and a confident air.

The Wapping History Wall is an interpretative art work that was based upon the artists' historical perspective of old Hobart's Wapping site. The overall format of the work referred to the suggestion of geological strata that emerge from the ground, inspired by Hobart's dominant and long extinct volcano, Mount Wellington.

Each of these strata carries forms of illustrative narratives and textures in a range of media that invokes historical reflections of the past. While fired clay was an important medium in this project, it was in the similarities of the working methods and properties of both slipcast clay and poured concrete that mould-making became the dominant working approach. It had long been apparent to me that liquid concrete and clay slip were of similar compositions. Both can be described as being made up of aggregates and water that require movement to keep them in suspension and a chemical reaction to cause them to set, thus becoming permanent.

This approach to mould-making was adopted from the outset – from the preparation and pouring of the concrete into the foundation footings on-site, to the off-site casting of the individual blocks. Each pre-cast concrete block incorporated a recessed plane that would allow the printed metal plates and the fired ceramic to sit within it. This required that a special clay body be made up that not only fulfilled the requirements of outdoor weather extremes, but allowed for the correct amount of shrinkage to fit into the concrete block recesses after firing. Press-moulds were made that incorporated numerous textural references from the local environment (for example, gravestones, ironwork, tools or shards). Clay was used in the form of traditional brickwork and floor tiles. In the latter instance, several hundred ceramic floor tiles were purchased and screenprinted with decal inks and fired to stoneware temperatures to provide the base for the water feature. This project was described in *Ceramics Art and Perception 36.*

The brief for *Morphology* at the Howrah Primary School, undertaken in 2002, called for an artwork for the walls of the 15.3 x 2m (49 x 6½ft), pre-cast concrete units that form a covered pathway between two separate schools. Howrah Primary and Howrah Infant Schools are situated some distance apart from each other but on the same campus. They needed to be seen as connected in some way to reflect the school's newly formed unity.

John Smith and I attempted to solve the problems of the campus' physical separation through visual textural integration. We did this by the gradual combination of the words that made up the two school titles within a grid format across all 15 panels. Like a playful word puzzle or Scrabble game, the letters form simple (from the infant

school end) to more complex words (the primary school end) that can be read both vertically and horizontally.

This project provided the opportunity to apply the techniques of ceramic slipcasting on a large scale through the use of cast concrete within a controlled factory setting to produce a series of pre-cast decorative units with architectural application.

A number of textural and letter-shaped form-ply (the standard industry medium for concrete casting) panels were CNC routered by a furniture factory. Each panel comprised a series of simple diagonal lines or letterforms that were secured on to the steel casting tables at the factory prior to each cast. Once the cast panel was removed, the form-ply mould forms were cleaned, re-laid and the next panel re-cast in a production cycle that produced all 15 panels over a three-week period.

Penny Smith, in her studio – work in progress.

C H A P T E R   S E V E N

Enhancing and Inspired by the Natural Environment

CLAUDE **A**LBANA **P**RESSET, from Geneva, Switzerland, has installed ceramic works in gardens with the purpose of adding a piece of poetry to the space. One of these works, *Black River*, is set near flowers in her own garden; another is the salt-glazed brown column with the story of a river from sky to ocean in the courtyard. It is the natural environment which has particular appeal for her. Invited to ClaySculpt, Gulgong, she built a garden seat based on the design of her grandmother's favourite chair. Built of separate blocks, these were salt-glazed after being painted with coloured slips; one of the blocks is inscribed with a poem. The form of a yellow shawl is casually draped across one corner. This chair is now placed under a group of trees facing the eastern hills, an ideal setting for contemplation. Another project was a turquoise river column installed in a stone and concrete space of a garden in Lausanne, Switzerland, in June 1998. She writes about further projects: 'My work with the concept of a clay carpet is a continuing one. These clay tile-carpets are part of a sand garden or placed in nature near a river to focus a place to rest, to meet friends; they could be settled on the flat roofs of buildings with sand or gravel. Ceramic is a suitable material for small gardens, terraces or patios, and has an intimate relationship for forms in the leafy space.' The idea of the clay carpet came from her intention to use all the various possibilities of colour, decorative techniques and texture possible in ceramic materials, to express luxurious ornaments made of stoneware to be placed outdoors under various climatic changes.

Presset says she would like to inscribe a poem, with its vocabulary inspired

PRESSET

BROVOLD-HAGEN

RUDD

DEJONGHE

LAMBERCY

YAMAMURA

McLEAN

SORENSEN

OPPOSITE: *Bernard Dejonghe, **Shark Tooth**, 1992. Glazed stoneware. Dimensions: 85 x 85 x 25cm (33½ x 33½ x 10in.).*

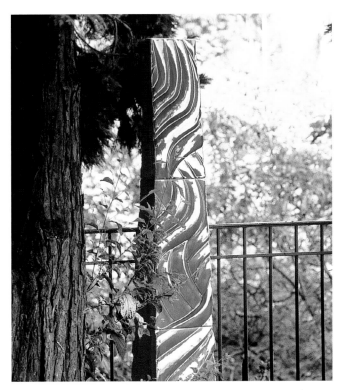

*Claude Presset, **Turquoise column**. Three elements pressed in plaster moulds. Copper and alkaline glaze. Oxidation fired at 1040°C (1904°F). Lausanne, Switzerland.*

*Claude Presset, **River of Water** (detail). Stonware bricks with coloured slips and celadon glaze held by a metallic structure. Reduction fired at 1280°C (2336°F). Installed in stairwell of Graduate Institute of Development Studies, Geneva. Dimensions (each brick): 20 x 35cm (8 x 13¾ in.).*

by nature, written on clay tablets which, by their way of fabrication, relate to specific houses, walls or architectures. The piece, *Black River,* was an attempt to express the flow of a river, which, by its black and matt texture, enables us to appreciate all the changes of seasonal colours, and the shadows or the light of the day. The turquoise river column, also made by pressing clay into plaster moulds, and using white slip with sgraffito, describes the lines of a stream on the modelled shape. The turquoise colour of the glaze was chosen to give depth to the river. Another sculptural environmental work situated in Lausanne takes on the shape and colour in a garden, and is destined to be a path for meditation and retreat for an organisation devoted to peace and religious understanding. Seven musical pots – made from smoke-fired thrown earthenware – were placed in the landscape architecture. These were made for J. L. Borgeaud for a project located in a grotto where drops of water produce music and rhythm. Water is a dominant theme in the work of Presset because she believes that water, its use

and preservation, will be a major issue for the future. A 2004 project, a work measuring 20m (65 ½ ft) in height, is placed in the six-floor high stairwell of a building still under construction, the Graduate Institute of Development Studies in Geneva where the students will research, among other things, worldwide water problems. The theme is, again, a river of water from the sky to the sea; its form is a double-sided column of carved, moulded and coloured stoneware. The 47 panels are held upright by a metal structure at the centre of a semi-circular space.

With four students in ceramics from Ecole des Arts Decoratif of Geneva, Presset participated in a summer event in Lausanne, Jardin '97, to create installations for small outdoor locations. The idea was to make a ceramic 'embroidery' with multiples and displayed differently according to the spirit of each garden. One project was to suggest a river in an established French classical garden. Black matt stoneware bowls, full of clear water, were arranged on a surface of black gravel. Another project in this series, an 'embroidery' made of 76 stoneware thrown pots planted with wild strawberries, filled a small courtyard. In an article for *Ceramics Technical 6*, Presset outlined the various student projects and the reasoning behind them. The students worked together to realise several projects, cooperating with authorities from the City of Lausanne and within the specifications of the Jardin '97 event.

Claude Presset has worked in Japan, Africa and India, studying the ceramics of the different regions and documenting what she found. A three-year project working with the Tiwi people in northern Australia has enabled her, on separate visits each of six weeks or so, to assist in the promotion of the indigenous talents of Australian Aborigines. As a teacher and ceramic artist working with environmental projects, her passionate interest is to discover the natural beauty of the landscape, its peoples and artefacts, and work with these elements in her own research.

KARI BROVOLD-HAGEN's sand-casting technique can be likened to the action of water during a flood. The Norwegian ceramicist says:

> In my ceramic work, as well as in my life, nature is my main source of inspiration. As long as I can remember I have been involved with environment protection. As a human being I am aware of the negative effects we have made to the balance of nature and the consequences, if we are not able, or willing, to change our course. We have the knowledge, but we must use it in the right way. My philosophy is to respect clay and nature.

Working with these two important perceptions has given her the opportunity, she believes, to draw on her experience to use ceramic processes for her personal development, 'hopefully, to become a better ceramicist. However, as an artist, I have the freedom and opportunity to make as many disasters in my studio as I like, depending on what I want to express. That is why I think that the process is as important as the object itself.' She writes:

> Sand-casting has afforded me a way of recapturing immediacy in my clay work. For 16 years, until 1988, the potter's wheel had been my most important piece of equipment. In common with most Norwegian ceramicists, I was trained at one of the important art schools in the country – the National Institute of Art and

Design in Oslo. After four years of study, I moved back to my rural home district, where I established my own studio. The 1960 concept of Scandinavian design had an influence on Norwegian ceramicists. The idea was to make beautiful objects as cheaply as possible to enrich the lives of as many people as possible. But the legacy of clean-lined functionalism led to a block in the creative development of my work, and I had to make a determined effort to sort it out. I decided to return to school to earn a master's degree in ceramics.

Brovold-Hagen began using the technique of sand-casting vessels in 1988, when she saw a brazier casting brass mortars at a local fair and she wondered if she could adapt the technique to porcelain.

> In order to be sure I didn't miss out on anything that could be used to solve the technical problems of the process, I searched out iron foundries where sand-casting is traditionally practised. Subsequently, I learnt to cast in

Kari Brovold-Hagen, tiles in Hvam Upper secondary school, 2004. Dimensions: 245 x 28cm (95½ x 11in.).

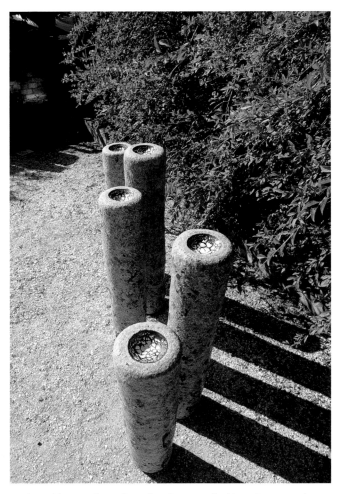

*Rick Rudd, **Set of Bowls**. Raku clay. Installed in private garden.*

bronze and brass as well. During this stage of the technique, new and unexpected expressions kept developing. This stimulated my curiosity and gave me the enthusiasm and the will to go on.

Kari Brovold-Hagen describes the process:

Moulds are made from various kinds of sand adjusted according to the effects you want to attain – the finer the sand the faster it dries. To the sand, I add bentonite, oil and water, in that order. When added in small quantities (approximately 3-5%) the bentonite acts as a binder and the mould retains its form. With the addition of oil, less water is needed; also, there is less dust in the air and the sand can be removed quickly and easily from the clay form. I use as little water as possible in the sand. Too much causes slow drying and cracks in the clay. Too little can result in the mould collapsing causing damage to the casting. When the sand can be pressed into a ball, the moisture content is correct. The mould is shaped from sand that has been packed

firmly into a wooden box. Tamping the sand avoids collapse when the wooden box is removed. Any tool (from the studio, kitchen or garden) can be used to shape the sand to the desired form. Before pouring in porcelain slip, I sprinkle a layer of talc into the cavity.

Because the sand absorbs a little water from the slip, the side that is open to the air dries more quickly – opposite to casting in a plaster mould. For this reason, I have electric heaters in the floor in my studio. To avoid the sunlight causing uneven drying, it is necessary to cover the windows with blinds during the summertime. Two doors can be opened to let the moist air out and allow fresh air in; this is beneficial for both the work and me. The floor inclines slightly to a flat drain so that it can easily be cleaned by hosing. The length of time that passes before excess slip can be removed varies, depending on the room's warmth, the sand's moisture content and whether a sufficiently thick layer of clay has adhered to the side of the mould. When satisfied with the casting, I ladle out the slip, just like soup, and then sponge away any excess that remains on the bottom. Once the cast clay has begun to harden, I open the wooden sandbox as quickly as possible; this allows more air in and hastens the drying process. Next, I remove the sand, little by little, from the cast form. Because the mould falls away from the cast object, there is no problem with undercutting. This opens up greater possibilities for variations in surface treatment.

Many artists using casting or handforming techniques with porcelain strive to achieve translucency and whiteness. Brovold-Hagen takes a different approach. 'While it is possible to sand-cast with those objectives, I don't aim for them because they are not important to my artistic intentions. My work is still what can be called applied art, but utility has become less important to me than decorative expression and by using sand-casting I have been able to retain spontaneity in my work.'

The commissions Brovold-Hagen has undertaken in Norway have included, Hebergheimen, Kongsvinger (1978); Sparebanken Nord, Årnes (1981); Nylænne Aktivitetssenter, Årnes (1985); the City Hall of Nes County, Årnes (1996); the Adminstration building at Kollsnes, Hordaland (1995); in the county of Hedmark, (1995); Brårud Primary school, Nes (2000), in the county of Hedmark (2001); and the House of Culture in Nes (2001). The latest commission so far is Hvam Upper secondary school, Nes (2004). She has also been involved as a consultant, advising on public works.

*Rick Rudd, **Bowl**. Raku clay.*

RICK RUDD has undertaken a number of commissions for garden pieces. His large works grace many sites in Auckland and his home town, Wanganui, in New Zealand. His training in ceramics was at Great Yarmouth and Wolverhampton colleges of art in England, where he increasingly became interested in sculptural work. The figure has also become of inspiration to him. His latest work takes the bowl and the vessel as a basis but he extends these into large-scale pieces in a progression of ideas, unlimited by size or space. Working slowly, he may take weeks to complete one form, nevertheless enjoying the physical and structural demands made upon his energy. Using local clays, often heavily textured with grog, he handbuilds his pieces in a process of coiling, pinching and scraping. His statement: 'I take the bowl and vessel for my inspiration and interpret them through form and texture,' is corroborated by Cecilia Parkinson and John Parker in their text *From Profiles – 24 NZ Potters* (1988). 'Rudd's training in ceramics was inclined towards sculptural rather than domestic ware and from 1978 to mid–1986 was raku fired, each piece an exercise in line and form. Since then it has been more figurative, with inspiration taken from the human body, but still with the emphasis on form and line.'

Rudd describes the process:

My materials are deliberately limited to three commercially prepared NZ clays, with grog added for texture rather than strength. At present I use only two glazes: a clear crackle glaze and the same one with 10% commercial black stain added. This small range of materials is enough to give contrast between smooth, heavily textured or shiny surfaces, with the natural colour of the clay showing in most pieces. Spring-steel scrapers are used to bring up the texture with the grog that has been added to the clay, and certain areas are then smoothed for glazing. Shapes evolve rather than begin as separate ideas and time is taken in developing new forms.

In a review of Rudd's work at the Auckland gallery, Masterworks, Howard Williams wrote for the *Auckland Herald* in 1993: 'Masterworks lives up to its name with this exhibition of nine works from a master in his field. Rick Rudd has a national reputation for his single-minded development of raku-fired ceramic sculpture which he now explores on a much larger scale.' Pieces ranged to 1.5m (5ft) high, fired in a purpose-built kiln. Williams writes:

Three works are formal or classical in conception. Square or tubular plinths taper gently upward, each to present a votive bowl supported delicately – even precariously – on egg shapes or spheres. The main colour is matt black or grey with a textured soft surface but the bowls have intense concentrations of crackle white glaze, or deep blue shot with black. A more recently explored direction comes in pieces where boulder shapes are stacked on top of each other seemingly defying gravity, again supporting dished bowls as offering containers.

After receiving a QEII Arts Council major creative development grant in order to experiment with new glazes and make a body of large works for an ex-hibition, Rudd was able to realise many of the ideas he sought. Writing in an article titled 'Is There Life After Raku?' in *New Zealand Potter 1/1994*, he stated: '

I have worked with clay for more than 25 years but have never tested individual compounds to see what happens to them. I began test firings to find out how materials react at certain temperatures. I made tiles with raised sides, mixed each of the different glaze components I could find and painted them on the tiles. I knew I would be applying glazes this way rather than dipping or spraying. I had decided to fire to a maximum temperature of 1150°C (2102°F), so I removed some from the kiln at regular intervals. I had no fixed ideas of what I was looking for except that I wanted textural glazes in black, white or grey. Once I considered a glaze test was worth taking further, I tested it on a spherical piece. After a year of glaze testing I found the direction I was looking for. Now I have a box of 500 test tiles and more questions than answers. The large works I wanted to make were more than a metre tall and some almost a metre wide, and were all

pinched and coiled. A few needed internal structures to support them and some were made as separate com-ponents and assembled after firing.

Rick Rudd claims that this journey has been inter-esting, depressing, elating, disappointing and exciting, but never boring. 'There are more large pieces I want to make and several more glazes to work on,' he says and he plans to place more of his large-scale works in the environment at the same time as developing his materials and processes. More recently he has been making a series of pieces called *Waterworks*. These are fountains, large pieces with water flowing over them.

'It is surprising to note how **BERNARD DEJONGHE**'s sculptures, whether large or small and set in nature, come into close contact with their environment,' wrote Michel Nitabah in 1993, for a catalogue on the work of this French artist. 'Having a close harmony with nature, it seems as if it was quite normal for his sculptures to be there and yet they challenge us aggressively where the artist takes possession of the landscape. Perhaps these factors help us understand the meaning of his work.' By placing his larger sculptures on the top of a mountain or on the bed of a river, Dejonghe draws our attention to the site and forces us to discover these places anew.

Bernard Dejonghe's sculptures are made from clay or glass which need heat to give them their final shape. The material when vitrified attains a free expression which releases the energy we feel in stones and rocks, weathered by the wind and water and dependent on the natural hazards of the climate. For this reason Dejonghe chooses simple shapes which come from the parallelepiped, the sphere, the cylinder or the cone, and where the surface marks show a direct relationship with the artist and the material.

Jean-Louis Maunoury, quoted in the same catalogue, believes there has never been a fixed state for matter. 'Therefore, lift up a stone of water, make iron translucent, liquefy the air, freeze fire, make crystals out of light. Bernard Dejonghe is like Vulcan at his forge, with his kilns and his computer, with the same age-old desire. It is from the dormant state of the gods that we get our dreams.'

However, Dejonghe says that he prefers simple

Bernard Dejonghe, working in the studio.

shapes. Writing at the time of his 1996 exhibition at Dunkirke Musée d'Art Contemporain, he noted:

> The forms that I have been experimenting with are always simple. More than just geometric forms – circles, triangles and lines – they are concentrated forms, human signs, that I repeat in differing variations depending on my moods or the possibilities available. Repetition can also be a way of neutralising the problem of form in favour of observing the varying phenomena of transforming materials – an

access to the notion of chance. The notions of pleasure and liberty count a great deal in this type of decision.

Dejonghe says that he does not begin a work with a predetermined form in mind, preferring to combine the conceptual with the material. In an article for *Kerameiki Techni 27* in 1997, Genevieve Boudon wrote that although Dejonghe's works have their roots in tradition and are related to the work of ancient masters,

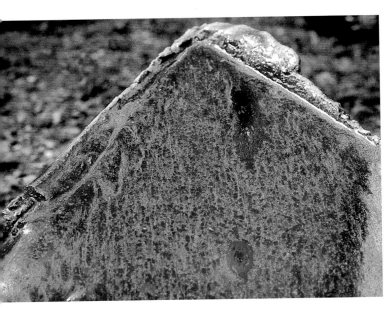

Bernard Dejonghe, **Red Pyramid**, *1981. Glazed stoneware. Dimensions: 30 x 30 x 40cm (11¾ x 11¾ x 15½ in.).*

OPPOSITE PAGE
ABOVE: *Bernard Dejonghe,* **Vertical Blue**, *1986. Glazed stoneware. Dimensions: 1.3 x 6 x 6m (4¼ x 19½ x 19½ ft).*

BELOW: *Bernard Dejonghe,* **Blue in Grass**, *1986. Glazed stoneware.*

the artist uses modern scientific knowledge and technology 'to address people of his era. The heavy material, the massive stonewares, these works have a boundless beauty which springs from specific elements of the material and their colour.'

Bernard Dejonghe has been working with ceramics since 1960. His studio in the Maritimes Alps in France, a dramatic landscape of huge mountains and intense sky, contains both his ceramic and glass workshops. He has won distinctions and awards for his work in both media, and his work is represented in museums throughout Europe and Asia. In an article in *Ceramics: Art and Perception 1,* Julia Davis writes of Dejonghe's response to landscape and his commissioned work which requires dealings with architects. She also outlined some of the techniques he employs. 'His ceramic works are made by pressing the clay into large wooden moulds. Long firing schedules and heavy equipment are needed. A large wood-firing three-chambered kiln, favoured for its irregularities and its power is used for his ceramic pieces and each stage of the preparation and installation requires a group of assistants.' Enjoying, as he says

'courting limits,' Françoise de l'Epine writing on Dejonghe (*Ceramics: Art and Perception 19*) calls him an artist-explorer whose works have the ability to open and outline the space they occupy. Dejonghe has undertaken numerous architectural projects and his research has often meant that several years are spent working with the same glaze, bringing it to its maximum intensity. 'I am looking for purity,' Dejonghe is quoted as saying by l'Epine in her article. She continues: 'He likes to smelt materials, to create timeless forms... that which interests him is not the superficial aspect, the beauty of a particular form or colour but the presence which emanates through the density of the materials and the refraction of the light as well as the energy which they give forth.'

Jean Luc Olivié, Curator of the Art Decorative Museum, Paris, wrote in the catalogue for Dejonghe's 1995 exhibition at the museum:

Art in the West has built its culture on the idea that man is placed in the centre of the universe, controlling everything and explaining things he does not understand in whatever manner suits him best. We have moved away from the fundamental values of nature, locking ourselves in an artificial and virtual modernity; we have lost the notion that life is equally physical and that, in all domains, we create meaning with the materials as much as with the spiritual.

Jean Luc Olivié quotes Dejonghe himself:

I have settled here, on this mountain, to experience an everyday life of nature and geological rhythms that help me find a sense of equilibrium. The studio is a space I built taking into consideration work patterns, circulation of light, and my own movement depending on my different activities and their required concentration. I do not like disorder in the studio. There has to be a certain control over the space, as with meditation, an ease that may take me further than the gesture itself. I don't work on the object for a result alone, but on an intuition, a force that surpasses the object and drives back the limits of its form.

My studio is in nature. Nature enters my studio. Silence and nature's sounds permeate my work. I am what I have done; it is as if what I've done runs before me. It's not me who defines or decides. I am what escapes me. There is a strong awareness of time due to rhythmic transformation of materials, gestures that become a reflection on time, on the length of time: precise periods when the

clay dries, stacks of wood cut years ago, the repetition of firings, the lengthy cooling of the glass after sharp rises in temperature. All of this easily takes place in silence.

Dejonghe has always been conscious of man being a part of the mineral universe.

> Since the beginning of my work in clay in 1968, I have always approached the material as if it were a field of possibilities, a base for experimentation and reflection. I give no more importance to concept than to the material itself: each contributes to setting something I call energies.
>
> The years spent working on these materials, that the uninitiated might call inert, have brought me the idea of constant movement in the universe: nothing is fixed. Ceramics and glass are composed of minerals that we mix and fire in different ways depending on what we're looking for or trying to obtain. The fusion of minerals has become the constant in my work, placed before form, colour, or installation on specific sites.

Something Dejonghe often thinks about is the question of exactness, similar to the *satori* in Japanese Zen: that particular moment when the condition is right. For what reason, and when, should we consider an object or an action correct, to what state of equilibrium or imbalance are we referring? 'The same glaze can be fired to different temperatures, at different speeds, in different atmospheres and give a thousand different results. There's a particular moment, or several brief moments, when our eyes or mind find satisfaction; there are even more times or states of mind when this satisfaction is not enough or too much. Why? What does this mean?'

For Dejonghe, the matter he works with is always subjected to fire, writes Jean Luc Olivié.

> For him, fire is not a law to respect or a constraint to be mastered but an accomplice to converse with. Energy is also mechanical, directly linked to consequences of gravity, whether it be a question of setting works into place by aligning them or curving horizontals, suspending them in space, raising them up vertically or any other gesture which, in the sculptor's studio, displaces weight, compacts masses in the confines of moulds, lightens wood into embers, ashes and smoke. This in-depth play with energies of fire that transforms, or forces that shape and displace masses even on the scale of landscape – intersects with the tradition of the 'Arts du Feu' and the problems raised by sculpture in the course of the 20th century.

PHILIPPE LAMBERCY, recognised artist and teacher from Geneva, Switzerland, was commissioned to execute a large stoneware mural for the City of Geneva Observatory in Sauverny. In the book *Ceramics of the Twentieth Century*, by Tamara Preaud and Serge Gautier, Lambercy's role as a ceramicist and teacher are noted, as are the large number of architectural works he has completed. Working with the existing vegetation of the site as an integral part of the composition, Lambercy's walls have always been conceived as part of the natural environment even though some of his walls extend 10m (33ft) into the garden. At a major retrospective exhibition at Musée Ariana, Geneva, in 1999, Philippe Lambercy was honoured for his 50 years as a ceramic artist. Roland Blättler, exhibition curator, wrote that Lambercy 'belongs to the generation of ceramicists who, during the '40s and '50s, in Switzerland as in other regions of Europe, had the courage to start from zero in using clay as an artistic medium in its own right. He is one of the pioneers of contemporary ceramic art in relation to his personal career – and among the first in Switzerland to explore the possibilities of high temperature stoneware – and, through his decisive contribution, to the modernisation of ceramic teaching.' Describing the situation in ceramics in Switzerland during the immediate post-war period as being associated with touristic souvenirs with a division of labour based on skills, Blättler noted that Lambercy sought 'a more creative approach to ceramics with a knowledge of the materials and processes involved: a global approach to ceramics that was not to be found in any teaching programme of the time. Starting out with only a rudimentary basic training, he undertook to teach himself the many aspects involved in an autonomous concept of ceramics.'

In 1952, Lambercy was appointed head of the ceramics department of the Ecole des Arts Decoratifs in Geneva, a post that he occupied until 1979, and where he played a major role in the revival of the teaching of ceramics in Switzerland. There, where instruction had previously been confined to decorative techniques, he created from scratch a school in accordance with his ideas of a broad approach to ceramic craft: students were expected to familiarise themselves with a complete range of technical procedures and the characteristics of various

*Philippe Lambercy, **2/Site**, 1997.*

materials while, at the same time, developing their own creativity. Under the influence of Lambercy, the Ecole de Geneve distinguished itself as a progressive educational centre whose reputation extends until today.

'Lambercy's career took a decisive turn in the early 1970s when he abandoned the throwing-wheel and the concept of a vessel in order to concentrate exclusively on creating free forms,' notes Bláttler.

> Inspired in his approach by the dialectic relationship between colour and form, the ceramicist developed, and continues to develop, an original sculptural language. The creative urge is stimulated through daily contact with the material and experimentation and his imagination is fed by thoughtful contact with the materials he handles and the processes he employs. This also applies to the new developments in his work, with their spectacular spatial expansion. It would seem that Lambercy, in his attempt to exalt and further reinforce the presence of colour, has released new energy. And this energy, conveyed by colour, now impels him towards a more ambitious dialogue with space. After more than 50 years of activity, Philippe

Lambercy never ceases to extend the field of his investigations. His work continues to gain in strength, carried forward as it is by a vital momentum – the energy of happiness and the joy of being a ceramicist.

YUKINORI YAMAMURA graduated from Osaka University of Arts in 1994 and became artist-in-residence at the Shigaraki Ceramic Cultural Park in 1996/1997. In 1996, he met the Norwegian artist Ole Lislerud, professor at the National Academy of Art and Design in Oslo, Norway. Lislerud invited Yamamura to work and study in Oslo, and this resulted in a number of large works being made, and an exhibition at Gallery JMS in Oslo was held. Exhibitions in Japan and awards for his work have made Yamamura a noted ceramic artist. In a statement of his work entitled *Texture Object – Chaos and Order*, Yamamura writes:

> Clay has texture – softness, hardness and cracks. This has fascinated me. My pursuit is not the texture of the object but the object of texture, piling up powerful forms

121

ABOVE: *Yukinori Yamamura,* ***Texture Object I****, 2000. Nishinomiya-City, Japan. Dimensions: 5 x 3.6 x 3.6m (16½ x 12 x 12ft).*

LEFT: *Yukinori Yamamura,* ***Texture Object II****. Acrylic paint on ceramics. Rådhusplassen, Oslo, Norway. Dimensions: 1.9 x 6.5 0.3m (6 x 21 x 1ft).*

OPPOSITE: *Yukinori Yamamura,* ***Texture Object III****. Oslo, Norway. Dimensions: 2.5 x 2.4 x 0.9m (8¼ x 8 x 3ft).*

covered with wet clay to make an object with vivid colour and weathered texture. I hope to express not only the passage of time but also something contemporary through my works. I would like to express something new and old at the same time. I always try to represent the contrast of objects between yesterday and today, today and tomorrow. I believe my works should reflect myself today.

In his acceptance of positions as artist in residence in many countries, from Finland and Norway to Thailand, the USA and Hungary, Yamamura feels he has been enriched by working in different environments. He says:

New surroundings inspire me and give me new ideas. In order to develop my work I will continue to travel,

meeting new people and seeing new places. Everything fascinates me and when I consider new surroundings I am inspired to develop my ideas. The materials are chosen to harmonise the surroundings, the people and the work. In that way I can express my identity in my work.

In an article in *Ceramics: Art and Perception 45*, Randi Gaustad, curator at the Oslo Museum of Applied Art, writes:

Yamamura's ceramics are made up of large architectonic elements that can be used to form spaces. It is primarily the surface structure of the forms that interests him. As far back as 1997 he created a large form with a surface that was reminiscent of a decaying tree trunk and which he named *Wood Texture*. The work he exhibited with Gallery JMS in Oslo in 1998, *Texture Object III*, has a surface modelled in such a way that it reminds one of a desolate and rugged mountain landscape. He says that he was inspired by both the Norwegian mountains and the rye crispbread called *knekkebrod* so common in Scandinavia. When it is broken up the dry crumbs have a certain resemblance to the surface structure of Yamamura's

ceramics. The 2 x 6m (6½ x 19¾ ft) long ceramic wall, *Texture Object II*, that he exhibited on the City Hall Square in Oslo, is made up of 14 large blocks joined together. For the first time colour was an important part of the expression. The wall was painted in strong acrylic colours, warm reds and oranges on one side, and on the other cold shades of blue and green. The interplay between the surface structure and the colours gave it a remarkable appearance and there were many who stopped to admire Yamamura's ceramic wall on Oslo's City Hall Square on that lovely summer day in August, 1998.'

MATT MCLEAN is a New Zealand sculptor who is conscious of working within various environments, natural and man-made. He thinks of art as a kind of adventure.

I am an outdoors enthusiast and can't help but be influenced by the geological features that I see when enjoying various sporting activities. Kayaking, for example, takes me down river gorges where a cross-section has been cut by the water and where the in-terrupted rock layers form their own weird calligraphy. In

recent years, I have juxtaposed clay from diverse sources in my sculptures and formed and fired them in dissimilar conditions. My current work is more elemental as I experiment with a wider range of forming techniques. When kayaking, cycling, even walking, one is constantly throwing oneself off balance, jeopardising one's security only to regain it with the next movement. I like my sculptures to show something of this. They often appear off balance and threatening to fall apart. I hope to intrigue the viewer by focusing on the internal structure which suggests why it hangs together. I hope too that people will

recognise them as metaphors for other aspects of life – human society, even the family, perhaps.

Matt McLean uses simple plastic clays, fires wood kilns and employs variations on conventional hand-building techniques.

Many of the individual forms I make are hollow like pots and are sometimes glazed. Projects are often built lying on their sides, however, on crude moulds made of earth, boards or tin – each material contributing its own characteristic setting because of their size, yet can look independent. 'Nevertheless, a piece will often relate to its new home in some unexpected way.' It is as if it has become a new independent being which, having left home, is having an adventure of its own.

Matt McLean's work has been reviewed on many occasions in the *New Zealand Potter* magazine. Helen Adams, writing in 1996, discusses how the works evolve as they are worked on, believing them to be non-fussy and unadorned, with a soft curvaceous quality. Some works, she finds, 'are deliberately solid, interlocking, suggesting shifting land masses that, however, sit contentedly in the landscape.'

US sculptor **BARBARA SORENSEN**'s working methods are simple and 'low tech,' she writes. She begins most of her work upside down, building layers of slabs upward, often around a central pole, for centring and stability, draping the clay as she goes, referencing the landscape and figure. Sometimes stones are embedded in the surface of the clay, bubbling and bursting in the firing process to emulate the volcanic nature of the earth's crust. Often the totems are built in several pieces and stacked, sometimes permanently joined after the firing, sometimes simply placed on top of each other and threaded on a pole. The pieces are loaded into a large gas reduction kiln and once-fired to cone 7. Steel rods and epoxies are often used in assemblage and installation.

Sorensen writes:

> Created in clay and bronze, my sculpture is about the figure, the landscape and how they relate to each other and their environment. My work ranges from geologic scale totems to small ceramic chests. It speaks metamorphically of volcanic movement within the earth's crust, how it emerges and moves, how it accepts change. Energy is ever-present. Rivers dance, rocks crack, mountains explode, streams chisel, fossils remain, foothills roll, goddesses emerge. As the circle continues, our lives erupt, we resolve issues, celebrating and accepting the nature of change. Mimicking these geologic movements in our lives, I mix, form and fire the clay from earth to stone. I recreate my life process by moulding and transforming myself.

The layers that Sorensen creates are reminiscent of antiquity, layers of time, layers of herself, draping the

ABOVE: *Matt McLean,* **Vessel Series,** *1999.*

OPPOSITE
TOP: *Matt Mclean,* **Lands Lives,** *2001.*
Dimensions: 200 x 150cm (79 x 59in.).

BELOW RIGHT: *Matt McLean,* **Rotor,** *1995.*

BELOW LEFT: *Matt Mclean,* **Lost Places,** *2000.*
Dimensions: 150 x 180cm (59 x 71in.).

imprint, I think of this as a kind of printmaking, the clay providing a record of all contributing influences. The downward side is hidden during making and is first seen only after firing and final re-assembling. My focus on interdependent parts gives me a kinship with bricklayers, or an orchestra, contributing to a greater whole; or writing, where letters combine to convey meaning.

In one body of work McLean dispensed with moulded structures altogether and concentrated on printing on clay using tyre treads as a means of shaping. He was inspired by road works and building sites where treadmarks tell the story of activity on the landscape. The fact that treads are commonplace yet evolved pieces of design was of interest to him. 'Although my work is informed by the natural and other kinds of environment, it is not usually site-specific,' he says. His works are usually installed outdoors in a landscape

landscape. 'I allow the sculpture to lead me where it wants to go. The stones I collect and add, percolate through the clay, and burst as they react with the vagaries of the kiln. They let the process show. The craters and bumps, both smooth and rough, are a representation of what is evolving from within.'

Writing for both *American Ceramics* in 1998 and *Ceramics: Art and Perception 42*, Sue Scott notes how the artist pushes herself to make larger than life-size works to fit into the environment.

The influence of the monumentality and drama of the Colorado mountains can be seen in the work of Barbara Sorensen, a Floridian who spends half the year in Snowmass Village, Colorado. In the wide-open spaces of the west, where the vistas go for miles, one is as aware of the space between the mountains as of their bulk. Yet in close examination of the mountains, one sees the individuality of each, defined by colour, shape and patterning. It is this duality of experience – both microcosmic and macrocosmic – that Sorensen seeks to convey in her work. One series of works, entitled *Sculpture as Environment*, was created over a period of three years and defines both its vessel references and its relationship to nature; this grouping takes Sorensen's basic underlying

philosophy to its next step in terms of size, scale and repetition of forms. The move was conscious, coming out of a desire to emulate the phenomena of nature and to activate the negative spaces between shapes.

Writing for the *Orlando Sentinel*, art critic Philip E. Bishop reviewed Sorensen's work thus: 'All her sculptures bear witness to the magical transformation of earth by fire. From a distance, in an outdoor installation, Sorensen's forms establish a different mode of being for the pot. These pots are the Rocky Mountain pinnacles holding up the sky.' The artist Rudi Autio has also commented on Sorensen's work saying: 'They have a towering and graceful presence. Some are precariously balanced on top of one another to lead the eye upwards … others are close as in implied space, like architectural ornaments.'

ABOVE LEFT: *Barbara Sorensen,* **Capistrano***, 2000. Stoneware, stones, steel and cement. Installation. CastleCreek Gallery, Aspen, Colorado.*

TOP RIGHT: *Barbara Sorensen, work in progress.*

ABOVE RIGHT: *Barbara Sorensen,* **Siren***. Stoneware and stones. Installation.*

CHAPTER EIGHT

Expressing Care for the Earth

R UTH DUCKWORTH BELIEVES THAT HER WORK has changed over the years. 'It has become less romantic and at times much harder. Can I, in my work, express what I feel about life? About being alive? What I feel about the earth and its creatures? What I feel about the beauty of the earth and its fragility? To me my life and my work are relatively unimportant compared with the drama of the planet. The health of the planet and how to keep it intact is what matters most to me. The earth is so fragile and beautiful, it needs so much love and caring and not just by me. Can I express any of that in my work?'

In an article in *American Ceramics 10/2* Michael McTwigan referred to Duckworth as having 'caring hands', saying that she was interested in trees because they were protective and that her manipulation of the soft, pliable clay, rather than chiselling and carving hard stone or wood, allowed her to work with feeling and spontaneity. Henry Moore expressed it well, he says, in his book of 1934, *The Sculptor's Aims:* 'Every material has its own individual qualities. It is only when the sculptor works directly, when there is an active relationship with his material, that the material can take its part in the shaping of an idea.' But Duckworth acknowledges that every generation's 'truths' are only half true. 'I often have to make my clay do what it doesn't want to do,' she says. 'In porcelain, you are fighting it. It wants to lie down, you want it to stand up.'

Ruth Duckworth wants her porcelain forms to show the imprint of the human hand. 'What originally fascinated me about porcelain was its fragility in the unfired state. A sort of testing of my ability to be caring and nurturing enough to

DUCKWORTH

INUZUKA

VIOTTI

SALA

MAKIN

ÓSKARDÓTTIR

BLASCO

WALFORD

OPPOSITE: *Sadashi Inuzuka,*
Offering, *1998. Ceramic, black granite. Outdoor installation. Gardener Museum of Ceramics, Ontario, Canada.*

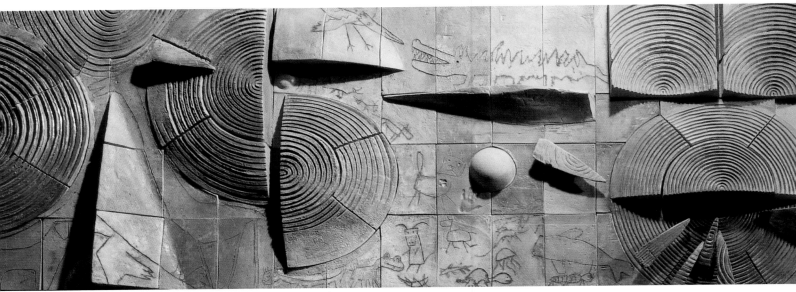

make a piece that would survive my handling it. How fragile can I make it and have it survive?' Duckworth is quoted as saying in 1991. Her early works, usually coil or slab-built, are, as the British writer Tony Birks has observed, nearly all asymmetrical: 'Not the studied asymmetry applied to a circular form before it dries – the calculated ellipse with its origins in the thrown bowl. Her work has the asymmetry of an apple or pear which grows in response to sunlight or physical circumstance. From nature's perspective, most living things are asymmetrical.'

Duckworth uses light to define and bring detail to form. 'Her training as a sculptor working in stone and wood reinforced her own predilection for a limited palette,' writes Michael McTwigan, 'but so, too, does her emphasis on form over colour. Many of her works are white with shadow and texture to provide contrast and detail. In those works where she juxtaposes dark against light for contrast, the colour introduced is usually black or brown. Rarely, a pink or other colour is introduced. Her murals and wall reliefs provide evidence for Duckworth's preference for form over colour.'

Duckworth recalls that she wanted to be an artist from an early age. But at the Liverpool School of Art, where she was a student for four years, she found herself restricted by the traditional rules of learning. 'Her work never wanted to be controlled in the narrow sense,' wrote Henry W. Rothschild for the Triennial de la Porcelaine, Nyon, catalogue in 1992. Rothschild believes

TOP: *Ruth Duckworth, **Mural for Dr. R. Lee Animal Care Centre**, 1984. Stoneware. Chicago. Dimensions: 7.3 x 1.5m (24 x 5ft).*

ABOVE: *Ruth Duckworth, **The Creation**. Stoneware wall mural. Hammond, Indiana. Dimensions: 5.3 x 5.3m (17¼ x 17¼ ft).*

that Duckworth shows persistence, spirit and genius with the work becoming simpler and more refined over the years. In an article for *American Craft* in 1991, Harrie A. Vanderstappen comments on some of Duckworth's architectural works: 'In 1964 Professor Harold Haydon invited Duckworth to teach at the Midway Studios of the University of Chicago, a one-year appointment that turned into a permanent move to the USA and heralded a new phase in her life and work. The earliest and most spectacular evidence of that phase is the monumental wall sculpture *Earth, Water and Sky,* 1968, commissioned for the entrance hall of the Hinds Laboratory for the Geophysical Sciences at the university.' This work, Duckworth says, 'made me look at the sky and think of the heavens, and that really put me into the context of the thought that all these forces and those of the world we live in grow from a common energy.'

The opportunity to execute large-scale works was one of the compelling reasons Duckworth remained in the USA, noted Harrie Vanderstappen. Over the next two decades the Hinds installation was followed by other wall reliefs in stoneware and porcelain. In *The Creation* (1984), commissioned by Congregation Beth Israel Synagogue in Hammond, Indiana, the seven days of creation as told in the Book of Genesis are sequentially depicted in text and illustration in a large spiral. Starting in the centre with the unformed universe, the story unfolds with the appearance of mountains, water, light and living things, and ends in paradise with the figures of Adam and Eve. 'This was an unusual excursion for Duckworth. She explored the phenomenal world and transformed it into one of her own, with textures, planes, fluid surfaces, gestures and colours. All function in an exceptional harmony of order in which the organic interactions of living things and their surroundings clearly follow the story inscribed in the spiral. A 2.4m (8ft) long porcelain mural (1979) is one of Duckworth's many works of the '70s and '80s in which clearly edged and shaped sheets of porcelain overlay rows of gullies. The thin sheets dominate, floating like clean-cut ice floes viewed from above. At intervals, they reveal zigzagging membranes underneath. Gentle bulging surfaces mix with a world beyond of crisscrossing clefts and bubbles, sinewy activities of a hidden energy.'

For another stoneware mural commissioned in 1984 for the Dr R. Lee Animal Care Center in Chicago through the city's Percentage for the Arts Programme, Duckworth uses broken spirals and partial spheres mixed with triangular intrusions in and over a square tile band, all in soft tones of blue, green and earth colours. Vanderstappen continues: 'While it appears on the surface to be unassertive, her work reaches form from worlds larger than life as well as from its miniature appearances. In both the small works and the large there is the same monumentality, a secure interaction between a life forever in flux and a form which catches that life when it stops for a moment to take a breath in the hands of Ruth Duckworth.'

In an article by Thea Burger and Kim Coventry for *Ceramics: Art and Perception 11*, Duckworth agreed that she liked working on a large scale. Between 1968 and 1990 Duckworth received commissions for more than 20 wall murals, 'each different in terms of theme and form but all in layered relief and all speaking of fertility, regeneration and the cycles of life.' The references in books and journals to the work of Ruth Duckworth are numerous and all reveal a care for the larger world of nature and the earth. Currently a touring exhibition and catalogue, curated by Thea Burger and Jo Lauria, is celebrating the achievements of this artist.

Since receiving his MFA from Cranbrook Academy of Art, Michigan, in 1987, the Japanese artist **SADASHI INUZUKA** has worked in clay, creating large-scale environments in which the metaphor of the insect and

Sadashi Inuzuka, **Hana**, 1991. Missisauga Art Gallery. Missisauga, ON, Canada.

Sadashi Inuzuka, **Exotic Species**, 1998. Earthenware, terrasigillata. Davis Art Centre, Davis CA, USA. Photograph by Stuart Allen.

his identification with what he calls a 'bug' allow him to address questions of nature and human nature, as well as his experience of living between cultures. He writes: 'My concern with space, scale, time and transformation evolves out of my process of working and dealing with materials. The ceramic medium itself, which involves the transformation of raw material through the forces of fire, air and time, carries much of the unspoken meaning of my work. I have always tried to create installations and freestanding sculptures which pose questions and allow viewers to find meaning in my work through their own experiences and interpretations. Recently, I have become interested in the microscopic world, particularly of bacteria and viruses. I am interested in their adaptable nature, scale and relationship to the human body and environment.'

In the catalogue of a 1990 exhibition at the Joseph D. Carrier Art Gallery, North York, Ontario, Canada, the curator, Denise Pillon, wrote: 'Sadashi Inuzuka's *Bug Dream II* employs dramatic contrasts in scale, texture and materials to create a landscape in which the contradictions in the natural and human worlds are expressed

symbolically. One of the expressive means by which the artist dramatises the union with nature is through manipulation of scale. By inflating the scale of elements of the natural world, Inuzuka invites the visitor to participate in an insect's perception of his environment. However, the design of the gallery entices the observer to explore the installation from higher levels and, in so doing, certain complexities unfold. Through his installation, the artist proposes that there is an underlying symmetry to the worlds of both man and insect.'

In the installation *Dear Lake* (1996), Sadashi Inuzuka required viewers to step up on to a platform in order to see his imaginary landscape. He had covered the entire floor with wet clay slip, which dried into lines and cracks during the following days, 'releasing messages of discord, portents of disaster'. *Dear Lake* alluded to an endangered lake situated in Deer Lake Park, where the Burnaby Art Gallery is located. Inuzuka wanted to draw attention to our interference with nature. 'Undoubtedly, from an ecological perspective, the solution to human-created environmental problems will require a fundamental rethinking and restructuring

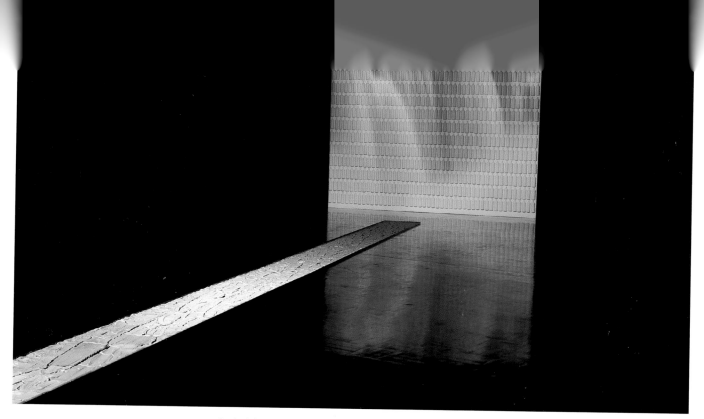

*Sadashi Inuzuka, **Water Trade**, 2003. Porcelain, video projection, stainless steel, acrylic, sound. Australia National University School of Art Gallery. Photograph by Richard Pedvin.*

of human processes, relationships and systems, including our social, political and economic systems,' he said in an interview with Grace Eiko Thomson, curator, for a catalogue on this work shown at the Burnaby Art Gallery. Inuzuka states that it is not his desire to actively intervene in nature, he is more concerned with questioning human experience in nature. 'Through the spectacle of art, Inuzuka evokes in the viewer ideas about her or his own spiritual and elemental connectedness with nature, making a space to consider the multiplicities of issues which surround the various meanings of nature.' Working on a similar theme, *River*, an installation at the Clay Studio in Philadelphia, directly addressed the plight of the Delaware River, a complex river system with saline and fresh-water areas which flow through a variety of habitats, both urban and rural. All of the problems of industrialisation and urbanisation are evident in the history of this waterway.

Sadashi Inuzuka was born in Japan in 1951 and studied at the International Institute of Art in Kyoto in the early 1970s. He migrated to Canada in 1981. Shortly after his arrival, he registered with the ceramics department of Emily Carr College of Art and Design, in Vancouver. His interest in aspects of human nature, which preoccupies him today, began as a negative experience when he was compelled as an immigrant student to deal with the complexities of his own nature. The artistic freedom he sought in migrating to the Western world was not so easily accessible. The four years at Emily Carr and two at the Cranbrook Academy of Art in Michigan were a difficult period of acculturation. Marginalised as an immigrant, lacking the classroom language of study and discussion between instructor and student, he kept his nose to the potter's wheel, positioning himself in control by producing prodigiously to compensate for the felt handicap and isolation. In 1987 he graduated from the Cranbrook Academy of Art, receiving a Master's degree in Fine Arts. Sadashi Inuzuka's training as an artist in Western institutions has not eliminated what is sensed by some viewers as a Japanese quality in his art and he admits that it is impossible to shake this off, that his work is related to Japanese aesthetics, even though he is undoubtedly influenced by Western processes and format.

*Sadashi Inuzuka, **Water Trade**, 2003. Porcelain, video projection, stainless steel, acrylic, sound. Photograph by Richard Pedvin.*

The natural world and our place in it has continued to be the subject of Sadashi Inuzuka's art, a subject he has been exploring over the course of his career, says Susan Jeffries, assistant curator at the Gardiner Museum of Ceramics, Toronto, Canada, in *Ceramics Art and Perception 51*. 'Working visually on such an important and complex topic, his installations explore biological diversity and, by extension, challenge our cultural values. It is in this arena where human endeavour touches and disrupts the natural world that he finds the greatest inspiration for his work. Dealing with an emotive topic such as the environment and its impact on man, and vice versa, is fraught with difficulties. The greatest is a tendency to seem to be preaching. Inuzuka avoids this problem by maintaining a certain detachment or distance from the topic. He does not challenge the viewer with grotesque imagery nor does he dictate

answers, an approach which destroys the impact of art, a visual intellectual discipline. Rather he focuses on the serene qualities of a natural order based on harmony. This beauty through order seems to transcend death but does not exclude solitude, loss and destruction.'

Inuzuka's installation, *Offering*, at the Gardiner Museum in Toronto, created for the exhibition Inside Out in 1998, is sensitively scaled to a large terraced area at the entrance to the museum and it also acts as a homage to the museum and its mission, the presentation and interpretation of its rich historical and contemporary collections. The black plinths, white vessels and granite recall the five essential elements, wood, fire, earth, metal and water, integral to the geology of the physical world and also part of the ceramic process. 'In all his installations there is a sense of architectural rhythm, repetitive symbols which reinforce and extend the themes inherent in the work. The sensual, intricate beauty of the assembled and often thrown parts of various fossil organisms and the sophisticated understanding of architectural space create an atmosphere which is timeless and calm but which, on reflection, challenges us to make good our responsibilities to the planet.'

In an interview with Sadashi Inuzuka, Bryce Kanbara, writing in a catalogue for the Embassy of Canada in Japan, 2000, asked Inuzuka about the development of his work.

My work has always been about the same theme. It is about the relationship between human nature and nature itself. And I am interested to discover nature in what is near rather than view it from a distance. I can look at small things and see large things in them. I am working on installations consisting of hundreds of ceramic forms. They are about mood and feeling, and they provoke questions about serious issues in society ... I have been making large installations since 1987. These combine ceramics with mixed media, and address issues of ecological imbalance and non-native species of animals and plants. Each work is an aesthetic and physical interpretation of scientific research, and the sculptural elements act as metaphors for the natural world and our relationship to it. In my work, I am concerned with the transformation of a given space into a more spiritual one which allows for meditation or reflection.

I am completely absorbed by the power of the material and the momentum of making. It is this merging of self with the whole which I experience as an artist, which I see paralleled in human society and the natural world, and which I wish to show the viewer standing in the space of my work. My most recent works are distillations of the intensity I relish in the massing of objects in a space. These isolated objects are studies in the subtleties of light, texture and form held in one spot, for one moment. I am returning to an attention to detail, to hidden things and lost seconds, and the possibility of making an enormous world within that.

Visitors to three galleries in Sweden during four months of 1990 encountered **ULLA VIOTTI**'s expression of concern for our planet. The text of the introduction to an article by Ann Mortimer (for *Ceramics Art and Perception 4*) on Viotti's work describes how Viotti, with tall 150cm (59in.) baskets, a wall of suspended forms resembling tools, arches and records of footprints, drew our attention to the fragility of the planet. A second article, this time by Kim Niklasson (in *Ceramics: Art and*

Perception 20) reaffirmed Viotti's stand. 'Her reliefs and sculptures have developed into an emotional testimony of struggle, death and destruction. During the past few years she has abandoned stoneware in favour of bricks. She has changed from traditional clay work towards personal new roads using a material that already in its composition seems to contain all ages. From clay she moulded bone shapes and human forms so that, when pressed together, it is as if her objects had been exposed to geological influence and interwoven for an eternity. Her art tells us, as do archeological objects, about relations, about vegetating life so that, despite its exposed position, it is like a river channel forging its way leaving behind the decaying bones of creatures that had once wandered the earth.'

All these ingredients are still present in her brick sculptures and, since 1983, she has been working with a number of brick factories including the coal firings at Petersen's Tegl at Nybolnor close to the Danish–German border. Her intense commitment as an artist has also meant that she has stubbornly worked for a renaissance of brick art. One of her first large projects was a 30m² (323sq. ft) work, commissioned by the Energy Authority in Malmo in 1991.

In the Swedish Parliament's new library in Stockholm, she was commissioned to design a 100m² (1075sq. ft) stone floor in which her genuine feeling for environment and art was realised. One of her unusual pieces is the brick sculpture *Tribute to King Bol*, placed so that it will crumble away. The round brick wall sculpture out in the open can be seen as a focus for her attraction to archaeology united with her belief in the future.

'The idiom is the same as her earlier work,' writes Niklasson, 'The tightly folded organic forms have been exchanged for the individual nature of the bricks. The *Telewall* in the Danish town of Aabenraa, Jutland, is a fine example of her ability to tackle the different demands of both setting and buyer. Glazed bricks form lines that associate with modern telecommunications, and the material in itself bears history's geological strata within. The work also summarises her experiences as an artist with official assignments. Since 1969, and after undertaking more than 70 assignments in public settings, she has developed an expertise in this field that has made her extremely sought after.'

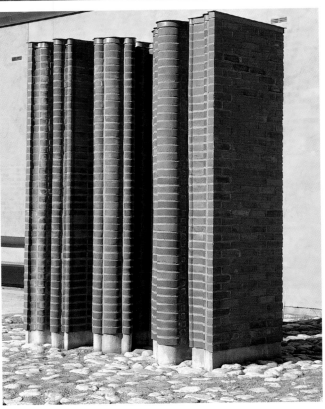

TOP: *Ulla Viotti,* **Cimbris**, *1998. Brick sculpture and grass installation. Simrishamn, Sweden. Diameter: 6m (19¾ft), height: 4m (13ft).*

ABOVE: *Ulla Viotti,* **Telewall**, *1993. Sculptural brick wall. Telecom, Aabenraa, Denmark. Length: 60m (197ft).*

RIGHT: *Ulla Viotti,* **Book**, *1996. Brick sculpture. Library Art Gallery Building Staffanstorp, Sweden. Height: 3.25m (10½ft).*

The brick sculpture *Telewall* was unveiled in 1993. It takes the form of a 60m (197ft) long winding wall. Viotti and a gang of bricklayers built brick by brick for several months. The wave-shaped wall is a sculptural communications link between the telephone company's head office and the museum in Aabenraa. The bricklayers estimate that the wall sculpture is composed of 18,000 bricks. Of these, several thousand have been moulded by the artist herself, numbered to be placed in the correct spot in the sculpture. It was estimated a single bricklayer would have taken approximately one year to complete the *Telewall*. Viotti describes her sculpture as follows: 'The coal-fired and individually shaped bricks were laid in a wave formation with two openings closed with forged iron grates. These openings are placed in conjunction with the sculpture's centre which comprises a semicircular-shaped sculptural space that can be used as a sitting area. At certain intervals along the wall facing the street are pilasters in various guises.'

A number of books and monographs have featured the work of Ulla Viotti, who has pioneered the contemporary field of bricks as an art form. *Brickworks* by Gwen Heeney (A&C Black, 2003) describes Viotti as one of the best-known practitioners in the field of green brick. Heeney, a monumental sculptor herself making large-scale work on commission, believes Viotti to be an artist who is dedicated to preserving the best of our civilisation.

For Viotti the interplay between architecture and art seems to have opened new roads for her creative expression. 'The brick lives under the artist's tutelage,' writes Niklasson. 'With an unbending will she conducts her brick sculptures as immense symphonies that penetrate the eyes in such a way as to remind one of an organ symphony's penetration of the ears. The tones are added, the counterpoint must be exactly placed and the sound rises slowly towards the light in order to bear witness to the indomitable people who inhabit the earth.'

Of Viotti's approximately 70 commissions for public environments, 20 are made from bricks. In 2004, Viotti completed the design for the entrance area inside and outside for the new hospital in Trelleborg, Sweden. Viotti's design won first prize in the competition. In the same year she finished the design for a parking place as a 'place of art' in Vellinge, Sweden, and in Athens, Greece, the new permanent International Olympic Ceramic Sculpture Park opened on 25th August with her brick sculpture, *Olympia Dwelling,* 3m (10ft) high. Twenty artists were invited, one from each country that had hosted the Olympic Games.

ELISENDA SALA is a Catalan ceramicist. In an article in *Ceramics Art & Perception 25*, Anne-Marie Marien-Dugardin wrote, 'The different tendencies, sometimes opposed, which can be seen in Elisenda Sala's work have a common denominator: her sensitivity. She received a thorough training at Massana School of Barcelona with the guidance of the potter Josep Llorens Artigas. But Sala had another vision of ceramics inspired by the fantasy of Miro's paintings. Miro was a close collaborator of Artigas. She had the chance of travelling to Sweden where she met Stig Lindberg, designer and artistic studio director of Gustavsberg. Her contacts with Lindberg were helpful and she was impressed by the pure and functional lines of this designer's work. It was he who oriented and led her to work again with the mural, confirming in her the concept that architectural ceramics have an important role in personal artistic creative expression. This role, however, she had already felt closely with the collaboration of Miro and Artigas, who had produced the *Sun* and *Moon* murals at the UNESCO palace in Paris in 1958.

Two subjects fascinated Sala from the start – several elements from the Romanic art discovered at Taüll, a small village in the Catalan Pyrenees and, even more, the Pantocrator's Eye in Saint Clement's church which radiates spirituality. The works that reveal this impact were called by the artist, *Taüll's Eye*. The stylisation of this eye showed itself in many of her works. The cross is another subject which Sala uses because of its austerity and the mystical symbolism of its beauty. At the same time, Sala enjoys wavy lines of water and the feeling of fluidity which emanates from it. From 1964 she created many ceramic murals including: *The Mediterranean Sea, Catalonia, Money and its Sources*, and in 1970, *The Cross, Leda: The Effort* and *The Swarm*. These are stoneware reliefs using volume and incised impressions; the largest of these works measures 14m (46ft) across. Sala calls this series her Mediterranean period and she chose clear blue, gold, some touches of dark blue and black on a white background. She also makes engravings. Now her art is marked with more exuberance and reveals her sensitivity towards the encircling world; everything she lives she translates in a personal way through her work and this conveys her impressions about the world and its needs.

GERALD MAKIN's ideas take initial form as small sketches, which may be developed into larger drawings or sketch models. With his columns he uses scale drawings and sometimes cardboard profiles of components. He writes from his home in Tasmania: 'I employ any working method that will enable me to realise the form I envisage. Coiling, throwing, slab construction and free modelling are employed to construct the main forms, often followed by adding small features or modifying surfaces by carving or using small stamps and moulds to give detail and texture.' Makin's ceramic sculpture is a synthesis of many things that interest and fascinate him.

> From an age that has left us little other record, there are the mysterious standing stones, stone circles and other megalithic structures in the British Isles and Western Europe. Brooding and bleak, they hint of some forgotten significance we cannot fathom. There is a power in them and food for the imagination. Then there are carved stones from past ages, particularly from the pre-Columbian Americas. The Mayan pyramids and temples are treasure houses of imagery, often disturbing, wonderfully designed

and crisply executed, though without the aid of metal tools. Older and more unfathomable are the figures and heads from Tiahuanaco from near Lake Titicaca, in the Bolivian Altiplano. From Africa and New Guinea and other islands nearby comes a wealth of the varied and lively carving in wood. These are some of the man-made things that are always somewhere in my mind when I make a sculpture.

But there are less tangible things, Makin concedes. 'I am conscious of the mystical influences inherent in the ancient Celtic oral tradition that to some extent I am party to. The world of the spirit, reincarnation, nature and the life of animals and plants, the leys or ley lines are all of significance to me. Then there are the forms of rocks and pebbles, shells, driftwood and many other things from the Tasmanian beaches and bush near my home in this beautiful island.'

Gerald Makin's objective is to create visual and tangible images that reflect some aspects of ourselves and the world that, for a time, we inhabit. He accepts commissions, large and small, for interior and outdoor works. In an article for *Ceramics Technical 15*, he explains that the motivations behind his work and the influences on him, are both real and mystical.

BORGHILDUR ÓSKARSDÓTTIR, a sculptor from Iceland, has always supposed that the reference to Icelandic nature existed in her works, but now these references have become still clearer and she has made a number of works where these elements are predominant, namely the relationship of the container and its content.

An example of this can be seen in the work *Farewell*, where the theme centres on transporting art and ideas between faraway places and different cultures. This work was created at Banff Centre for Arts in Alberta, Canada, where she resided as a guest artist in 1993.

Óskarsdóttir has been combining glass and ceramic materials to explore her ideas of landscape and our place in it.

> When I started using ceramics in my art I did not use glazes, but sought to link glass with ceramic. Around 1980, I experimented with cast glass as an independent medium, using ceramic forms as moulds. In the beginning of this experiment with cast glass, I chipped the ceramic moulds away from the solid glass forms after the firing. Then I

*Gerald Makin, straight row of columns. The column in the foreground is titled **Joie de Vivre**.*

fixed the glass units to other ceramic forms. One day, when working with the process of casting glass, I noticed beauty in the interaction of opposites in the ceramic moulds and their glass content. The ceramic moulds which before had only been employed as containers for casting glass and then discarded, now became a part of the total existence of the work.

The work *In Memory of Life*, erected in 1994 and placed in Fossvogur Cemetery in Reykjavik, Iceland, is a memorial for children who die before birth.

I made the picture on the memorial inspired by a silver foil, a tiny fragment, which was found in an excavation at Skálholt, Iceland. On the fragment, which dates from the Middle Ages, is the head of an angel and a part of a wing. I started by enlarging the image and forming it in clay, which I divided into six moulds for smelting the glass. The cast glass was then arranged in the picture of the angel. The clay moulds were, however, placed without sequence on the surface of the memorial.

Star Myths is a work which Óskarsdóttir made in 2003 for a swimming hall in Reykjavík. Here, the theme is the starry sky. She cast stars of glass in different sizes, but the earth-bound clay moulds, in which the stars were formed, had no purpose in this work. She says, 'I placed the glass stars in appropriate holes on large plates, together with drawings and texts, relating to the constellations in the Northern Hemisphere. The drawings, the plates and the walls of the swimming hall were painted in light blue, and behind the plates, electric lighting was installed.'

Iceland – Special Offer is her most recent work, made in 2004. 'I formed, rather accurately, the coastal lines of my native country, Iceland, on a large clay plate. Then I cut the country into pieces, to form nine moulds of clay. Glass was cast from these moulds. The country became an outer as well as an inner being.'

This work was made for an exhibition tour, the first venue being Wroclaw in Poland in September/2004. Five Icelandic artists held this joint exhibition with the working-title *Market*.

'When considering Spanish contemporary ceramics, one must recognise the influence of **ARCADIO BLASCO** and his work on a generation of young artists. Born in Alicante in 1929, he is a key artist because his ceramic work, without rules and prejudice, has enabled European ceramics to head in a new way.' This is the opinion of Carmen González-Borrás, art historian and curator, writing in *Ceramics: Art and Perception 52*. 'In the beginning of Blasco's career, around 1950, his works had a character of investigation and an element of risk. They were made in Spain, a country that was culturally isolated from the rest of the world because of Franco's dictatorship; as well it was a country with an unhealthy financial situation after overcoming a civil war. In 1947, Blasco had moved to

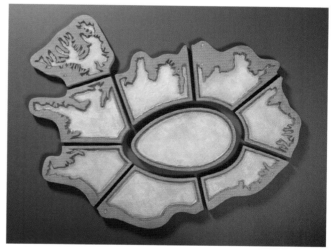

ABOVE RIGHT: *Borghildur Óskarsdóttir, **Iceland – Special Offer.***

BELOW RIGHT: *Borghildur Óskarsdóttir, **In Memory of Life**, Reykjavik.*

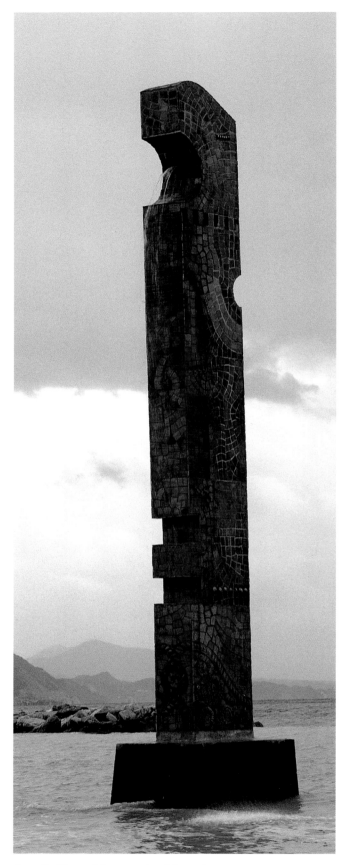

*Arcadio Blasco, **Monumento al Pescador.***

Madrid, the capital of Spain, in order to study painting. After finishing his studies, he was granted a scholarship in Italy, where he became a successful painter.'

Blasco joined a group of artists who revolutionised Spanish art in the following years. He began to work in ceramics as a means of artistic expression, and what mattered to him was the sculptural possibilities that it could hold. He enjoyed the cracked surfaces, the aggressive treatment on the surface and colour, the choice for the abstract that followed the concept of experimental painting. 'In 1969, Arcadio Blasco sculpted a series of pieces which he called *Propuestas Ornamentales* (Ornamental Proposals). They were large-scale sculptures, with iron outside and ceramics inside, sculpted with terracotta. It is possible to walk into the pieces or lock oneself inside, given their size. With this series Blasco represented Spain in the Venice Biennial in 1970,' writes González-Borrás.

From 1984 to 1989, Blasco began to make large-scale sculptures for public places.

He uses two systems: first, coating cement pieces with ceramic, and, second, building sculptures through modules by placing one over another. Large-scale architectural sculptures are some of the most significant works in Blasco's career. He works alone and for him it is an exercise of discipline in which he has to learn new skills as a ceramic artist. The result is a sculpture fully integrated with the landscape, for example *Homenaje a la dama de Elche* and *Homenaje a Castelao* (Tribute to Castelao) or *Monumento al Pescador* (Monument to the Fisherman), which has one part of the work resting in the sea. For Blasco, this starting point is sometimes in a small fragment of a work of art. The result is a work with a valid archaeological content and references the person and time.

Nowadays Arcadio Blasco combines the production of *Nuevas Arquitecturas* (New Architecture) monuments and travel, and he is often invited to participate in ceramic-related courses and events. Blasco is a mature artist, yet bold and inquisitive. He searches for innovation in terms of form and concept, and his creative talent and passion are expressed as he sculpts in ceramics. Blasco has also been active in public works which involve the community. One such project – *A Monument to an Important Man* – is an equestrian clay

Arcadio Blasco, **Monumento al Pescador**. *Dimensions: 8 x 4m (26 x 13ft).*

statue made by young people from the neighbourhood of Palomeras, Vallecas, Madrid, under his direction. Blasco writes:

> The teamwork raised the necessity of relying on fellow workers to carry the proposal through to a successful conclusion. The work in materialising an idea from a group representing everyone's effort can result in the satisfaction that a creative coexistence gives. The young people presented the idea, they studied its development and contributed to transforming their energy into the work. The method we used is one similar to that used, even nowadays, by our large earthen jar makers of Colmenar de Oreja. Pieces which were easily handled by the children were made by patting them so as to give them the necessary density and strength; then they were fitted into each other around a wooden brace that served as a bracket. Later the pieces were filled with concrete to give heaviness to the sculpture. The older children were in charge of polishing the surfaces and placing the ornamentation, although the tasks were organised by roster in order that the experience be total. At the base of the figure the shield of Madrid was incised along with the names of all those who had a direct participation in the final work. The work has become an exultant commemoration of the creativity which was its *raison d'être.*

ANDREW WALFORD has installed tile panels in KwaZuluNatal based, he says, 'on the theme of trees of Natal.'

> My commission for the International Conference Centre in Durban was inspired by Zulu crafts and I employed Zulu women to make the small tiles. My first major tile panel was at the Government Head Office in Ulundi in 1990. I was inspired by a most unusual Minela tree near the site. The theme which dominates the panel involves the use of branches or *uthango* which surround a traditional kraal. The unifying blue lines represent the underlying mythological undercurrents of Zulu legend and the areas of light and dark porcelain and stoneware clay textured with iron oxide represent the collective unconscious feeling of the people. The two small circular discs with a white pattern in the centre are representative of the earlobe decoration which is a part of the Zulu tradition. The fluting pattern at the top of the panel represents the thatching of the large beehive huts that abound in this area.

Another panel is inspired by the Umkuhlu tree in Pietermaritzburg.

> As always with art projects in South Africa the budget is cut back dramatically after the works are commissioned.

*Andrew Walford, **Isiktoti**. Panel installation.*
International Conference Centre, Durban, South Africa.

This panel stretched my skill as an economist as well as ceramicist. I went to the old Victorian town of Pietermaritzburg and explored the town through the eyes of a child, with the assistance of my youngest son, Zeke. The boot scrapers at the city hall and the motifs on all the old lamp posts is the elephant, *ndlovu* – after all it was not long ago that elephants roamed here. Then it struck me that man and, in particular town planners, just move in regardless with their straight lines and squares but the pigeons are oblivious, they just fly where they want. There is also a dignified Natal Mahogany tree at the site. Because of lack of funds and long low walls with three lift openings, I put segments on these including a copy of a modern Zulu craftsman's signs, Chicken Man Mkise and No Stiletto Heels. The distinctive seeds of the tree are represented in the circular motif. The imposed square represents town development over natural environment, and the line of unglazed tiles is reminiscent of the typical Maritzburg red brick. I fired the panel in one firing to 1380°C (2516°F) and put the panel up myself in two days.

The panel installed by Walford at the International Conference Centre in Durban was based on the theme of a wedding cape, *Isikhoti*, and came from the layered beaded capes of the area. He writes: 'I used layers of stoneware and porcelain, the pattern of pigmented clays pressed in and textures on the surface represent the *krantzes* at sunset. Thembi Madlina and Benedicta Shongwe decorated small tiles made by Edmond Gumede with naïve birds, animals and people.'

Walford is immersed in his environment, its land and its people.

Living and working in Africa is important for me with its contrasts of primitive beauty and intrinsic starkness. My iron brushwork on porcelain epitomises this African essence for me. Here in Nshongweni, KwaZuluNatal, in my mountain-top studio perched on a ridge overlooking a natural game reserve, I am surrounded by indigenous

Andrew Walford, **Umkuhlu Tree**. *Pietermaritzburg.*

forests teeming with birdlife, gnarled thorn trees, gigantic boulders covered with moss and lichen, and sandstone cliff faces reflecting the ever changing light. I can watch the sun go down over the dusty hills, colours changing from dark rust to the palest of pinks. Dusk falls suddenly in Nshongweni: francolins, bushbabies and owls with occasional snuffling of bushpigs create a backdrop of sound.

Walford's studio is surrounded by wild pear *dombeya* trees, clumps of huge yellow and green bamboo, and ponds with koi.

The contrasts of glaring relentless sun, shadows and dramatic winds and rain storms all impinge on the senses and inspire me in this wilderness. Nature is rich in diversity. If only I could catch a glimpse of it in my work and just freeze a millisecond of its essence. What really pursues me is the colour of the clay fired in a reduction atmosphere, where a glaze has fused well with the piece

and areas of interest remain like weathered rocks. I dig my own stoneware clay and mix it to my own needs. I use indigenous wood ash and glazes, mixed and sifted by hand. Up the hill from my studio, sugar cane is grown and when burnt and harvested, leaves bands of black and sienna following the contours of the rolling hills. This I use in my *Shongwe* shapes. I am surrounded by the Zulu crafts of beadwork, which I incorporate in my tiles. Fine wooden spoons, wooden milk pails, *isithebe* grass mats with subtle, intricate designs, are what inspire me and I have called this 'Zen Zulu' – the minimalist essence of Japanese Zen with pure lines, economy of form and reverence to material drives me onward.

Andrew Walford exhibits his ceramics internationally and is called on to give workshops on a regular basis, both in South Africa and overseas.

CHAPTER NINE

Narration, Scale and Figuration

'CONSTRUCTING FROM THE INSIDE', an article written by the Hungarian ceramicist **IMRE SCHRAMMEL**, was published in *Studio Potter 16/1*. Schrammel wrote:

> Fate was gracious to me and offered the opportunity to execute ceramic murals. My first mural, constructed in 1976, decorated a wall of the Vác theatre. In this 60m² (645sq. ft) mural, I tried to compose a drama of orographic formation, the result of the conflict between forces of nature and nature's raw material. A second mural was a ceramic relief for a theatre in Pécs. This was a 15m (49ft) long mural on a bridge between two buildings joining the outer façades. The theatre itself, built at the turn of the last century, was richly decorated with romantic ornaments and figures, and I decided to consider it as a stage setting located on the street of a historic city. My task was to link the existing buildings.

Schrammel produced a number of drawings before starting active work on this commission. He wanted to find the optimal solution from among the technical possibilities and create a 'form and matter' appearance that harmonised with the technique he had chosen.

> I decided to take the viewpoint of a film director and select actors. I installed a stage for them. The actors were well-known and mythological figures: the Willendorf Venus; a baroque Christ popular in Hungary; a wooden dress-dummy; a statue of an ancient Hungarian king; the mask of a famous Hungarian actress; and a Minotaur and his lover. I made copies of the Venus, the Christ and the head of the king. I made a

SCHRAMMEL

DIONYSE

KLIX

FLYNN

PORTANIER

SILER

BROWN

HOWDLE

NOVOTNÁ

OPPOSITE: *Carmen Dionyse's workshop showing her scuptures of three elements **Aer, Terra, Aqua**.*

*Imre Schrammel, **Recling Figure**. Stoneware.*

mould of the face of the actress and of the dummy. The Minotaur and his lover were shaped by hand.

The 15m (49ft) long façade was divided into five scenes for technical reasons – Schrammel did not have a large enough space in his studio. Taking the designs of the relief from the theatre façade, he composed the figures to be placed in this setting. The whole surface was made in negative forms so as not to lose any liveliness through the necessary handling process. When the relief was ready, it was installed on the façade and unveiled in 1986.

One conclusion I reached, was that the motives of the actor were the same as those of the painter, sculptor or ceramicist. The other conclusion was that clay is a living material. We cannot consider it simply as a raw material, but must accept it as a partner if we want authentic answers to our questions. The third conclusion was that there is a mystic correlation between the material world and the imaginary world. There is an additional important

question that ceramicists must address: that is, the relationship between the building and the art object decorating it – today's art needs to develop an organic unity with architecture and its environment. I have always strived to adapt my work to a given building but have had difficulty in finding an overall solution. Now that I have approached the Pécs Theatre in this way, I think I am closer to a positive solution.

Imre Schrammel believes the ceramicist also works in the same way as an architect; he or she encloses space with walls. The body of a living being is a structure of cavities, separated from the outer world by a skin. If a ceramicist takes any living creature as a model, he or she comes up against the principle of constructing from the inside. Such a sculpture changes shape according to the same forces as living beings do. In addition, it adjusts itself to the environment, just as the environment adjusts to living beings. This mutual formal interaction can be the starting principle for a new partnership between artist and architect.

In an article on Imre Schrammel, Sylvia Hyman, writing for *Ceramics Monthly* (1996), outlined the details of the Vác mural construction: 'In Hungary where Romanesque, Turkish Baroque and Early Christian architecture abound, the integration of art and architecture is being revived. To create his latest mural, Imre Schrammel mixed 14 metric tonnes of clay in the basement of the Academy of Applied Arts in Budapest, carried it to three upstairs classrooms, spread it over the floor and attacked it with clubs and with his body.'

This commission resulted from a competition to which Schrammel had submitted several small plaster models that suggested the mural. Starting in mid-July, when classes were not in session, Schrammel, Associate Professor of Art at the Budapest Academy, began forming the 20m (66ft) wall relief. When he decided that the heavily textured surface approached his original concept, the clay was sectioned to facilitate drying, firing, transporting and mounting.

More than 700 pieces were made, and each was recorded with a number on an overall plan. When sufficiently dry, the pieces were hollowed from behind to an even thickness of 2cm (¾in.). The larger sections had one or two additional reinforcing walls to prevent warping. The mural was fired in an oil-burning kiln – its

*Imre Schrammel, **Pécs Theatre Façade**. Stoneware.*

1m³ (35cu. ft) ware chamber (12.2 x 12.2 x 12.2m/40 x 40 x 40ft) required 35 firings to complete the forms. Subtle variations of reduction provided the only colour treatment of the finished surface. Installation required working on scaffolding because the mural was installed 2m (7ft) above floor level.

Schrammel, educated at the academy where he now teaches, was a student in the 1950s during the period of Stalinism; his was a conservative, academic education. A major influence has been folk art – not in an attempt to imitate it, but to discover its basic meaning. He has sought an approach that comes from a natural direction through the use of the medium itself.

The theme 'ceramics in the environment', the alliance of ceramics with architecture, that is, ceramics harmonised with architecture, is a theme that has occupied the longest period of Schrammel's professional life. His works, which have received prizes worldwide, represent pieces completed in this field. Among these are the ceramic panels covering the walls of the building of the 'Enchanted Castle' situated in the Budapest Amusement Park. Schrammel writes:

The building itself can be taken as an 'architectural comedy'. I endeavoured to express this comedy aspect applying two styles for creating the cornices of the façade. Due to the fire protection regulations the building has been constructed using a steel framework and we attached the ceramic panels to the steel beams and columns by welding. The salt-glazed panels were fired to 1300°C (2372°F).

A book on the life and work of Imre Schrammel was published in 2003 to celebrate the artist's 70th birthday. In a text written by the art historian Hedvig N. Dvorszky, Schrammel is recognised as having epoch-making and sculptural knowledge, a researching mind and, as an observant naturalist, has been able to reap the rewards of a life in art.

Hans-Ulrich Roller describes the ceramic works of **CARMEN DIONYSE** in *Ceramics Art and Perception 8*:

They carry us into a world that exists apart from and beyond our commonplace reality. It characteristically opens up boundaries, it offers choices and implies demands that surpass artistic pleasure as mere aesthetic consumption. Dionyse does not belong to any stylistic movement or artistic group. She goes her own way, self-assured and she has come to occupy a singular position on the international ceramics scene. Her many-sided training at the Royal Academy of Art in Ghent, Belgium, provided her with the option to turn to ceramic techniques. She feels that ceramics is the material best suited to give shape to her artistic ideas because of the specific expressive possibilities it offers. After years of confrontation with the contemporary international language of style and form, she succeeded in placing the image of man back into the centre of her creative work, and she quickly developed a form and an expressive vocabulary that has proved to be unmistakably her own.

Placing her work in a number of public and private environments, she has concentrated on the study of the figure. Many of her works are life-size and refer to history and culture from a variety of sources, ancient and contemporary. In an interview with Chrysoula Tagari for *Kerameiki Techni 23*, Dionyse reflects on her interest in Greek mythology, which began when the artist was 18 years old. 'I developed a way of reading these myths,' she says. 'I discovered a world ruled by men who only thought of war, how to destroy or steal … on the other side, I saw those who were persecuted and abused by the strong.'

Frank Nievergelt, writing for *American Ceramics 12/4* also noted the influence of myths and time, 'The three-dimensional forms of her works combine with the graphic aspect of the surface obtained by her use of clay, metal salts, engobes and glazes. Dionyse, whose sculptures encompass man, his earthbound existence and the transitory character of all worldly things, uses ceramic materials in an evocative way to make a statement about human nature.' Nievergelt finds enclosed energy, eternal humanity and tension in her figurative pieces. Roller continues:

The look in her figures' eyes must be considered of pivotal importance: it is the impelling mediator between the inner self and the exterior, between the essence of what is

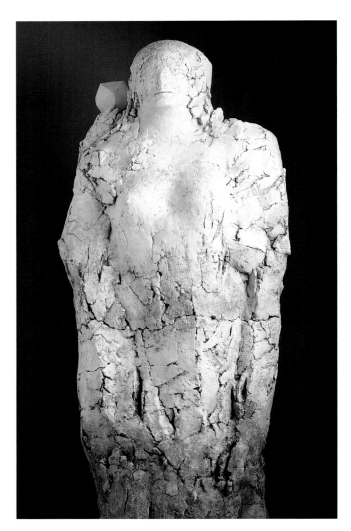

*Carmen Dionyse, **Aqua**, 1994. Height: 220 cm (87in.).*

represented and its observer. The range of expression is wide. From an utterly inner-directed negation of the exterior world, to a compelling, powerful, challenging gaze at the other. But expression is also conveyed by the covering of the figures, which ranges from explicitly invoking the cultic, the priestly and the severe, to being merely hinted at.

Dionyse uses both earthenware and stoneware clays. Each piece is slab-built and pressed from the inside out. Textured areas are sometimes darkened with oxides. A variety of coloured glazes is used and the work is fired in an electric kiln at different temperatures between 1280°C (2336°F) and 900°C (1652°F). It is not uncommon for each piece to undergo multiple firings; some works have been fired more than 15 times to achieve a particular surface and effect.

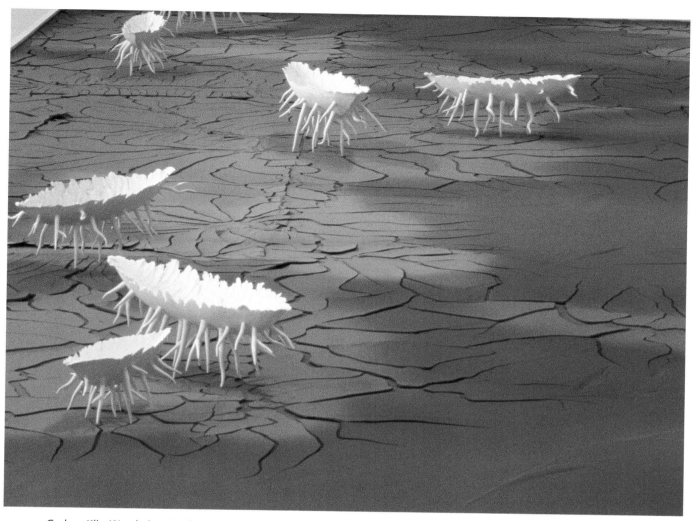

*Gudrun Klix, **Wandering Hands**, 1999. Porcelain forms in terracotta slip. Installation. Object Gallery, Sydney. 7.2 x 3.6m (23½ x 11¾ ft).*

GUDRUN KLIX has moved home many times: as a child from Silesia to West Germany, then from Germany to the USA and later, as an artist, to Australia. Klix is fascinated by the consummate differences that she discovered, and the key to it all, she believes, is the land. She needs to walk, explore and physically interact with each new homeland and learn about its people. According to Moyra Elliott writing in *Ceramics: Art and Perception 40*:

It is her way of connecting with the place, a means to form a touchstone and in a sense, to internalise it. This is her route toward making a claim for herself: to be able to call a place home. Klix's work has reflected these issues for a number of years. One of her recurring motifs has been the boat form. A metaphor used to explore personal issues, the references for Klix are migration, loss of homeland, the ongoing quest for a new place to call home and the search

for new identity markers. Her previous work on mythologies and feminine iconography is still interconnected with the form of the vessels and she sees a continuum rather than any great change in direction.

In Gudrun Klix's 1999 installation at Object Galleries, Sydney, the floor space was flooded with red clay slip. This varied in thickness and the cracking was similarly varied as it dried slowly over the duration of the exhibition. This cracked slip referenced the Australian desert landscape – the red interior. For Klix there are also wider resonances in this cracked earth with ecological issues as well as the severed personal bonds. The boat-like forms, made in moulds with their interiors stroked by the hand, are delicate and fragile. Elliott writes:

They resonate the tenuous hold the migrant has in the

CERAMICS IN THE ENVIRONMENT

*Gudrun Klix, **Airscape/Landscape**, 2004. Installation.*

OPPOSITE
LEFT: *Michael Flynn, **Totentanz/Dance of Death**.*

RIGHT: *Gilbert Portanier, **Bouclier**. Underglazed colours on white clay, fired at 1030°C (1886°F). Diameter: 70cm (27in.).*

new land. They are stark in their whiteness. This also speaks of the dry Australian interior and desert-like conditions. Importantly and additionally, these vessels have grown roots. The roots, white and bony, are suggestive of trees searching through dry soil for moisture and nourishment. They hold the boats high above the land so that they barely touch the cracked clay, not penetrating; alien objects in the landscape. Like immigrants they fleetingly touch the ground, but that touch is without substance; tenuous in their glancing connection with the soil.

Klix suggests, through her work, that definitive answers are not within our grasp. She also proposes that a connection with the land and developing an understanding of its indigenous population is the key to searching them out. By endeavouring to understand the land and its people, a linkage can be made, culture to culture and generation to generation.

In a more recent installation held at the University of Sydney in 2004, Klix carried this theme further. *Airscape/Landscape* is a work based on a number of journeys she made into the desert by four-wheel drive vehicles and taking flights over the red centre. In this work she looks closely at the features and structure of the land itself, which then become the narrative reference points for the work.

The installation is comprised of individual ceramic units placed on the walls in such a way that layers and planes are created. This arrangement provides a sense of space and directional movement. On the floor steel boxes containing materials collected from the landscape – rocks, charcoal, salt pan, bark and red sand – provide a sense of grounding. Overall textures, colours and forms are strongly evocative, taking the viewer on a journey far beyond the gallery walls.

'**MICHAEL FLYNN** is primarily a figurative sculptor,' wrote Alison Smith for an article in *Ceramic Review 172*. 'Flynn manipulates the stone-like resilience of the medium as if attempting to fossilise the emotional force which propels the naked body into expressive motion.' Several site-specific works have been commissioned in recent years, including a fountain in London and altarpieces for a church in the Czech Republic.

In an article, this time for *Ceramics: Art and Perception 26*, Angelika Gause wrote:

Michael Flynn's sculpture, although it is clearly figurative and within the European tradition, is difficult to assess in terms of the usual criteria or categories. Neither Flynn nor his work fit into any accepted overview. His work, just as his personality, is ambiguous and controversial. It is not straight-forward in the literal or the figurative sense. It is complex, full of scars and cracks, both ambivalent and ambiguous. It provides no answers but raises many questions, seeking in this duality the essential human condition manifest in apparent contradictions or in connections between seemingly unrelated aspects. Initially, the stark vitality of his objects is foremost: action and emotion fossilised in clay.'

Although his work is based on traditional iconography and symbolism, Flynn selects the images for the multiplicity of their possible meanings and presents them in new or unusual combinations. 'The intention is to instigate a process by which the onlooker questions his own beliefs and the associations which arise from this confrontation,' believes Gause, and continues:

In a series of nine reliefs, Flynn took classic themes from art history and imbued them with a contemporary relevance. The classic historical depiction of *Totentanz/ Dance of Death*, calls for death in the form of a skeleton to

lead those he has chosen in a kind of round dance. It shows people of diverse worldly and spiritual standing forced reluctantly to follow. Formally such a sequence depicts a series of figures, each representing a particular social level and each accompanied by a dancing skeleton. This is how Flynn has presented his own 'Dance of Death' figures. However those in this series represent a contemporary world order. Different mythological and folkloric meanings are brought into play. Although perhaps not always initially apparent, much of Flynn's work centres on the symbolism of death. His methods, however, his use of ambiguity, the evocation of existential query are, at the same time, an expression and a symbol of our disoriented and sense-seeking times.

Michael Flynn is the author of *Ceramic Figures*, which gives an overview of contemporary artists working with figurative imagery.

GILBERT PORTANIER, a French ceramic sculptor living in Vallauris, wrote about his approach to ceramics for *Ceramics: Art and Perception 21.*

Everything I do leads directly to the following and then the next, to the next. I have an appetite for work, a need to work; there are always more things to accomplish. I constantly have a feeling of discovery. It never ends, it never pauses. I never feel well unless I am working. I came to ceramics in a roundabout way … I discovered the earth, the clay as a possible raw material, as a kind of body. Earlier I painted but when I came to Vallauris in 1948 I discovered clay, the earth into which one plants, a medium for one's sense of touch. When I first began to paint, that medium was an intellectual enterprise. In ceramics I discovered that there were many possibilities: colour as in painting but also form. There are endless ways of working in ceramics; there is the kiln, the wheel, the brush, the manner of handling the clay … all have a role and all work together.

Influenced by everything, Portanier says, by other artists and by circumstance, by people he meets and by nature, he believes his ideas come, however, from within him. 'There are things which one discovers when at work and there are other things that come out of the

Gilbert Portanier, group of sculpted elements in ceramic, forming a fountain in a 9 x 4m (29½ x 13ft) basin. Atrium centre of the Estrel Hotel in Berlin.

subconscious or by happenstance and creep into one's creative endeavour. I study and analyse these and then, being fully aware of them, I use them in my production. What at one time was an accident can then develop into a style. Consequent accidents lead to yet different ideas. In this way a technique comes about which I then learn to master.'

To master your craft, Portanier believes, there must be a projection into the future. He has become interested in making forms both small and large. The question is not whether it is small or large in itself, but the dimension. The quality is the essence of the piece and that distinguishes the small piece from the large one.

With a small piece it is speed that counts, the tiniest touch is immediately apparent. The outside influence becomes clear at once because small pieces make no demands and practically all options are open. One learns from making small pieces. The big pieces, almost as large as people, are forms which you can actually embrace; fight with, which one can compare with oneself. They have an impact. I believe we can satisfy our needs for communication only through art.

The true artist does not look so much to the outside world, he looks inward and develops. Those who look to the outside think they will find something out there that is missing inside them. But they can never find it because the more they look, the fewer chances there are that they will find something in themselves.

Phillipe Chabert, chief conservator and director of the Musée d'Art Moderne de Troyes, in a catalogue essay on the work of Portanier, and reproduced in *Ceramic: Art and Perception 52*, draws our attention to the impact of Portanier's work and its relationship to the painters working in Vallauris.

Ceramics offered painters an opening to a form of expression which they thought they could turn to their advantage and it also presented them with a challenge. It provided them with a chance to tackle a new medium, new volumes, new surfaces and, above all, it invited them to rethink the whole question of the place of artistic creation. Portanier has created his own vocabulary: 'Once the form was completed and fired, it blossomed, as did my pleasure in the painted decoration. I covered the piece, like ivy; I played with the form; I used my brush to upset the balance, falsify the symmetry, open windows, build balusters; what I saw from beneath my fingers was the living being, figuration, volutes and arabesques; a people of faces and shadows.'

There is a joyful quality about Portanier's work, visible in his sensuous love of colour, his wealth of forms and his unrestrained emotion. The joyfulness of Gilbert Portanier's ceramics is evident from both the forms and the decoration. The well-organised friezes are offset by independent motifs; a dynamic figurative design goes beyond the limits of perception, obliging the spectator to walk around the object. The unadorned areas invite us to use our imagination.

Portanier freely combines matt and glazed surfaces, curves and reverse curves; he destabilises the object by moving motifs outside the picture space: everything moves in Portanier's art. He knows that suggestion is richer than description and has experimented in working with series in order to explore all the potential in any one theme. He has ventured into the world of masks, for example, producing bust-masks, masks with legs, all types of masks which may disguise, conceal or help the wearer to escape.

In 2004, Gilbert Portanier celebrated his 60 years of life as an artist, drawing attention to his works placed in public spaces, as well as his private commissions throughout Europe.

PATRICK SILER, US sculptor, has always liked the idea of large paintings, 'ones which are so broad and high that you could walk into them. When I had the idea of making a ceramic wall, I wanted it to be on this scale. In the late 1950s and '60s I was immersed in the mystique of abstract expressionist painting, trying to create forms with a paintbrush, to create the illusion of space, to sculpt, bend and manipulate it on a flat canvas. This was my challenge and my passion.' Siler received his MA in painting from the University of California, Berkeley, and there, in 1965, he first saw a ceramic wall, made by Harold Paris. 'Harold threw his clay on a wall, punched it, tore it, modelled and caressed it into a most arrestingly complex configuration of abstract form. They were large blocks of clay expressively modelled into intriguing abstractions. The excitement, in a large measure, lay in the expressive freedom, directness and childlike freshness of the work.'

The San Francisco Bay area was an exciting environment for a young artist and Siler was able to work with Jim Melchert, Ron Nagel, Peter Voulkos and Jun Kaneko. Through these people he learnt about the work of John Mason, Ken Price, Steven DeStaebler and Mike Frimkiss. The emphasis was to make bold, strong, large-scale works, 'big in feeling, big in spirit and heart'. There was an emphasis on pushing the limits of the ceramic media and processes. 'Although many of us were not ceramicists, we were excited by much of the new ceramic work. We thought that as modern artists we could break many of the rules – and sometimes we could and sometimes we couldn't. We were interested in what ceramics could be, not what it already was. So when I began making ceramics in the mid-1960s, I had healthy stimulation and inspiring models to follow.'

From the beginning, Siler's ceramic pieces contained patterns on them, images and pictures, combining these pictures with three-dimensional form. He says:

The images I use on my ceramics just occur to me, sometimes from listening to music, listening to a conversation, the words of a song or by observing people. I like to combine subjects which seem to have no relationship. I combine the image-subjects on my pieces by intuition – whatever physically or formally looks good – and I try to create tensions between the objects with no perceived message of a moral, social, psychological or political nature intended.

ABOVE: *Patrick Siler,* **Airheads Enjoying TV**. *Tile panel.*

LEFT: *Patrick Siler,* **Flying Saucers Invade Earth**. *Tile panel (detail).*

Creating strong forms and interesting shapes is important to Siler, as is the formal arrangement of elements on a piece. He says he is interested in giving the individual figures, animals and objects a shape which, on closer observation may take on some outlandish or strange twist. 'The subjects I like to deal with involve the everyday activities of the average person eating, sleeping, working, driving, dreaming, loving, in ecstasy, in torment. I like the idea of transforming the mundane and everyday into the moving, the profound and the powerful.'

CHRISTIE BROWN, from London, UK, explores a personal iconography concerned with universal themes of attachment and loss through the use of narrative and the body. Her main medium is ceramic but she sometimes uses bronze, plaster and wax, materials with a long-established relationship with clay, with casting and the use of moulds. Ceramic artefacts and other ritual objects from burial sites and the associations of clay with myths of creation provide rich references for her. She writes about her work,

> Exploring the metaphorical associations of the casting process through press-moulding, my work exploits the clay's capacity to receive an imprint, to record a trace, and connects to ideas about mimesis and replication, transformation and fragmentation. The work is informed by debates within psychology, anthropology and archaeology and the preoccupation with material culture.

As an artist and a university professor she perceives a need for ceramics to question its decorative utilitarian history and to engage with broader discourses and disciplines. She is actively seeking alternative spaces in which to present her work:

> In 1998, I was commissioned by the organisers of the Wapping Project in London to make a body of work in response to the large industrial space of the Wapping Hydraulic Power Station. The subsequent exhibition in 2000 entitled *Fragments of Narrative* required me to respond to scale, memory and a specific site. This resulted in a group of life-size ceramic figures, inspired by characters from myths of creation such as Prometheus, Pygmalion and Galatea and the Golem which also connected to the original use of the space as a source of animation. Other smaller figures and several heads were placed in various groupings around the building as if part of an archaeological dig. The wall piece, entitled *Resource – Clay*, was composed of many fragments cast from earlier moulds of figures that related to the people who worked in the power station and the form was inspired by the tradition of *ex votos* where gifts are offered with prayer as a form of healing in certain cultures.

*Christie Brown, **Kalos Thanatos**, 2003. Brick clay. Height: 120cm (47in.).*

TOP: *Christie Brown, Installation of* **Fragments of Narrative.** *Figures range from 111 to 170 cm high. Brick clay.*

ABOVE: *Christie Brown,* **Prometheus.** *Brick clay.*

Writing about Brown's installation, *Fragments of Nature*, Edmund de Waal (*Ceramics: Art and Perception 46*) looked at the reasons behind the work: 'Figuration is the art of enacting our multiplicity of our own personality, a way of impersonating ourselves … in figuration we can make a space in which to engage with the dangerous play necessary to understanding who we are.' In this way, de Waal believes, Christie Brown's figures make us review ourselves in relation to what we see around us.

'Intense but abstracted, powerful yet calm,' are the descriptions given to Brown's work in *American Ceramics 12/3* by Rosemary Hill, while Tony Franks, writing in *The Scotsman* finds the works 'brooding' and 'individual and isolated'. Ruth Pavey, in *Crafts* (Nov/Dec 1999), uses the words 'poised, strong and intriguing' finding within them, as does Brown herself, 'a deeper emotional range than is obvious from their exteriors'. Brown's work has been shown at the studio gallery at Kingsgate Workshops (London) in a show entitled *Between the Dog and the Wolf*

(so called since it explores boundaries and change) and her most recent project is as artist-in-residence at the Petrie Museum of Egyptian Archaeology based in University College, London.

Since I am looking for other contexts in which to present my work and have always been inspired by ancient Egyptian culture, I have begun to study this extraordinary collection of small-scale everyday artifacts which connects the viewer to the individual rather than just the grand world of the Pharaohs. Whether responding to a site or to a group of artifacts, my central preoccupations remain the same but the external reference is not only an invaluable stimulus to my practice but helps me develop the work in a more objective way within a contemporary context.

BRUCE HOWDLE, a sculptor from Wisconsin, USA, reports that many of the commissions he has produced require detailed planning from conception to installation.

After the drawings are approved, I build an easel 13.6% larger to account for the shrinkage of the clay. The clay formula contains a high amount of perlite – to open the clay body so as to allow moisture to escape during firing, – and sawdust – to eliminate warping. I have sought, over the past 25 years, to develop my skills as a sculptor who works with clay and to enhance the ability to express myself through this medium. As a result, I have derived a profound respect for the earth and what it has to offer. Clay's malleability allows me to create the images desired to their likeness and this is based on extensive research for each mural that I create.

What Howdle appreciates most about working with clay is the surface spontaneity that takes place; this he finds expedient in finishing the design before the clay dries. It is fired with a sodium process that softens the clay surface, preserving the mural's design and creating a durable piece. This process also allows the clay to maintain its natural colouration where needed as well as the ability to apply additional colours as desired. Many of the murals used two to nine tonnes of clay. Nothing is more exciting, he says, than to look upon a large span of

*Bruce Howdle, **T D S Metro in Madison WI**, 2003. Height: 5m (16½ft), width: 1.75m (5¾ft) with additional 4.75m (15½ft) that wraps around corner. Commissioned by T Wall Properties. Photograph by Skot Weidemann.*

Bruce Howdle, Installation at Brighton, Colorado, USA, 2002. Comprised of 745 pieces glued on 22 modules. Municipal Court Facility and Police Department. Dimensions: 2.7 x 8.1m (9 x 26 ½ ft). Photograph by Frank Ooms.

clay, to sculpt it in a week with larger-than-average tools and ready it for firing and installation.

> I have been a ceramic sculptor in Mineral Point, Wisconsin, for the past 28 years. I have produced and installed 30 major works of freestanding or wall-mounted sculpture in both indoor and outdoor settings in six US states. I have designed work to fit large concave surfaces and to wrap around building corners. Other works have been mortared into place under my supervision. In Sportsman's Park I worked with a Chicago mason to lay the mural like brick. At Menasha, Wisconsin, a mural was glued and jointed on twelve 2.4 x 3m (8 x 10ft) concrete panels, then craned up and bolted to the wall. For a Brighton, Colorado, installation I glued 745 pieces to 22 wood panels which were wall mounted to steel studs. In some cases, I have designed work that at a later date can be disassembled and moved elsewhere.

Working as a sculptor since 1976, Howdle has had much acclaim for his work. Kevin Lynch, writing for Wisconsin's *Capital Times*, believes that 'Howdle exemplifies the contemporary artist who lives in a small rural town while producing work that contributes to the vitality and future of urban life.' Alongside each mural, the client usually hangs a statement of the artist's intent, giving details of inspiration, history and process. In this way the public is informed. Howdle says: 'The statement can be interpreted in more than one way. Everyone is an individual, through their background, education and environment. However different we are, we work for a common goal. Murals can be timeless, showing aspects of the past, present and future. In this way we can preserve our heritage.'

Bruce Howdle enjoys working with commissioning organisations. After extensive study of the history and functional use of a space, he produces concept sketches, finished drawings and small clay models prior to final design acceptance. The sculpted clay for the project is cut while wet into firing-size pieces and carefully numbered on the back for reassembling. After glazing and firing, if the work is not to be mortared in place, he mounts the pieces in sections for transportation and hanging. He likes to take the finished artwork to its site and he installs it himself.

HANA NOVOTNÁ says her early work was inspired by objects from everyday life. Sculptures called *The Chair, The Table with The Carpet* and *The Stairs* were created from her authentic world, a world not visible to all. Later she became inspired by nature, making such works as *The Nest* and *Back to Nature*. She writes of her work:

> The topic of nature was new for me in many respects. The shapes from reality that had been formed for many centuries had, in their purpose and structure, an aesthetic attraction for me. For the works inspired by nature I used raku techniques that I associated with natural colours as well as a rough appearance. In this way I introduced the real world into the clay. The nature-inspired works, such as *The Nest* gave me a new respect for the environment, and there my former inspiration from reality took on a new look and sense.

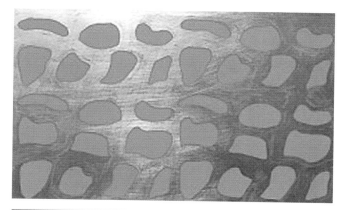

TOP: *Hana Novotná, **Empty Places**, 2003. Detail of porcelain slab, lustre glaze.*

ABOVE: *Hana Novotná, **Nest**, 2002. Raku clay.*

In her work from the past few years (2002/2004) she uses light and shadow to create shape and colour.

> I try to cooperate with the intensity and changes of light and time, I perforate porcelain slabs and enclose them in a metal sieve. The light coming through the sieves is drawn into shadow and together creates one shape, one object. This is a connection of something changeable and something stable. Slabs covered with simple metal drawings called *Reflection*, change under the light from the non-visible to colourful pictures. For it to function it needs our activity, motion and intensive light.

At the beginning of this cycle of work, Novotná made many drawings and objects from paper. The silver drawings on the surface of the porcelain slab, *Empty Places,* are contrasted with places that are left untouched. The reflection of the light on each area is different. Empty places suddenly become filled, the changes in reality of the object are influenced by the light and shadows, between the metal surfaces reflecting light, the empty spaces absorbing it within, and this gives space for the imagination.

Hana Novotná graduated from the Prague Academy of Applied Art in the ceramics studio with Václav Serák, and also undertook study at the University for Industrial Arts in Helsinki. In an article in *Ceramics: Art and Perception 37* on the work of Hana Novotná, the curator and art theorist, Milena Klasová, discussed the ideas behind Novotná's ceramics: 'Hana Novotná's sculptures are introjections of the world into clay and determine her space. The are tri-dimensional dreams; with their help she fights against losses and emptiness and builds up an intimate setting pure, formally clear, ordered and simple.'

CHAPTER TEN

Monumental Concepts

I N THE LONG VIEW, the history of art is synonymous with the history of public art: pyramids and cathedrals were built before the appearance of art museums. Today it is often the word 'art' that is emphasised before 'public'. But the origin of the concept is of vital importance for public art processes with their evident conditions: the purpose, the function of the place or building as a whole, the collaboration with other artists and with those who use the place. We are living in a time of change, the market is becoming more global, communication is digitalised. How does it affect us? Are there new collective meeting places being established? Can we still talk about a public space, belonging to everyone? Even in those categories of art where the material and how it is treated plays an important part in the result, we gain if we look with fresh eyes. Can ceramic be used in new applications? Materials used in new combinations? Can artistic expressions be widened in temporary or permanent contexts? These are some of the thoughts of Lillemor Petersson, an artist from Sweden, who for four years (2000–04) was a member of the board of the National Public Art Council, whose task, besides supplying buildings which house government offices with good contemporary art, is to support projects in other areas as well. This could concern population centres, traffic areas, schoolyards and more. But its overall mandate is to make contemporary art accessible to the broader public. The Council commissions art for a particular building or a particular site. They are also an important purchaser of 'movable' art, to be placed in offices or hospitals. In 2001 the Council initiated a project which focused on 'Building Ceramics', with the aim of exploring

PETERSSON

HARRISON

ANDERSON

MESTRE

GARRAZA

CARLÉ

NANNING

TRUMPIE

HUDSON

OPPOSITE: *Carlos Carlé,* **Megaliti per Barge** *(detail), 2000. Stoneware and marble (quarzite). Italy. Dimensions: 5.2. x 1.1 x 2.8m (17 x 3.6 x 9ft).*

ABOVE: *Lillemor Petersson, **Sun Wheel**, 1995. The Hidden Art Forest, Ostersund, North Sweden. Width: 11m (36ft).*

RIGHT: *Lillemor Petersson, **Brick Summer** (detail), 1994. Sculpture in a central city garden, Gothenburg, Sweden.*

fields of application for ceramic art and to support cooperation between smaller, more flexible ceramic producers and artists and ceramicists.

LILLEMOR PETERSSON, Swedish sculptor and professor emeritus, former head teacher in ceramics at Konstfack University of Art in Stockholm, has been a regular contributor to the field of environmental ceramics. Two statues in fired brick, 9m (29½ ft) high, grace the courtyard outside the entrance of the Department of Civil Engineering at the University of Technology, Gothenburg. Their monumental shapes remind us of the spans of a bridge, the tall sections crowned by an arch. Petersson's sculptures seem to be growing out of their surroundings; on the ground they are enclosed by a cup-shaped circle laid with large paving stones and at the side there is a red carpet of fishbone – patterned and massive paving bricks spread out towards the entrance. The benches, shaped as circular segments, are placed to underline that this is an area for people to gather. The sharp detail, thoroughly worked and individually dealt with, is accentuated in that each brick is articulated with relief, carvings, paintings, scribbles and stampings – among other things one can find the bricklayer's name. 'This is a unique example of how an environmental piece of art can collaborate, have

an influence on and contrast with its surroundings and at the same time live its own life,' writes Håkan Wettre, former Head of Gothenburg Art Museum, on the work of Lillemor Petersson.

During one year's work at the Bohus brick factory in Munkedal, Petersson worked directly with clay. She writes:

> Educated and experienced as a ceramicist one knows quite a lot about clay and its character. Over the years one's curiosity and respect for this material only grows, its evidently never-ending possibilities for expression and its plasticity. Ceramicists in Sweden often work with imported clays which are fired to stoneware at about 1300°C (2372°F). The clay goes through mixing and glazing in a complicated process and the firings give varying results. At the brick factory we met the same ceramic processes but in large scale. The brick clay, direct from the ground and mixed with gravel, takes its colour from the iron in the earth. It is unglazed and the firing temperature is around 1000°C (1832°F). And in spite of large industrial and automatic methods, it is with the same excitement that one waits for the result after a firing. The circulation of flame in the kiln, the reduction atmosphere, the weather and wind give surprises and create each brick as an individual object with its own variation.

The practical shape of a brick and the generous amount of them at the factory creates a desire to make something, either in the one piece or in combinations making larger surfaces – walls, columns, arches. With differently shaped bricks, the body of the building can be

enriched – the single bricks with small details, large reliefs or with a register of modules for varied surfaces; soft bending in the wall, an undulating movement or ornamental modulation – brick walls do not always have to be square-shaped, or hard. In the soft clay there is a possibility of forming round or square-edged shapes, small or large. For the artist there is a possibility of contributing early in the building planning, either the work as an individual piece of art or embodied in the whole.

Petersson writes that people have made bricks and built with them for many thousand of years. Nobody knows for sure when the first bricks or 'baked stones' came into use. Sun-dried stone must have been earlier than the fired. Also grasses were added and fired in the clay body to make them stronger. Egyptians and Romans developed manufacturing techniques to a high level. Walls from Roman times, 2000 years ago, are to be seen today. In northern Europe, however, bricks weren't made before the 12th century.

For a large brick wall on commission for a new county museum in the town of Uddevalla, Petersson enjoyed a cooperation with the architect. Most of the bricks for this work were built up with two and three double bricks. All the work was made with wet bricks taken directly from the extruder in the factory, Petersson using her experience of working with earthenware. What was different in comparison to her other ceramic works was the weight – each brick weighs 3.5kg (7.7lb) and 10,000 of them were used in the wall. And they

needed to be moved many times. The subject for this wall is an ode to the local landscape with its seaside, its cliffs and traditions.

Petersson exhibited *Missile*, made from sculptured bricks, in Scandinavia during 1987 and 1989. Large red-firing bricks were cut in ornamental profiles, fired and some refired in a raku kiln; the largest form is 3.5m (11½ft) high. 'It has such a beautiful grey colour.' Other works include a 30 x 4m (98 x 13ft) brick wall at St Görans hospital in Stockholm, made in 1989. The wall follows the street and on the opposite side there is an old church which is built with a variety of bricks. Most of the 7000–8000 bricks were fabricated at the brick factory where Petersson worked for about three months.

Many hundreds of the bricks were handmade, and the crosses and all special shapes had to be individually cut. There are cuts through the wall to give the shadows and many are glazed or painted with blue, green and white slips. The pieces were made with a red iron-rich clay often mixed with high percentage of lime to lighten the clay towards a pink tone and then fired at about 1000°C (1832°F). Almost all the firings were made at the brick factory using tunnel kilns fired with oil.

Another piece comprises blue crosses on a bed of spruce. One hundred terracotta figures in front symbolise the resistance against a motor road through a nature area in the neighbourhood. The crosses are fired once, unglazed but painted with a clear blue slip. This work was exhibited in Sweden in 1995-96. In the town of Ostersund, north Sweden, another work, *Sun Wheel,* is an 11m (36ft) broad labyrinth built on a steep slope on the hill in the Hidden Art Forest in 1995. It is large enough to be seen from the air. 'The work in the forest landscape took two years. The main piece on the hill is the wheel. Of the 10,000 bricks about 2000 were handmade and decorated in a factory.' Petersson collected 8000 bricks from different places, 'some were old and pleasantly shaped. The labyrinth has a complicated placing on the sloping ground and it was difficult to find the right shape for its base. To find out how it sat on the slope we had to compose the whole work upside down. Friendly people let me borrow a large yard at a stone-cutting factory. There all the bricks were assembled in order and then numbered. This part of the project took three months. This place has now become popular with visitors.'

Wherever he has found himself – at the Archie Bray Foundation in Montana, Wisconsin's John Michael Kohler Arts Center, the Omaha Brickworks Workshop (now the Bemis Foundation) in Nebraska, the Banff (Alberta) Centre School of Fine Arts, or the Watershed Center for the Ceramic Arts in Maine – **ROBERT HARRISON** has left his mark.

> His need to inscribe upon the landscape clear evidence of his presence is nearly a compulsion. And yet, in the structures Harrison builds out of brick and tile, adobe and stone, wood and shards recycled from pots jettisoned by his fellow ceramicists, there is something impersonal, egoless, even universal.

Rick Newby, writing for *American Ceramics 9/3*, draws our attention to the commissions that Harrison has built in the environment. Invited to Australia to take part in the ClaySculpt project in Gulgong, NSW, Harrison, in conjunction with Bruce Anderson (Australia), built *Gulgong Square*, an environmental piece using adobe, iron and stone.

Earlier commissions include *Turtle Creek Archway*, Kansas, *St Lawrence Passage*, New York, *JB's Arch*, Colorado, and *A Potter's Shrine*, Montana. Born and raised in Winnipeg, Manitoba, Canada, Harrison has always felt a connection with the natural landscape. From his parents'

interest in the environment, he learnt to take pleasure in the natural world. Newby describes Harrison's career as a ceramic artist under the tutelage of Robert Archambeau at the University of Manitoba in the early 1970s as being 'attracted to the roughly elegant traditions of Japanese pottery'. Harrison found himself fascinated, too, by American painters and sculptors, and by Robert Smithson's heady theories and spiral jetties of the possibilities of architecture. Harrison's eclectic tastes led him far from his pottery roots, and halfway back again. When he entered the University of Denver's graduate programme in ceramics in 1979, Harrison was ready to step outside the tradition of vessel making and begin to explore other possibilities in his ceramic work. Today, Harrison sees his move from pottery to sculpture as a natural evolution, saying that he 'always loved clay as a material'.

Harrison wanted to work in a larger scale and he found that sculpture offered him what he needed. He began by creating ceramic installations, but filling the walls and floor of a gallery with figures was not enough: he wanted to mark the earth itself. One of Harrison's dreams was to build a monument to the potters and ceramic sculptors who were his comrades at the Archie Bray Foundation. In 1985, just as he was completing his residency at the Bray, he received a grant from a local film society to construct *A Potter's Shrine*. He says 'Over time, I

RIGHT: *Robert Harrison,* **Queen City Gateway,** *1997. Site-specific architectural sculpture. City of Helena Public Art Commission. Helena, Montana. Dimensions: 7.5 x 7.5 x 3m (24 ½ x 24 ½ x 10ft).*

OPPOSITE PAGE
LEFT: *Robert Harrison,* **Black Mountain Colonnade,** *1994. Site-specific architectural sculpture, Helena, Montana. Dimensions: 8.4 x 4.2 x 2.1m (27 ½ x 13 ¾ x 6 ¾ ft).*

CENTRE: *Robert Harrison,* **Medaltarch,** *1999. Site-specific architectural sculpture, Medalta International artist-in-residence programme. Medicine Hat, Alberta, Canada. Dimensions: 6.6 x 1.8 x 3m (21 ½ x 6 x 10ft).*

RIGHT: *Robert Harrison,* **Shedway,** *1989. Watershed Center for the Ceramic Arts. North Edgecomb, Maine. Site-specific architectural sculpture. Dimensions: 3.6 x 1.8 x 0.6m (11 ¾ x 6 x 2ft) each side.*

had begun including images in my work – in particular, the circle and the spiral – that were more life-affirming, that suggested growth and renewal.' Perhaps, Newby suggests, he was subconsciously turning away from what he now views as the rigidity and coldness of modernism, and towards a more playful, sensual and humane stance.

Rick Newby, again writing on Harrison's work, this time for *Ceramics: Art and Perception 10*, on an installation in Adelaide, Australia, reminds us that Harrison's temporary gallery installations have paralleled the developments and obsessions to be found in his site works: 'Usually developed at the instigation of gallery directors in the US, Canada and now Australia, Harrison's installations – despite their obvious connection to his outdoor pieces – allow the Canadian-born sculptor to exercise a side of his nature impossible to fully indulge in those works situated out-of-doors.' Harrison notes: 'When I am working outside, nature always surprises and delights me, the effects of moisture and extremes of temperature on my materials, the look of the work depending upon the angle and intensity of the sunlight. Indoors, I find a different pleasure; I can control all the elements, especially the lighting, and instil a sense of heightened drama, an almost magical or spiritual atmosphere.' Harrison finds himself drawn to resonant sites and spaces, and his works, both indoors and out, echo and honour the cathedrals, ruins of Roman temples and Celtic megaliths Harrison visited during a tour of the British Isles and the European continent in 1987. 'I see my installations,' says Harrison, 'as sanctuaries. When you enter them, I want you to enter another dimension.'

BRUCE ANDERSON is an Australian ceramic artist who has increasingly turned his attention to architectural enhancement. In an article for *Ceramics: Art and Perception 5*, Dean Bruton writes: 'As maquettes for architectural work, Bruce Anderson proposes that sculptural form may be part of postmodern architecture and at the same time be craft-based.' Bruton believes that Anderson raises questions concerning the nature of good taste, high craft and recent trends in architecture, saying: 'Emphasis on exploration of new materials, and expanding the knowledge-base of materials, has resulted in a novel solution to the problem of sequential sculpture. The height and arrangement of his terrazzo constructions is not as ominous in its confrontation as say, Aboriginal burial poles or the Easter Island statues might be. Instead, the pastel colours and airy textures convey a playful mood.'

The influences of Indian temples and his own spiritual endeavour are referenced in his architectural works and Anderson regularly visits India as part of his continuing study of Eastern religion. The Hindu temples of Asia have inspired his terrazzo and cement spiritual spires. Bruton continues, 'The theme of the superficiality of life seems to be overlaid with the concerns of '60s absolutist idealism. Anderson's balanced forms seem to propose that the Western world might transcend everyday reality through monumentality.'

ENRIQUE MESTRE has always showed interest in his immediate surroundings, in the place where he lives and, through it, seeks the meaning of his existence. He has focused his attention on the perfect geometrical lines of fields and fragments of certain types of domestic architecture in order to explain his own experiences, emotions or memories. Roman de la Calle, Professor of Art Theory and Aesthetics at the University of Valencia (Spain), writes about the work of this Spanish ceramic artist:

> There are neither sudden leaps nor haphazard variations in the rigorous line of sculptural research by Enrique Mestre. It is precisely this personal touch – the intertwining of unconditional and unwavering coherence and his increasing demands on himself and uncompromising attitude with his own work – which have led to Mestre's tendency to simplification. His is an increasingly purified formal simplicity born of a complex synthesis of simultaneous factors.

The demands that Mestre makes on himself and the fastidiousness of his working methods are a part of the artist's aesthetic approach. His sculptural practice and his

architectural works characterise his basic outlook and demonstrate monumental concepts. Matter, form and space determine the physical limitations of the works, Calle says, increasing their mystery and the scope of their possible spirituality.

Hollows which are partly hidden from sight or merely suggested become momentary conductors of light and allow us to discover all the apertures perforating his forms, and fully credit them as architectural structures housing secrets of their own. The artist's muted colour schemes and carefully controlled textures are intentional strategies – generators of volume – meant to highlight the shelters for space, perhaps as a metaphor of life itself. Mestre's architectural purpose to his work has revealed new and inspiring objectives, at the same time the artistic language he uses has become enriched.

In 1996 Javier Diaz made a series of videos under the *Ceramic Mediterranean* title. In the video on Enrique Mestre we learn of the techniques employed by Mestre in the making of his work. Mixing his own clay he then uses a slab roller to form 2cm (¾ in.) thick slabs from which he assembles his architectural structures. Mestre makes a full-scale ground plan after sketching out his ideas, many influenced by Moorish architecture. The techniques are exacting. Often he models a volumetric form so that he can see the interior spaces clearly, Mestre is careful to work the sections with the grain of the clay, and individual pieces are carefully dried after texturing and polishing the surface. Mestre likes sharp edges, filling any gaps with soft clay and smoothing the form with a wooden block. Slip is used to create different colours. Mestre has organised his studio space so that the work processes are streamlined and efficient; large pieces are moved by means of a forklift truck. Firing is gas reduction using large trolley kilns with swing doors; the work is fired to 1280°C (2336°F).

'Of Places and Memory', an article on the sculptural works of **ANGEL GARRAZA** (Spain) by Kosme de Baranano, published in *International Ceramic Art '96*, reads: 'The series of works that Angel Garraza presents under the title of *Sites and Places* brought together a common thread: the memory and the mystery of travel as a recollection. Garraza, the sculptor, dividing up a field – on the ground or on the wall – signs that conjure and recall, rewriting in ceramics one's memories and sensations from other sites and other places that are out of the ordinary.' Garraza believes it is sometimes difficult to communicate feelings and memories but making information available to others is demanding and should be precise. In his works it is not the memory of something that happened that is revealed; rather it is the impressions that such events leave behind.

Writing in *Ceramics: Art and Perception 22*, Antonio Vivas, editor of the Spanish magazine *Ceramica*, says:

Ceramic artists like Garraza lift ceramics to mainstream art. His need for expression and the language he uses in

forming it enables his ceramics and sculptures to evolve. For Garraza, inspiration comes from confronting the work and, given time, obtaining the results he seeks. His ceramic oeuvre is unmistakable and the dynamics of his creation conforms to a personal language. His evolution has been as a consequence of a constant rhythm, spaced aesthetic changes, in essence a compromise between his expression and innovation.

While Garraza is captivated by the creative potential of ceramics, he searches out the multiple possibilities

ABOVE: *Angel Garraza,* **Sitios y Lugares,** *2002. Bilbao. Dimensions: 5 x 12 x 5m (16½ x 39¼ x 16½ ft).*

LEFT: *Angel Garraza, Installation, ceramic.*

OPPOSITE
Carlos Carlé, **Dolmen,** *1989. Centro Storico di Padova, Italy.*

CARLOS CARLÉ writes that *Megaliti per Barge* and *Dolmen* are two examples of the most interesting sculptures in an important period of his work, and represent a stage in a creative pathway that is still evolving.

> My work has always included primitive atemporal prototypes, inspired by elementary geometric elements that may be traced back to the original forms of artistic expression. This pathway is marked by works such as these, evocative and monumental figures that connect to a remote past, to primeval examples, still missing an artistic connotation yet rich with a spirituality linked with rite, religion, magic and celebrative of festivals.

These works are static, simple yet mysterious, imposing and absolute, although lacking any historical or literary content, Carlé says that he feels their significance — silent testimonies, memories whose message becomes conscious and universal.

In the Breton language, *Dolmen* means stone table, and is a megalithic form of the Bronze Age.

> The essential form of this work of mine, which discards the redundant, the ornament, is defined in the man–space relationship. Therefore, it links to the currents of contemporary art, from minimal art and from ambient art. A sculpture is like an empty vase surrendering itself to the viewer expecting to be filled with meanings. I am no theorist, I don't like using words to express myself, I prefer doing it with stoneware, with earth. In the words of Henry Moore, 'I do not understand why sculpture should be explained in words, words pertain to literature. Neither figurative arts nor music want to explain the world. Arts pass through the senses, and have no practical goals . . .'

Born in Argentina, Carlos Carlé settled in Liguria, Italy, in the mid-1960s, in Albisola. This town has been recognised as the birthplace of 20th-century art ceramics because of the artists who worked and settled there. Cecilia Chilosi, in an article on Carlos Carlé for *Ceramics: Art and Perception 49*, wrote that Carlé had 'a mastery of his materials and control of form' and that worldwide recognition and the appreciation of critics have defined his role in modern sculpture. She cites his respect for nature: 'Carlé is a gatherer of stones. Time has modified their structure, water has smoothed and rounded them, friction has carved and scaled them, modelling their surfaces … he reaches monumental results.' Other critics

that exist within it. Sculpture has allowed him to detach himself from the seduction of the medium but he uses the rich elements of it that are available through the processes and the materials. The red or black clay, the subtlety of porcelain, the glaze or the fine texture that comes from an expanded mica, the atmospheres possible in the wood-burning kiln, convert themselves into potential instruments of expression. Vivas writes:

> His study of architecture and archaeology and his interest in culture have produced the subtle contrasts of light and dark and his compositions of earth reds and smoked blacks; he uses an intimate language that produces an aura of antiquity. The sculptures of Angel Garraza are monumental and he makes his mark with his ceramics, physically and literally, going beyond the possibility that painting is like a dream, sculpture is like truth and ceramics is like fire.

have given equal praise. 'Carlé considers ceramics as a way of writing on which you can directly impress your emotions in matter,' wrote Maria Thérèse Coullery, while discussing his vital strength and expressiveness. Antoinette Fay-Halle, chief keeper at the National Museum of Sèvres, finds Carlé's ceramics expressive and artistic. And the art critic Luciano Caprile, writing in 1997, talks of Carlé's work as enduring signs of the 'mystery of the sacred and the infinite. With him, satisfaction is on the threshold of the unknown, of a message that has to be accepted, not as a revelation but as a gift.'

BARBARA NANNING's work in ceramics has generated acclaim throughout the Netherlands and worldwide. For a 2003 exhibition at the Singer Museum in Laren, the Netherlands, a book, *Barbara Nanning – Evolution* was published to celebrate her achievements. Since finishing the ceramics programme at the Gerrit

Rietveld Academy in Amsterdam in 1979, Nanning has consistently pursued her work with remarkable success, and her ceramics straddle the boundary between the applied and the fine arts; she is always in search of contemporary expression. Nanning is inspired by nature, in all forms of appearance and growth, and in recent years, colour has played an important role. She uses clear, brilliant colours and pure pigments.

Increasingly, Nanning completes monumental commissioned works for both outdoor and indoor locations. For these works, she makes extensive use of computer techniques to visualise, design and construct the installations. Working together with industry, she continues to develop techniques to achieve form and detail in what are ambitious projects. A recent example is the series of 14 monumental gilded flowers completed for the ceiling of the first-class dining room of the MS *Zuiderdam* and the MS *Oosterdam*, two Holland-America Line cruise ships,

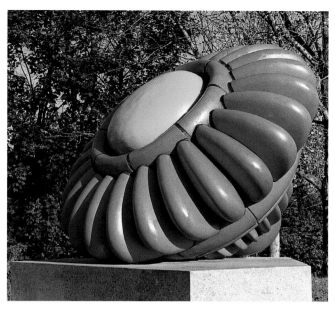

OPPOSITE: *Barbara Nanning,* **Flowerbuds***. KLPD, Driebergen, during installation.*

ABOVE: *Barbara Nanning,* **Eternal Flower***. Alsmeer.*

commissioned by VFD Interiors b.v. Utrecht. Since 1990, alongside her ceramics work, Barbara Nanning has worked in glass and over these years her art has become complex.

Evolution, a term for mapping out a piece of artistic history, describes Nanning's 2003 work and is documented in the book that is quoted here; it also appeared in *Kerameiki Techni* and the Dutch magazine *Residence.*

> The oeuvre of Nanning is a continuum of objects that can be classified into groups, as of species and families. Her latest objects follow from the preceding ones. Ideas often continue to have an effect for a long period of time, but never in a strictly linear way. Sometimes the forms are hybrid, emerging like some caprice of nature in an entirely new guise – and in isolated cases, via a large detour after much searching and experimentation. But they almost always come into being without a shred of hesitation; they are confident and bold.

Nanning writes, 'Between 1979 and 1983 I placed the emphasis on applying colour to turned pots. I based my methodology on the colour theory of the Bauhaus, in particular that of Johannes Itten. At the same time, I was fascinated by the traditional forms of the dishes and bowls made by the Indians in Mexico, the vivid, intense colours of the textile and the plastic utensils.' Nanning's work took a leap forwards in 1988, when she constructed composite forms out of cut-up cylinders. Worthy of note is that her desire to work in monumental formats grew apace. Her first sculptures for public spaces date from this period. With the *Fossilforms,* she added no colour and left the fired stoneware clay for what it was. She found the inspiration for these works during a study trip to Cappadocia, a chalk-white Turkish landscape with dwellings hewn from the cliffs and weather-eroded masses of rock. 'The barrenness, the monochrome quality, the purity appealed to me enormously. These impressions led to unglazed, turned pots and vases, which were circumvented with rope, causing bulges to arise between the constrictions. In a subsequent phase I cut out the bottoms and laid these turned forms on their sides, so that a pot or vase became a free object.'

The *Galaxy* series, with its centrifugal systems of planets and heavenly bodies as its inspirational source,

appeared in 1990. It caused a breakthrough for Barbara Nanning in the world of Dutch ceramics during the Keramiek '90 exhibition in south Holland. Her installation in the Museum Het Prinsenhof in Delft was something new in the established world of clay and glaze. Monumentally turned ring-shaped objects, as well as the use of pigments, was far away from what purists within the world of ceramics considered authoritative and sanctified. Nanning was no longer using glazes and engobes, but pure paint pigment – a cold finish on cold material.

Nanning also began assembling stoneware components with epoxy resin. The technique she developed is laborious but precise. She feels that a skin of lacquer, pigment and sand connects the world of the painter with that of the ceramicist. Colours that until then belonged only to the world of painting were reintroduced in another world. Within the infinite range of colours that Nanning now had at her disposal, she chose a limited pallet of pure, unmixed pigments. Vivid colours such as clear red, intense yellow, deep blue and brilliant purple give an unexpected, almost unreal dimension to her work. Mixed with fine sand, the colour cocoons the object and softens its contours. 'My fascination for everlasting motion, the revolving of the planets, stars and molecules and my desire to record the essence of this motion has resulted in vividly coloured objects comprised of truncated curves.'

Various trips to Japan laid the foundation for Nanning's ceramic work from the mid-1990s. Inspired

*Barbara Nanning, **Hanging Flowerbud**, 2004. ABN AMRO Bank, Amsterdam z-o. Dimensions: 2.7 x 1.2 x 1.8m (8¾ x 4 x 6ft). Weight: 240kg (529lb).*

ABOVE AND RIGHT *Barbara Nanning's* **Flowerbuds** *under construction.*

by centuries-old Zen gardens she said:

> The objects are earthy and stand on their own, they rise up from the earth. The straight lines are reminiscent of ploughed fields and Zen gardens. I take these rational forms and combine them with organic forms from nature, grafting feeling on to reason in this way. Dynamics with a static resting point. There must, I think, be a balance, a harmony between the positive and the negative, the static and the dynamic, inner and outer forms, growth and gravity.

What initially began around 1996 as a few isolated objects inspired by flower buds and seed capsules gradually developed into a separate group. Compactly composed buds evolved into lush flowers with leaves that seem to wave in the wind. In their turn, the flowers transformed into underwater beings swaying along on the currents.

Buds were also the departure point for several monumental commissions, such as for the Gemeente Aalsmeer (Municipality of Aalsmeer) and for the Korps Landelijke Politie Dienst, or KLPD (National Police Service Agency) in Driebergen. In collaboration with architect Paul van Leeuwen and the Hague-based company Struktuur '68, life-sized sculptures were built and assembled from glazed segments. The *Botanica* series acquired an air of grandeur with the prestigious commis-

sion to decorate the previously mentioned first-class dining rooms of two luxury cruise ships. The ceilings resemble an inverted field of flowers. The lustre of the 'Fleurs de Mer' installations comes from the fact that the flowers are gilded, either with gold leaf or a combination of gold leaf and platinum. For these and many other of her monumental commissions, Nanning makes use of advanced computer designs. She has developed types of finishes new to the industry that can be applied in large-scale projects.

'After each of my trips – Mexico, Turkey and Asia – I returned to my studio with a profusion of new ideas about colour, form and texture that has profoundly influenced my work.' Nanning sets down her inspiration in dozens of sketches, drawings and photographs that function as a memory aid. Direct sources of inspiration can be seen, but because she always combines different things, the results are never literal. Nature, both organic and inorganic, is a constant source of inspiration. She examines crystals, jellyfish, flowers and micro-organisms with an almost 19th-century fascination for form, structure and geometry. Nanning combines regularity with fluidity, order with chaos, the hard with the soft, the rigid with the informal.

Often there appears to be an inspiration from the Far East: onrushing waves such as those represented in the woodcuts of Hokusai, raked Zen Buddhist gardens, age-old gnarled tree stumps and motifs derived from lacquerware and kimonos. Such an interest in the exotic is typically Dutch. A tradition was nourished for centuries by trade relations with the Far East. Nanning gives it contemporary interpretation: 'The perfect workmanship, the omission of the superfluous, the composure for doing it the right way are elements that I have brought back from Japan to my studio. The Japanese cultivate a greater depth, a more intense concentration when making their products. Colours and forms are a true inspiration for them.'

A press release written for the exhibition *Evolution* summarises Nanning's art practice:

Barbara Nanning combines tradition with innovation, Eastern opulence with Dutch austereness, freedom with structure and reason with emotion. Her work is a mix of unequal quantities without becoming complex; a fusion of carefully chosen and at times seemingly contradictory elements, which in the end look so self-evident that no one wonders about the unusual combination of ingredients. She unites classical artisan methods with an innovative use of materials to achieve an entirely unique language of form, one which often develops in the making process, the turning of clay on the wheel and the blowing of glass. At a later stage she processes those forms by cutting and assembling them. This applies to both the ceramic and glass work. Her language does not comply with the existing one, but breaks new ground and forms a universe.

In an article in *Ceramics Technical 9*, Christian Reinewald writes about some of the commissions Barbara Nanning has undertaken. 'Nanning knows where she is going,' he says. 'With monumental commissions her course has become realistic. The sculptures of flowers are recognisable but are clearly shaped from a more abstract constructivist approach. Nanning designs her works on the computer choosing an Autocad system with a render programme.' With the 3D functions she obtained good visualisation of different possibilities and combinations for the cross-sections and side views of the objects, she explains. One such work was placed at the entry of a major road and catches the attention of the pedestrians, bikers and passing traffic. The monumental stylised flower was realised by Struktuur '68 in Den Haag and placed in position in 1997.

The studio for ceramics Struktuur '68 was founded in 1968 by Jacques van Gaalen and **HENK TRUMPIE** in the centre of The Hague, Netherlands. This enterprise was in response to the growing need among visual artists to realise monumental work in ceramics and incorporate individual artistic quality into a large-scale production system. Artistic experiments are time consuming, expensive and therefore not interesting to industry but because of its specialist approach, Struktuur '68 has the opportunity to assist artists with handwork and experiments. The studio has been involved in the manufacturing of large sculptures in public and private spaces, inside as well as outside. Up until now the studio has collaborated with about 200 Dutch national and international artists, resulting in about a thousand successful monumental commissions.

Apart from the three-dimensional aspect, the malleability of clay proves to be attractive to artists. By the application of glazes, a form can be realised in the most varied colours. Trumpie says:

Ceramics possess a natural and perpetual value. Through the use of different clays and because of the fact that the kilns make it possible to reach high temperatures, ceramics are no more vulnerable than other materials. Struktuur '68 collaborates with expert construction and transport firms needed by artists making monumental works. Struktuur '68 is more than a studio for ceramics, it invites contacts with architects and initiating institutions at the museum and gallery level. It enables artists to engage in discussion and collaboration. Its mediation between commissioners, architects and artists is primarily directed towards the improvement of the quality of ceramic art. The six employees have thorough technical knowledge and experience at their disposal and they are always willing to search for new solutions, to advise and to be of assistance.

In a book on the work of Struktuur '68, published in 2003, Trumpie is reported as saying that working with ceramics requires imagination. When clay becomes part of an artist's thinking, it takes on an independent significance that cannot be linked to any other art form. Paul Hefting, in an essay in the same book, noted that in the Netherlands the collaboration between artists and architects began at the end of the 19th century. The result of this was visible and led to many innovations. Individual patrons played an important role at that time, leaving a legacy that is still relevant today. Struktuur '68 answered the call for monumental ceramics, writes Hefting. 'Anything was possible, every experiment viewed for its feasibility, each innovation embraced.'

Stephen Hudson, **Topographical Fictions** *(detail of installation). Tasmania.*

STEPHEN HUDSON is a Tasmanian-based sculptor whose work aims to question our perception of and position within an increasingly mediated world. A major award winner at the World Ceramic Biennale Korea in 2003, he continues to exhibit and research these themes. Hudson's interest in the history and materiality of clay is aligned with his fascination with the development of cities and his work is strongly influenced by contemporary architectural theory. He writes in an artist statement for his 1999 exhibition Models of Models: Representations of Souvenirs/ Souvenirs of Representation, 'The issues that have emerged in my work are those concerned with the lived experience of the city and, in particular, the influence that representations have in our perception of that experience.'

In his large-scale installations Hudson explores the complex and often contradictory interconnection between the self and the world – each influencing the other through their representations. He writes:

In our everyday lives we make use of and are confronted by countless representations – from simple diagrams to the more complex representations of the media. In turn, we represent ourselves to the world by means of how we choose to express ourselves and also by our use (or abuse) of the city. My interest is in the degree to which this interrelationship determines our social experience as well as the continued evolution of the city itself.

Central to this body of work, which is based on images of ideal cities, is the manipulation of certain elements of conventional representation such as perspective and scale. Dualities such as real/imaginary, past/future, inside/outside have also been combined in order to undermine the representative nature of the work. Most significantly for Hudson, however, has been the role of the architectural model or miniature in his project. Existing as both physical objects and simulation, Hudson claims that miniatures and models blur the distinction between the real and the imaginary. His interest in the miniature has not arisen, however, from

*Stephen Hudson, **Models of Models**. Installation detail.*

*Stephen Hudson, **Models of Models**. Installation detail.*

the fact that they present a perfect, uncontaminated version of the world; more important has been the notion that our experience of and interaction with miniatures reflects in an exaggerated manner the paradoxical interconnection of the self and the world that he mentions in his statement. 'The miniatures have been manipulated and distorted, so that the viewer's relationship to them is unstable and, therefore, the respective positions of both are questionable. The aim of my work is to highlight the illusionary nature not only of the world, but also of ourselves, by the disruption of conventional representations and expectations.'

Hudson has now become interested in digital technologies and computer-generated images. He says, 'With the combination of advanced science and digital technology we are now offered a variety of dramatic representations from the innermost terrains of our bodies to the outermost dimensions of the universe.'

For his 2002 exhibition, Topographical Fictions, Hudson based much of his work on the iconic image of

DNA's double helix. Again, the intention of these large-scale installations suspended on the walls is to disorientate viewers by suggesting a sense of projection into or out of the virtual world beyond the computer screen. In addition, the marbled surfaces, achieved by the application of decals, highlight the virtual nature of these images by referencing computer rendering.

Of his most recent work, Hudson has this to say:

In particular, I am interested in the spatial consequences of the digital revolution, which has dramatically increased the parameters of human perception and experience. This research utilises aspects of architectural practice and theory, whose parameters have likewise increased, as a major reference point. While art and architecture have always shared concerns in respect to space and representation, in the digital realm the intersection of these disciplines is particularly apparent. As a visual artist, my interest is in the way virtual spaces are being created and represented, and how virtual and real environments inform one another. It is my aim to conceptualise and represent this complex environment.

CHAPTER ELEVEN

Form as Language

PETER **MASTERS**, A CERAMIC ARTIST originally from Canada and now living in Australia, asks:

Is there value in art being in public spaces? Relatively few children are taken to an art gallery – a play maybe, a concert most likely, a film most certainly, but a gallery interior is unfamiliar territory, and in school at tertiary level, gallery visits are exclusive to art students, a precious minority. Thus most adults are ambivalent toward or even intimidated by art galleries – they are not comfortable in places like that. In a given year, only approximately 22% of Australians over 15 years of age visit public art galleries, according to the *Sydney Weekly* (15 February 2000), so for the majority to be exposed to art, it needs to be more accessible. This then is reason enough for the public or corporate sectors to commission art for public spaces – within or without buildings.

How are the roles of the architect designer/artist affected? The architect, designer and artist take on an enormous responsibility to not only serve the demands of enhancing the space (and usually with a far too limited budget) – but to create an environment both inspirational and inoffensive – and almost impossible, produce a work with integrity, within the spatial demands, restricted budget, and public/corporate body expectations which ultimately must be governed by public reaction.

Within these parameters, Masters believes site-specific work need not be compromised, and it can and does have a major impact on its environment, such that the space becomes not only a more friendly place but somewhere, other than the gallery confines, to have a dialogue with the artist and his intentions.

MASTERS

SHIN

HANSEN

DELRUE

KVASBO

MADOLA

BALDA

KERASSIOTI

HSU

OPPOSITE: *Sangho Shin,*
***Dream of Africa** (detail), 2002.*

Peter Masters, one of 12 sculptures installed on columns in the terminal at Cairns airport.

*Sangho Shin, **Dream of Africa**, 2002. Sculptures at the artist's home and studio.*

Assisting Peter Masters with a public art work, this time for the Cairns International Airport terminal, Augustine Fleischer wrote that the whole project took eight months to complete.

The project consisted of 12 sculptural works, which were attached to the columns adjacent to the terminal walls. Writing in *Ceramics Technical 6*, she describes the commission from the start to the details of installation. She concludes: 'The making and installation of these works continually challenged Masters and myself. It provided Masters with an opportunity to extend the concept of his sculptural work in ways previously unrealised. That all 12 sculptures were successfully produced in such a limited time testifies to the skill, patience and craftsmanship invested in these works.'

The work of **SANGHO SHIN** is dedicated to incessant challenge, experimenting constantly in search of the new, believes Yangmo Chung, former director of the National Museum in Seoul, South Korea, writing for *American Ceramics 14/1*. Shin works in two styles of ceramics, one the traditional Buncheong ware, the other sculptural work: animal figures that are commissioned for public spaces. Chung writes that 'Shin makes artworks of pictorial beauty and power.' Several books have been published on the work of Sangho Shin. The art critic Bok Young Kim, writing in Shin's *Dream of Africa* monograph of 2002, describes Shin's understanding of clay, his pushing of the boundaries of his medium and his painstaking efforts to realise his creative imaginary world. Shin himself says that his animal heads are created from his imagination although he has always had a liking for the primitive in art. In an article in

*Shin Sangho, **Dream of Africa** (detail), 2002.
Dimensions: 71 x 67 x 57cm (28 x 26 ½ x 22 ½ in.).*

*Shin Sangho, **Dream of Africa** (detail), 2002.
Height: 66cm (26in.).*

Ceramics: Art and Perception 44, by Jaeon Lee, Shin is quoted as saying:

> First, I try to reveal a language, a sense of beauty or an individual structure and pattern of the clay on the basis of my aesthetic motivation toward nature and freedom. Secondly, I try to minimise any technical difficulties and material shortcomings, for example, I don't have to limit the size of work just because of the limits of the kiln. What I have to do is to enlarge the kiln, develop techniques and prepare clay with good plasticity. Thirdly, interpreting and presenting the space where my works will be shown is crucial. This gives the maximum aesthetic satisfaction to viewers.

Lee believes that the ultimate purpose of Sangho Shin's work is to express nature and freedom. Shin states: 'Like the form of pottery, the lines drawn on the surface should be able to express their own images – to create impromptu and accidental lines. I use a bamboo or metal knife. Using such tools, I dig, refill and scratch in order to show my experience and to harmonise the pictures on a ceramic shape.' More liberally expressed figures show the culmination of a sense of nature, believes Lee, who goes on to say:

> Shin uses complex clays that have good adhesiveness and in that way he is able to increase the size of his work. The freedom from a limited size increases the challenge and boosts his energy towards the clay, and makes it possible for him to make giant pieces. A sense of the artistic in ceramic art cannot be recognised until it adjusts itself and understands and reflects the changing times. And, then, its social and historical usefulness may be appreciated accordingly. Shin's work suggests a new possibility and vision of ceramic art.

ABOVE LEFT: *Jørgen Hansen,* **Pillars of Movement**. *Work in progress. Taastrup Theatre, Denmark.*

ABOVE RIGHT: *Jørgen Hansen,* **Wearisome Paths**, *2004. Vibary, Denmark. Height: 3m (10ft). Using 6.5 tonnes of clay. For the celebration of 475 years since the beginning of the Reformation in Denmark.*

OPPOSITE
LEFT AND RIGHT: *Jørgen Hansen, firing of sculpture, and detail of finished piece.*

The ceramic art of Sangho Shin has been collected by major museums throughout the world. He is currently Dean of the School of Industrial Arts at Hong-Ik University, and is a member of juries and committees of important contemporary events in Korean ceramic art.

JØRGEN HANSEN is interested in people's feelings, what is behind the reasons and the questions, saying, 'In my work I want to come close to people's lives, to interfere perhaps, to move people.' When undertaking commissions, he likes the possibility of interposing something of himself in a public space, changing people's attitudes, making them change their thoughts about everyday life. For him, this provides a direct possibility for communication. 'Projects and commissions are a way to use my ideas and material

from a new angle and tie them to a destination. For me, it is a welcome challenge where I can see new horizons and discover new tools.' In 1995 he visited Australia to assist Nina Hole in building *The House of the Rising Sun* at the ClaySculpt project in Gulgong, NSW. This was just one of the environmental sculptures in which he has been involved.

Jørgen Hansen has made a number of ceramic works in the environment since 1987 when, at Ebeltoft, he built *Dragon*, a 1.5 x 7m (4.9 x 23ft) work in salt-glazed stoneware. In 1988, he built a five-piece lawn sculpture at Aarhus and, in 1997, at the Taastrup Theatre, Denmark, he built three outdoor sculptures each 3.5m (11.5ft) high. Other works have been commissioned for schools, churches and hospitals in both his native Denmark and abroad.

Hansen calls one of his works *Cathedral of the Soul*. He describes the work as 'an oval almost round, inside a bigger oval form. The outside is composed of vertical uniform elements.' This work of sculpture was made for the protected Saint Olaf Church square in the centre of Aarhus city, where the first church in Aarhus was built on the beach in 945. The sculpture is built of two tonnes

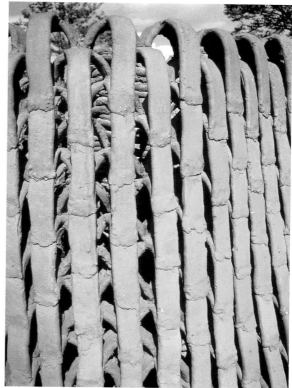

of earthenware clay, composed in a way that will make it crumble and fall apart and thus let the old church square open again. The work was made in one week with the assistance of students from the school Clay-Art in Aarhus. Marianne Eilertsen, writing about the sculptures that Hansen built in Taastrup, *Pillars of Movement*, described them as 'radiating an aura of simplicity and matter-of-factness, objects that just existed.' (*Ceramics: Art and Perception 36.*) These works were part of a series of sculptures created at the Tommerup Tileworks on the Danish island of Fyn. Eilersen believes that Hansen deliberately places himself in a position in which the clay and work processes can challenge him. 'Themes which involve movement, change and humanity, are those which preoccupy Hansen in his sculptural work.' Fire is also an important element and his ability to use fire as a factor in making the sculptural work permanent at the same time as providing a spectacular event for the public has resulted in invitations to a number of different countries, including the south-west coast of Ireland and Perth, Western Australia.

Jørgen Hansen intentionally veers away from perfection and prefers to supply the sculpture with a certain incompleteness, says Lisbeth Bonde, art critic and journalist.

In this way, there is a reference to process. The sculpture entitled *Verwandlungskreis*, erected in 2002 near what was once the Berlin Wall, shows that Hansen is becoming increasingly more interested in the sculpture's interior, and the clay glowing from the firing is playing a part that becomes more important in his work.

In viewing Hansen's sculptures the public can witness a process that normally occurs within a closed system, namely inside the ceramic kiln, where the porous clay is transformed into something hard and everlasting. The process laid bare is a spectacular sight. The sculptures are both conceived and executed on a grand scale since they manage to fill quite a considerable place and can weigh many tonnes. What is also characteristic of these works is that they are site-specific in much the manner of other three-dimensional works in recent art history, which means to say that they have been created for a specifically chosen spot and that they enter into dialogue with a particular cultural history and architecture. They can constitute a passage and function as a connecting link between two historic epochs, as exemplified by *Rejsen* (The Journey) in Fredericia, which is intended to unite a modern residential neighbourhood with the city's original centre.

Chantale Delrue, *Foyer*. Fairview Primary school, New Norfolk, Tasmania.

'**CHANTALE DELRUE** came to ceramic murals and floor and pavement pieces from a well established background as a painter and ceramicist with many group and solo exhibitions in these media to her credit, both in Belgium and Australia,' writes Diana Klaosen in an article for *Ceramics Technical 18.* Klaosen continues:

> Delrue studied ceramics at tertiary level in Tasmania with the idea of making a living as a potter but decided being a production potter was too restrictive for her. Later, having undertaken a number of painted murals as public art commissions, she became aware of and disconcerted by the relative lack of longevity of these painted forms. This led her to investigate mosaics in the early 1990s because of their durability. As she observes, 'It is a long, difficult process but the tiles last longer than our lifetime and it is the only art you can walk on.'

An early mosaic project was the 1991 embellishment of a Hobart pedestrian thoroughfare, Mather's Lane, with Delrue leading a team of about 100 people: senior citizens from an adjacent club, children from a crèche and members of the nearby Catholic Women's League participating in the art making, as well as the council workers who were officially employed on the task. Other public mosaic commissions followed: for schools such as the Trevallyn Primary School in Tasmania; and for cities such as Glenorchy, which commissioned ten pavement panels to celebrate 100 years through its stories and its people, combining depictions of major events with tales from everyday life and achievements.

Delrue's work incorporates her environmental and ecological concerns. She has a strong sense that the viewing public should be uplifted and heartened and that public art should generally bring happiness. As a political statement she may depict the flora and fauna of a region, as in her pavement piece and mural for the Australian National University (ANU) with its entwined spirals portraying European – imported – animals and plants alongside native Australian creatures and plants. This work, entitled *Evolution/Involution,* addresses the integration of native and European species and is a ground-based piece that is part of the ANU's sculpture garden featuring works by Australian and international artists. Delrue's mosaics combine aesthetic criteria and abilities with a sense of the artist's conceptual considerations, and her personal symbolism and imagination. Klaosen believes that the immediacy, accessibility and the universal appeal of Delrue's ceramics are vital for public mosaic art works.

TOP: *Torbjørn Kvasbø,* **Water Basin**. *Work in progress.*

CENTRE: *Torbjørn Kvasbø,* **Water Basin**, *1995. Work in progress. Gulgong.*

BOTTOM: *Torbjørn Kvasbø,* **Cube**, *Nordic college project. Dimensions: 1.7m (5.6ft).*

The Norwegian sculptor **TORBJØRN KVASBØ**, says:

I don't like undertaking commissions, somehow they never seem entirely finished. Between the thought and the clay, understanding and emotions, clay and emotion give us the best prospects. However, I work thematically with form, that is, I have been engaged with specific forms as, for example, houses, chests or coffins and troughs over a long period of time, over years. Through this focus I find closer associations with life, form, texture, structure and colour. Form as language, that is, expression, by means of local clay is used to catch as many ideas as possible. The raw clay and quickness of heating gives me a starting point for a fast work, up and down, to a form and gives just enough for identification: here my stories stop. I effect nothing, I just make and try to gather as much force and power as I can in the clay form.

Kvasbø uses nature as his source of inspiration, in particular from what is near where he lives. 'This has to do with my growing suspicion that what is man-made is not always true and reliable. Stories are not to be trusted, history is theory and subject to any changes that might fit whatever purposes. Clay in this respect is the most reliable material that we have. Clay doesn't change, and ceramics change slowly.'

'Between Nature and Civilisation' was the title of an article by Gunnar Dunbolt, published in *Ceramics: Art and Perception 13*. Kvasbø's work is described by the author, an art historian, saying that the clay's open flexible nature is exposed by the artist, and that there is no attempt to disguise the materials and the processes. 'Natural materials are transformed into art, only to be broken down and returned, eventually, to nature. History and conviction have become important in Torbjørn Kvasbø's work.'

As Professor of Art at the Academy in Stockholm, Torbjørn Kvasbø has been involved in many projects. In one he was assisted by more than 20 students from the Nordic colleges of art, all handpicked for the project. Kvasbø designed a three-tonne solid brick 1.7m (5.6ft) cube, using pugged slabs (but not cut into bricks) of earthenware brick clay. Half of this cube fell and scattered in a pattern on the ground. The whole sculpture was collapsed into a 5m (16½ft) long, 2.5m (8¼ft) wide, partly constructed, partly disintegrated form that was pleasing to him and 'is far the strongest I ever made. I built a 25mm (1in.) fibre kiln around it, supported by wire mesh, and fired the sculpture with wood for three days, up to the melting point of the clay at 1120°C (2048°F). The firing brought out every imaginable colour and texture from the brick clay.'

When exhibiting with the Danish ceramicist Nina Hole at Galerie Norby in 2003, Kvasbø worked at the Tommerup Brick Factory in Denmark where Esben Madsen assists artists with large-scale pieces. He worked at Tommerup for a month before the show. Invited to Gulgong's ClaySculpt project Kvasbø designed and made a large water basin that covered an island in a water catchment, firing it on site. He says, 'I felt humble in this old and strange continent, and wanted to introduce as little harm as possible. Another project I built was a wall patterned after the special fences we have in Norway. I have 150-year-old wood fences like this around my own house.'

'Between the Temple and the Altar' is the title of an article on the work of **MADOLA**, a ceramic sculptor from Barcelona. Daniel Giralt-Miracle, Director of the Museu d'Art Contemporani de Barcelona writes:

> Thanks to their experimental nature, the historical avant-garde have allowed a freedom in the use of artistic methods and concepts that would have been unthinkable according to Renaissance canons or Neoclassical standards. Taking this freedom as her starting point, Madola opened up an exploratory path rooted in the language and tradition of ceramics, a tradition to which she holds firm because it is the expressive medium she knows best and finds most stimulating. Her current work moves between the sculptural and the architectural. If at first she articulated an architecture inspired by pavilions, columns and pediments tending towards a conception of ceramics which assimilated the magnificence of architecture, the work she now presents penetrates the oldest and at the same time most mythic dimension of constructed forms. The nakedness of her pieces, their compact forms, the proportion of the parts to the whole, their monumentality, find in these referents mythic values which Madola incorporates into her vocabulary through an architecture made to measure, as an extension of the resources proper to ceramics.
>
> She pushes the medium to the limits of its expressivity, testing the technical and spatial possibilities allowed by the kilns she works with. It is almost as if she wanted to transmit to a series of pieces, which go beyond the

Madola, **Font Vermella**, 2003. Stoneware.

> ceramic dimension of their material base, part of the religious symbolisms which accompany the temples, the sanctuaries and the altars of the great historical cultures; these pieces are thus converted into totems of memoirs or the architectures of myth.

Writing on a particular project, a plaza for the City of Barcelona in *Ceramics: Art and Perception 11*, Madola described aspects of her planning:

> Colour was intended to be the most important element in the project. The colours used in the realisation of the plaza are yellow, blue, white and black – colours traditionally used in the ceramics of Castilla la Mancha and the production centres of Talavera de la Reina and Puente del Arzobispo. The project pays homage to all those who have used colour in their works in the urban space, especially Gaudi and Joan Miro. The configuration of the plaza has both horizontal and sloping areas. My idea was to rep-

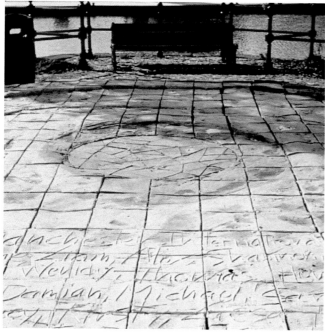

TOP: *Madola,* **Castella**, *1986. Project for the City of Barcleona.*

BOTTOM: *Madola,* **Meditarranta**, *1996. City council, Catay Square Manchester, England.*

resent an island, crossed by a water curtain. I used the metaphor of a river for the river of cars crossing the plaza. The traffic transformed it into a moving space that resembled water flowing on its normal course. The combination of all these views is designed to bring us closer to a symbolic world integrating the elements of water, colour and lineal rhythms – a sense of movement and life that transforms an unattractive urban space into a place of fiction.

The construction and structure of the fountain required different levels of realisation. After topographical considerations based on the model and the sub-terranean laying of all services, the foundations were constructed in concrete. Alongside the centre of the fountain, two pools were installed to be filled with water and act as receptacles for the water curtains. The centre of the fountain was divided into two zones: one is a passage, surfaced with concrete, the other covered with ceramics, fired to 1280°C (2336°F) and coated with varnish. The irregular forms have four different levels of thickness corresponding to colour and patterned with pictorial symbols.

Rosario De Casso, curator at Museo Espanol de Arte Contemporaneo, Madrid, and responsible for curating an exhibition of Spanish ceramics calls Madola's work 'constructionist'. 'Madola's work reverberates with the Mediterranean and its light. Of Catalonian origin, she has always lived near the blue sea from whose reflections one can confirm the validity of her ceramics. Her passion is expressed in vigorous strokes, in the vitality in the volumes, in the ambition of fulfilled and mature forms. It is charged with impulse and instinct and has the strength which binds irresistibly.'

Born in 1955 in Plattling, Germany, **RENATE BALDA** studied art at Nuremberg Academy of Art under Professors Weil and Sack-Coldilz. She is self-taught in ceramics and she continues to paint, often using coloured clays as a painting material. Her ceramic surfaces are bent to form cylindrical shapes, which also act as a basis for her painting. 'The cylinder does not move,' she says. 'It remains static, neutral; it is simply there.' Yet in reality it has an inner movement that keeps it lively. There is a dialogue with the fireclay surface, the rough textures, polished here, smoothed away there. 'Clay is my material now, for painting too, and I know that this is the right road for me to travel.'

Dr Carmen Gonzáles-Borrás, a Spanish art historian and curator living in Germany, is a regular contributor to art and ceramics journals. Writing for *Keramik Magazin* she describes Renate Balda's paintings and ceramics thus:

> Clay gives her that special dimension; even when she uses paper or canvas as the bearer, she uses pigment and clay to model the surface. Where her cylindrical shapes are concerned, the advantage for her is the immediacy with which her hands come into contact with the surfaces. These surfaces can be caressed and protected, or they respond with their roughness. All it takes is a small impact on the clay and it expresses itself – small pieces of slate or tiny stones pressed into the surface, the mixing of other materials, spots of coloured glaze – all help make the clay cracked and fissured.

Renate Balda's cylinders correspond to her idea of the course of life, slow and calm, without any great highs or lows, without any major incidents, yet at the same time they are full of emotion, traces of time and events. 'To follow the different surfaces is to follow the different moods of clay, like sounds of life,' she says. Describing some of these works, Gonzales writes:

> It will be colour which characterises them, whether painted or enamelled. For others, it will be a certain processing of their surface: texturing using fireclay or through the marking of the surface. Sometimes it will be all the techniques combined, for in order to be useful to the artist, many different influences are concerned, including the interrelationships between the cylinders. Balda's intention at this particular moment is also crucial, as are the responses which the material itself is capable of making. The intellect alone is never right. There is always the chance turning of events during the process.

The cylinders can be arranged differently. On the way from her house to her studio just a few metres apart, some of her cylinders stand on top of each other on iron tubes, like columns. When she is indoors, she can see different fragments of these columns through the window. Then she composes with her eye, as though the window were a frame for the picture which she then completes in this moment. In her imagination, she combines these elements with the landscape and the light, all of which serve as a sculptural exercise. Those who collect her work do the same to suit their individual environments. 'A brief glance is akin to

ABOVE: *Renate Balda,* **Columns** *(detail).*

OPPOSITE: *Renate Balda,* **Columns in Landscape**, *2003. Height: (tallest) 2.1m (6 ¾ ft).*

*Maro Kerassioti, **May, to Maroussi by train**. Maroussi train station, Greece.*

breathing for my heart and mind,' Balda observes. More important than the work is the artistic process, the moment in which she makes every component. 'We are not dealing with standard production work here. With the process of stamping each element and the resulting dialogue between feeling and the response to the material, my work appears as an archaeological product of memory. I hate concepts. What impels me to work, what drives me, lies within me, is always there, and forces me to surrender to its will.' Renate Balda is painting with clay and modelling with colour in an attempt to express her feelings, while at the same time using natural processes with the value of chance as an essential element.

MARO KERASSIOTI is a ceramic sculptor living in Athens, Greece. She writes:

Creating a large-scale mural is a challenge for every ceramicist. The collaboration with the architect is not always easy, but it is more than necessary. The ideas of the two artists have to coincide, colours and shapes have to match. For the needs of the 28th Olympic Games, which took place in Greece, 2004, the management of the train company had decided to construct new stations in Athens and reconstruct the old ones. Therefore, they held architectural and artistic competitions for all of them. Maroussi – a suburb until 1940 incorporated within Athens and now a separate municipality – hosted the main Olympic stadium, athletic installations, the press village and many manifestations both of the cultural and the Athletic Olympiade.

Since it was founded in the mid-1800s, Maroussi has had one of the oldest and largest train stations, with a famous steam train known as the *Smudge* or the *Monster*, because of the cloud of black smoke in which it appeared and disappeared. It was the liaison between the port of Piraeus and Kifissia, the summer resort for wealthy Greeks.

Known as the suburb of potters, more than 50 workshops were functioning between the years 1900 and 1960, Maroussi was also famous for its excellent natural water, the beautiful gardens and the celebration of the first day of spring, the first of May. 'Many families used to go there by train, among them mine, to gather flowers from the fields and make the nicest possible wreath in order to ornament their front doors, while the children were free to play. From this memory came the

*Hsu Yung-Hsu, **Implicit Light of Ai Ai**, 2003. Dimensions: 6.25 x 1.43 x 1.15m (20½ x 4¾ x 3¾ ft).*

title and the inspiration for my work, four relief ceramic panels of 10m² (108sq. ft) each, I called it *May, to Maroussi by Train*.'

The colours, the joyful feelings of her childhood, but also – and most important – her first-hand knowledge of the juggler-potters and their miraculous wheels came to her mind spontaneously. 'I could only see the station as a pleasant passage for passengers to cross, whether coming or going home, ornamented with round shapes.' The design of this station is audacious and with strong colour combinations, 'I had to choose my palette from colours equally strong or otherwise muted ones and thus invisible. So I had to abandon my first thoughts about pale tones and abstract designs, and let myself play like a child with all the hues of the rainbow.

'The round shapes and the holes of the metal construction seemed to match perfectly with the shape and colour of the May wreath, and the circular movement of the potter's wheel. Therefore they appear repeatedly on almost every wall, in combination with vertical colour lines and winding interventions as hints for the continuous movement of the passengers. I used stoneware clay, porcelain engobes, oxides and stains and the low reliefs vary from 2 to 5 cm (¾–2in.).'

Maro Kerassioti's finishing touch was the use of a three-layer anti-graffiti product 'to protect the panels from any ambitious painter who would like to see it look his way.'

The Taiwanese sculptor **Hsu Yung-Hsu** uses ceramics for his large-scale chairs and figures because he finds it is a tangible and giving material. He says the fragile quality of ceramics helps demonstrate a 'nervous and uneasy expression', especially when his sculptures are placed in an open field. Yet in this setting ceramics complements the natural environment. Hung Tsui-Hsia, an art critic, writing about Hsu in *Ceramics: Art and Perception 45*, sees ability combined with experimentation in these large works. 'Hsu hopes that he is an observer of social pulses. He wants to use his eyes to understand the interaction between man and society. Therefore, no matter the theme of his ceramics he has been working to a consistent idea – to transform clay to a living expression, and let it speak and say what he wants it to say.'

OPPOSITE PAGE
ABOVE LEFT *Hsu Yung-Hsu installing the sculpture with the aid of a crane.*

BELOW LEFT: *Keeping the sculpture in balance during installation.*

RIGHT: *Hsu Yung-Hsu,* **Myth***, 2004. Shigaraki Ceramic Cultural Park, Japan. Dimensions: 1.12 x 0.92 x 3.4m (3¾ x 3 x 11ft).*

Hsu Yung-Hsu says he is intrigued by the sense of uncertainty in ceramic processes yet it is a material in which he can express his views and feelings. He says he sees through human concerns of traditional society where everybody seems to be wearing a hypocritical mask. While they are hoping to share other people's life experiences, they are afraid that those people would see through them as well. These paradoxical plots can be seen in all corners of society. They are also found in the language of the works of Hsu Yung-Hsu.

Hsu makes use of the fragile properties of ceramics to create the body language of dancers and present them in virtual and realistic space. In 2000 one of his works, *Seats*, Hsu Yung-Hsu symbolises the different roles played by the public in society. Through the opportunity of an open-air exhibition, he hoped to alter people's conceptions towards ceramic art. Hung continues: 'Through ceramics, a material most intimate with human beings, Hsu hopes to extend his understanding

and his unease towards social phenomena. The internalised feelings of Hsu Yung-Hsu are transformed to monumental works and through these, he intends to arouse and bring about a kind of shock, sympathy and a new visual appreciation to his audience. He lets four dimensions, that is the viewers, the work, artists and the space stimulate an interaction. He combines internal spiritual thinking with external presentation, and presents them to demonstrate the artistic qualities of the time.'

Professor Fu-Shou Lu of the Fine Arts Department at Kaoshiung University, Taiwan, writing in Hsu's 2000 catalogue, says that Hsu's passion allows him to be absorbed in his work. 'There is no doubt of his patience and tolerance in overcoming any obstacles he may encounter. His ideas seem endless.' Hsu has been invited to participate in exhibitions throughout Asia and has received awards for his large-scale ceramics.

CHAPTER TWELVE

Admiration for the Human Spirit

MARIA GESZLER HAS ALWAYS BEEN a keen photographer and, over the years, she has made a number of portraits and landscapes which depict the human mood. She places these figures in the landscapes she has visited in different seasons. 'Using the negatives of these photographs I can make a screenprint which I transfer to porcelain. Then these can be reproduced as whole figures. My challenge is to make a three-dimensional form out of a two-dimensional photograph and explore the possibilities hidden in this technique. Expressed in terms of sensibility, my wish has been to create an ethereal object, capable of inspiring emotion and provoking thought relevant to its symbolic and dramatic content.' (Geszler's statement was written for the catalogue of the Triennale de la Porcelaine, Nyon, in 1986.)

As with her figurative ceramics she hopes to express the human sprit in all her sculptural work. Some of these are clay-pipe forms, some hanging singularly, some in multiples. She writes, 'Musical instruments are constructed copies of ourselves. I turned to the simplest form, a pipe, a flute, seeing it as a human icon. The pipes may lie, stand or hang from the ceiling, they are always the same, alone or in hundreds.'

After graduating from the College of Applied Art in Budapest, she began work as a designer in a ceramic factory. 'I noticed the smoke of the freezing towers, the lines of the factory's broken windows, the conveyor belts, the workers and the loneliness of the huge badly lit factory halls. I started to photograph these impressions and transferred them to porcelain. I was led by

GESZLER

HIGBY

PAIKKARI

KUCZINSKA

GLICK

HEENEY

SCHULTZE

GAZZARD

HYMAN

COURT

KEIGHERY

OPPOSITE: *Klaus Schultze. Part of a sculptural ensemble in Bremen, Germany for a technical high school, 1979–80.*

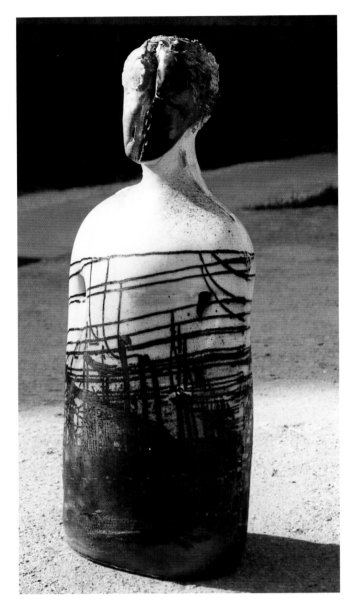

Maria Geszler, **Poetry of the Industrial Landscape**, 1996.
Porcelain, silk screen, salt firing, wood kiln.

Maria Geszler has won many international awards for her work and has completed commissions for works in the environment. She plays an active role for the International Ceramic Studio in Kecskemét, Hungary, where many of her large-scale works are made.

The firing of her works in wood-burning kilns fights, she says, 'against nature, cold, strength, fatigue, heat and defeat. This struggle is an organic part of the forming of my thoughts and credo – whether I will be capable of inner visions, of their articulation and realisation. For me salt-glaze is not technology, salt-glaze is content.' Geszler wrote in a statement for the book: *Salt-glazed Ceramics: An International Perspective*, published in 1996:

> I felt I had at last found the technique of rounding out the hard lines of the photograph by this method. Salt-glaze envelopes the porcelain mass, changing the colour of the cobalt oxide to pure silver. This effect gives my printed porcelain windows a surrealistic content. I begin the firing slowly, adapting myself to the weather, the kiln and the quality of wood. After reaching 1000°C (1832°F) the pace of the firing increases until 1300°C (2372°F) is achieved throughout the kiln. I salt three times with sodium chloride, at 1250°C (2282°F), 1280°C (2336°F) and 1300°C respectively. I use only a little salt for my porcelain pieces and calculate for the ash. I reduce the kiln strongly. I fire for 16 to 20 hours and prefer a kiln that I can manage by myself. I always fire my works myself. My objects are my life.

WAYNE HIGBY is concerned with landscape imagery as a focal point of meditation. Space, both real and implied, is of utmost importance to him. He writes. 'I strive to establish a zone of quiet coherence – a place full of silent, empty space where finite and infinite, the intimate and immense intersect. The material and immaterial oscillate. In combination they become the alchemical philosopher's stone.'

One of Higby's major commissions was described in *American Craft* in 1997: 'The distinctive but minimalist headquarters of Arrow International in Reading, Pennsylvania, gives no hint of the major works by leading craftsmen that grace its interior. Yet from the architectural design stage, Marlin Miller Jr, President and CEO of the medical supplies firm, had discussed his intent to commission works with Michael McKinnell of Kallmann McKinnell & Wood, architects for the building. Together they began a process of looking at Miller's private

two feelings: admiration and appreciation at the sight of human spirit and technique, and fear and anxiety at the sight of the huge, creaking steel plants.'

Portraits – portraits on porcelain – became her diaries:

> For decades I have experimented to express my personality in simple, concentrated minimal art forms, its technical difficulties and its content. These figures I imagine living in the landscape, hiding in the bushes, lying in the grass, standing in water. In an exhibition hall, on pedestals, however, I see a dissonant phenomenon. That is why I try to set them in natural surroundings.

Wayne Higby, **Intangible Notch**. *Arrow International Reading, PA, USA.*
Dimensions: 400 x 300 x 35cm (157½ x 118 x 13¾ in.). Photographs by Brian Oglesbee.

*Wayne Higby, **Earth Cloud**.*
Photograph courtesy of Helen Drutt Gallery.

collection as well as artists' slides, finally narrowing their selection to five – Cynthia Schira, Gerhardt Knodel, William Daley, Anne Currier and Wayne Higby.

Each artist was reviewed by Miller and McKinnell at the artist's studios, where they had the opportunity to evaluate and discuss the final direction of the work. The artists' original proposals were all accepted. Higby entitled his work *Intangible Notch*. It is 4m (13ft) high, 3m (10ft) wide, 35cm (14in.) deep and incorporates a niche. It was installed October, 1995. He writes: 'I made 700 tiles each approx. 20 x 10 x 0.5cm (8 x 4 x ¼ in.) thick, all cut by hand, biscuit fired, glazed one at a time and individually raku fired. A single glaze was used overall. The orange to green glaze is a signature glaze, colour variations occur because of the timing of the raku process. The project took one year to complete.'

In an article on the work of Wayne Higby for *Ceramics: Art and Perception 6*, Robert Turner wrote:

Landscape as image was in a degree a constant motivation for Higby, and the raku process provided the visual texture, warmth and colour he sought. By 1969, he had digested that historic feast [a reference to Higby's early study of art history] sufficiently to move toward forms permitting a more personal association, to landscape and childhood. The motivation for the dimensionally and visually dynamic works was to achieve form directly through landscape. Composed of a complex of physical geometry and visual drama, sensuous and even luxurious surface, exquisite as

abstract drawing and intriguing and fulfilling as idea, the unity is masterful – the ambiguity of real space entered. This comes out of risk. The compelling image has to be uncovered, a new level reached for new information.

Seriousness combined with passion about issues and about his work mark Higby as person, artist and teacher. In a kind of credo for fellow artists and teachers, he says that 'imagination, moral consciousness and craft (the principle of doing things well) are required to meet challenges as informed human beings'. In this way he perceives the artist as a bridge, a connector between daily decisions and inner feeling and identity.

Wayne Higby has worked on a second project for Marlin Miller and Kallmann, McKinnell & Wood. Since 2001, he has been involved in the production of a porcelain wall for the entrance to the theatre of the Miller Performing Arts Building on the Alfred campus, Alfred, New York. The working title, *Earth Cloud*, refers to the concept of a transitional meeting between earth, gravity and sky – floating free. This emphasis on the dynamic tension between the material and immaterial lies at the heart of all Higby's work. *Earth Cloud* measures 15 x 9m (50 x 30ft) and is made up of 7000 tiles with an overall weight of 8 tonnes (18,000lbs). Installation was completed in 2005.

Writing about his approach to his work in an article in *Ceramics: Art and Perception 28*, Higby noted:

Gradually I began to realise that my work in porcelain established a monochromatic state of sculpture in which illusionary image, surface and dimensional form are fused almost completely. Therefore, my ongoing quest for a balanced interdependent condition of reality and imagination has been facilitated. In addition, this monochromatic condition along with the complex layering of the surface as a result of particular ceramic phenomena (cracking, crazing, melting, dripping) has created a sense of distance or removal in time from the actual moment of the image content. I realised that this work operates more like a memory of a landscape.

This approach towards the evolution of a final product led Higby to a better understanding of skill as a tool or gift for making it right, not perfect. Following material and process – in essence, nature – is a way, he believes, towards awareness and insight.

TOP: *Pekka Paikkar,. installation at Arabia Museum Gallery, 2004.*

RIGHT: *Pekka Paikkari, **Firesculpture**, 2003. Height: 5m (16½ ft).*

PEKKA PAIKKARI, a Finnish sculptor, prefers the classic forms of ceramics. Ritva Röminger-Czako, an art curator from Bonn, Germany, writing in *Ceramics: Art and Perception 56*, reveals how Paikkari looks to add new dimensions to his ceramics.

Apart from clay, he uses other materials for the ceramic process for making large-size objects and installations. He knows his material well and appreciates it for its long tradition because it is closely connected to the earth and the human being as well as being a challenge for the artist. From the start of his sculpting career, the conventional rules of ceramics have not been enough for Paikkari. He wanted to work with clay in large proportions, freely in a space, and without podiums and cabinets. By the mid-

1980s, his first large ground objects and installations were made. He is not looking to create beautiful and finished pieces but wants to show their transitional state. His forms are therefore 'unfinished' and 'unsteady' with surfaces rough, cracked and open.

Pekka Paikkari likes to use motifs based on vessel, bottle and brick forms that are traditional in ceramics and are familiar to everyone. 'They are part of the collective memory of the human being,' writes Röminger-Czako.

The intellectual concept and the working process occasionally mean more to the artist than the final work. The process is expressive and experimental in which it plays an important role. Fire is respected by sculptors since

*Pekka Paikkari, **The Flow of Time**, 1997.*

it can make or break their work during the burning process. Paikkari has learnt to work with fire and knows how to control it. Nevertheless a piece of work can come from the kiln broken into shards but, even then, it has a power of expression in and of itself and can record an important moment.

From 1999 to 2000 Paikkari made several versions of the installation *House of the Brick Maker*. It shows a room made from bricks, and containing large ready-made plates and vessels – arranged as if encircling a place of ancient memory. The latest works are bottles, more than 3m (10ft) high. These are monumental vessels displayed sometimes together in one installation, as they were in Rastatt, Germany, in May 2002. For his exhibition in Helsinki in 2003, Pekka Paikkari chose a gallery whose premises formerly belonged to the porcelain company Arabia, a place where bricks and clay were produced in the past. The exhibition, which had the title The Stage, pays homage to both place and the Finnish ceramics tradition. Paikkari also pays tribute to the famous Finnish architect Alvar Aalto, for whom bricks played an important role when creating new forms.

For **MARIA THERESE KUCZINSKA**, the subject of her works concerns the condition of man. For centuries human imagination has been the source of current visual expression of innumerable generations of artists and this imagination still remains one of the most relevant subjects of art. She writes,

> When we regard the sculptures of the Cyclades, of Tanagras, or the works of Donatello, we discover, as through a mirror, the fragility of our existence and the strength which lies in the continuation of life; we realise that, in spite of the belief in our importance in daily life, we are but an element of an eternal rebirth. Our image, however, is perpetuated in our art, bearing witness to our spiritual presence, and to our physical beauty, to our determination or our heroism.

Kuczinska would like this belief to remain impressed in her works – that is, the tracing of the rapidity of present-day life as well as respect for our past, of nature, as well as her faith in the positive aspects of our humanity.

> When I am working, I endeavour to remember that scale is an integral part of sculpture. Its physical size has an emotional signification, but its monumental aspect does not depend on its dimensions but on the vision which lies

John Glick, five-piece wall mount. Stoneware, glaze.

in its conception, in the mass of the sculpture, in its proportions and the contrast of its forms. Clay is an ideal material in which to express the excitement experienced by an artist in his search for aesthetic solutions. The nature of clay, its sensuality and its dynamic character allow me to work in such a fashion as to reflect the creative process, posing questions rather than giving a definite answer.

Firing is not only a technical process in ceramics, says Kuczinska; it indicates the frontier between two important aspects of art: a creation and its perception. The object is finished, but is still living: firing fixes the traces of hesitation left by the artist, even his faults, offering others the continuation of creation, sharing in discovering the energy in such a material as clay and in the decision-taking. 'The final presentation of my works, therefore, includes elements such as the intuitive moment when my hands leave the clay, the closing of the studio doors and the silence which envelopes the sculpture awaiting its firing.'

Since establishing the Plum Tree Pottery in 1964, **JOHN GLICK** has enjoyed the exploration of the rich world of functional pottery. He says he enjoys the interaction with people:

It would seem that those who follow my work have become accustomed to the changing nature of my ceramics over the years and have supported it with kindness and sympathetic generosity. Without this sense of harmony that flows between us, the survival of my studio would be in question. But, as it is, my inclination to be inquisitive is happily matched by an equally willing public response. I believe it is the kind of relationship that has nurtured enduring art activity in other times in many cultures.

His work in the studio is enhanced and balanced by accepting a number of invitations to lead ceramics workshops in the USA and other countries, and through writing, lectures and tours of his studio. He also offers apprenticeship training as a way to help young potters learn about techniques, philosophies and goals in a full-time studio pottery.

Mantels and large wall-mounted pieces are part of Glick's repertoire and have been sought after by his followers. Here he describes the approach he takes:

In 1989 I began making slab-formatted works that explored the issues of landscape and realism. These works have continued to evolve towards a more sculptural con-figuration that incorporates familiar objects (fruit, vessels,

Gwen Heeney, **Bid Ben Bid Bont**. Sculpture finished and installed.

letters and shell-like forms) on a mantel that acts as a background or environment for the collage of individual elements. After 1995, I began to develop aspects of the mantel that would allow me to explore the metaphorical or story-telling aspect of the mantel format – childhood memories and those collections of personal treasures we have tucked away somewhere in a recess of the mind. I make the mantel parts as either single or diptych, or at times larger configurations. When it is time to begin an actual grouping or collage, all the separate parts are assembled and an instinctual, additive, trial-and-error process unfolds until the mantel and contents tell their story. I trust to a career-long instinctual approach and it serves me well – an exploration and the element of surprise that permeates this part of the process.

GWEN HEENEY has been a ceramic artist for more than 30 years, and has spent the past 15 years working closely with a number of brick factories, and making large-scale commissions. In that time she has also taken her MA in architectural ceramics at the Royal College of Art, been a research fellow at the University of Wales, Institute of Cardiff, on architectural ceramics and spent a summer working in Sweden on the same subject. She was also the organiser of the successful Yellow Brick Road symposium. She currently teaches at the University of Wolverhampton.

The themes behind Heeney's brick sculpture dictate her making process. The large-scale, site-specific artworks aim to reconcile figurative compositions with function. The work is of human scale, constructed out of a familiar material – vernacular brick, which has the resonance of the home and the domestic environment. 'I operate on a variety of levels,' she reports 'on the one hand fulfilling my need for personal expression, on the other allowing me to appeal to a wider public through my use of symbolic imagery.' One of Heeney's sources of imagery is taken from popular mythology with its narrative themes of social identity and meaning. These stories are ideally suited for questioning contemporary issues related to, for example, gender roles and the nature of the modern family with its associated problems of structure and function. Much of her work articulates such tensions and attempts to resolve a conflict of emotions. In *Bid Ben Bid Bont* both sides of the two-headed Janus (the Celtic god) vie for dominance while pulling at a rope, a symbolic umbilical cord. 'I aim to relate a visual tension within the work. Myths are a constant source of such imagery and encourage an anthropomorphic realisation, which in turn provides an opportunity for

a broad range of interpretations. The symbols are multivalent.'

Heeney is also the author of *Brickworks* featuring artists using bricks to create sculpture.

'Art from Bricks' is the title of an article by Peter M. Bode for *Ceramics: Art and Perception 7*. Bode wrote:

The German ceramicist **Klaus Schultze** discovered, when visiting Sienna, Italy, a town with beautiful brick architecture, that one can make almost anything with this material. Brick, made from fired earth, is not only handy and at hand, but lends itself to the most varied of forms because of its small modular size. It is astonishingly adaptable and does not limit ideas but an ideal plastic building material. Klaus Schultze has freed this material from the limits of its usual geometry and opened it up to a round sculptural possibility through his adaption of the brick as an art product.

How he found his way between ceramics and architectural art is described by Schultze:

After a difficult three-year apprenticeship in Konstanz, I went to work with a potter in Paris in 1952. In 1956 I established a workshop there and soon there was plenty of work to do, even exhibitions came out of it. I was satisfied, but when a painter friend worked or painted a piece of clay spontaneously, or my son modelled automobiles, I became jealous of their freedom with the material. So I threw great heads and busts, which I subsequently cut up and put together as puzzles. In this way, a new and, until then, unresearched world opened up to me. I had an idea to use the essential or basic element of throwing and turning, namely the cylinder for sculptures, and I combined round and straight parts to human measurements. This was much stronger than before but there was still a problem of the clay. I had been working with clay which fired to 1000°C (1832°F) because I wanted a particular colour but for larger pieces this clay shattered and I realised that large sculpture for open spaces could not be built with this kind of clay.

Schultze turned to the use of frost-resistant brick for his purpose and has built sculptural ensembles successfully in public spaces. His recurrent theme is the variation of human meditation; the attitude of a figure – lying, sitting, embedded in the ground or rising out of the ground, a gigantic being with open arms which have endless time, listening to their own existence. These groups stand in many French and German localities, and enrich the urban scene of water, earth,

Klaus Schultze, private commission, 1997. Bavaria.

OPPOSITE:
Marea Gazzard, **Bindu***, 2004. Handcoiled and burnished clay sculpture. Dimensions: 110 x 50cm (43 x 19½in.) and 120 x 55cm (47 x 21½in.), attached by stainless steel to marble base. Dimensions: 75 x 75 x 150cm (29¼ x 29¼ x 58½in.).*

architecture and walled benches; the sculpturally and colourfully integrated plazas form a protective and warming environment. Bode continues,

> Whether it is a 100m (328ft) long wall of figures in Paris or the enlivening of a pedestrian area in Grenoble with up to 18 sleeping and sitting giants, his art always shows an expression of quietly delighted relaxation. These are human gestures and traits which one can recognise despite simplification. In contrast to the impact of material and execution, nothing threatening emanates from these sculptures. The archaic, statuesque element of pictorial frontality from ancient cultures is a dominating intention. That also goes for the cubist abstract heads and busts in the smaller format.

Klaus Schultze continues to be an active participant in the world of architectural ceramics: as artistic leader at the Gmunden Symposium in 2003; participating with his wife, the ceramicist Nica Haug, in the Nabeul Festival in Tunisia; visiting professor at Townsend University, Baltimore, USA, working with students to build brick benches; participating in the Sieversdorf symposium, Oderbruch, near the border of Poland; and a monument for the city of Friedrichshafen for victims of the Nazis. In addition to these public commissions there have been private orders and exhibitions at Galerie b15 in Munich and at Darmstadt, Germany.

MAREA GAZZARD, an Australian ceramicist and sculptor, is the subject of the book: *Marea Gazzard: Form and Clay* by Christine France. France discusses the sculptures Gazzard has completed in both the public and priviate environment. One work, made in clay and then cast in bronze and completed in 1988 is noted:

In the centre of the Executive Courtyard which adjoins

the Prime Minister's suite in Parliament House, Canberra, are five quietly monumental, hill-shaped bronzes which cast changing shadows and evoke an atmosphere of serenity. Situated at a distance from the constant activity that characterises a centre of government, the forms appear perpetual, emerging from the ground and shaped by the spaces which flow between them. Entitled Mingarri: The Little Olgas, they represent another centre – the physical centre of Australia, a centre of Aboriginal culture. At the same time their strong overlapping forms, almost painterly surface and changing shadows possess a universal quality, quite independent of national symbolism. Their presence defines a place of calm, a place where decisions can be made and where visiting heads of state can meet. They are witness to both the past and the future and symbolise the unique position which their maker, Marea Gazzard, has held in shaping Australia's recent art history.

Writing the introduction to the book, France continues,

Gazzard's art began with pottery and has concentrated on presentation of form for more than 30 years. In this time she has produced works of archetypal presence which have attracted both art and craft audiences, and eroded the status distinctions which existed in Australia prior to the '70s between the major arts of painting, sculpture and architecture, and the so-called minor arts such as pottery, fibre, metal and woodwork. Gazzard's role in establishing recognition of craft practices, many of which were the domain of women and lay outside the mainstream, extends beyond her own work back to the early '60s when she started lobbying for the formation, interaction and improved standards for those involved in the crafts.

Reviewing Gazzard's book, her attitude and the impact of her work, Joe Pascoe wrote for Ceramics: Art and Perception 18: 'This book establishes why Gazzard is one of Australia's most important artists, presenting her life and work in an elegant and unassuming way.' Noting her record of achievement and the humanist ideals she espouses, he says, 'Gazzard's artworks exude a noble simplicity that communicate her many interests.'

For an exhibition titled Edge, shown at the Utopia Art Gallery, Sydney, in 2002, a monograph on the work of Marea Gaazard was published. In a discussion between Gazzard and Christine France, the latter commented 'Marea Gazzard is an artist whose personal vision and dedication to excellence have consistently produced works of elemental simplicity. Her interest in form has led her to study the strong feeling in certain archeological works as well as the simplicity of modernism as a means of synthethising complex ideas and feelings.' France reaffirms this with comments from reviewers of Gazzard's works and the book. 'Splendid, powerful and heroic … they emphasise the passage of time and inevitable destinies,' wrote Elwyn Lynn in The Australian. 'Compelling – Gazzard's work is of disarming simplicity,' wrote John McDonald in the Sydney Morning Herald, advising us not to underestimate her achievements. Gazzard admits to having a reservoir of ideas that return later, often with different emphasis, stimulated by new ideas. France sums up: 'With a flow of energy and subtlety, Gazzard has produced objects of volumetric power and universal quality.'

Marea Gazzard was commissioned to represent Sydney (as an Olympic host city) by making a work for the permanent International Olympic Park of Ceramic Sculpture in Maroussi, Athens, 2004. That sculpture is now in place. The work stands 120cm (47in.) high and is handbuilt and burnished ceramic.

SYLVIA HYMAN has been working with clay as a material for art since 1958. Sculpting, teaching and exhibiting, Hyman has always had a message for the future while depicting memoirs of the past. In Vanderbilt University's Divinity School publication The Spire, the Professor of Classics, Susan Ford Wiltshire notes that Hyman's 2003 Genesis 7 sculpture represents some of the oldest stories saved in cuneiform on clay tablets. These stories are retold, in all their versions, again in the enduring form of clay in this piece, which was commissioned for the Professor of the Mary Jane Werthan, Chair of Jewish Studies at the Vanderbilt Divinity School.

In an article in Ceramics: Art and Perception 56, Vince

OPPOSITE
ABOVE: *Sylvia Hyman, **Diversity of Thought**, 2004. Stoneware and porcelain. Dimensions: 52.5 x 55 x 41cm (20 ½ x 21 ½ x 16in.).*

BELOW: *Sylvia Hyman, left section **Re-Generation**, 1996. Vanderbilt University Collection. Dimensions: 157 x 75 x 15cm (61¾ x 29 ½ x 6in.).*

Pitelka substantiated this claim. He quotes Hyman as saying, 'As I look back, I see the work I am currently doing as the culmination of all my life's experience. I hope my work will cause the viewer to think about the meaning of reality. Contemplating reality is like searching for truth, which is what any meaningful work of art should do.' Pitelka writes:

> In her case, that could be part of a manifesto. Through the intervening quarter century, the assemblages have become far more complex and convincing, employing carefully worked clay to impersonate a broad range of baskets, wooden boxes, tubs, corrugated cardboard cartons, drawstring pouches, folders, wrapped packages, postcards, diplomas, certificates, blueprints, doilies, shelves, trays and even birthday cakes and fortune cookies. Hyman's work is convincing in its illusion but is unpresumptuous and accessible. The initial ordinariness of what we see invites us to be close with no barriers.

Like much trompe l'oeil in both two and three dimensions, the objects seem common and often are, but this work is invested with content and meaning that sneaks up on you. In general terms, it addresses issues of communication, traditional means employed for dispensation and passage of information, and does so in ways that toy with concealment and secrecy, suggesting importance while rarely revealing specific meaning. Letters, scrolls, envelopes, blueprints and sheet music are only partially revealed in boxes or baskets, as illustrated in Diversity of Thought, which is installed in the main reading room of the Education Library on the Peabody/Vanderbilt campus. They trigger significant memory and reaction, catalysing meaning specific to each viewer, and thus become intensely personal. Hyman refers to some of this work as 'coded messages' or 'mixed messages' as she hovers between whimsy and mystery.

The subject matter and careful composition invite closer examination that reveals the mystery, simultaneously challenging and appealing to our senses. Some art answers questions, some asks and among the more provocative pieces are several addressing the dispersion of Old Testament stories through multiple cultures. In Noah and the Flood we see an ark-shaped basket, filled with paper-thin vellum scrolls, shaky and frayed on the edges, the surfaces alive with calligraphy in English, Hebrew, ancient Akkadian and Arabic. The illuminated Arabic text seems charged with significance and meaning far beyond any promise of literal translation.

Sylvia Hyman was commissioned by Vanderbilt University Medical Centre's department of Cultural Enrichment in 1996 to create a piece of work for the Eskind Biomedical Library honouring Annette and Irwin Eskind. The piece is titled Re-Generation. In 1999, Hyman was commissioned by Cultural Enrichment for the Page-Campbell Heart Institute at Vanderbilt to make a piece of art that focused on healing. Her piece, Healing Heart, depicts natural forms springing forth from a heart-shaped vessel in the form of a ceramic relief.

CAROLINE COURT is trying to push the definitions of site-specific sculpture.

I work in permanent installations from the imperatives of a specific group of people. The involvement of the group can be as simple as group members carving their marks into unfired bricks and using the resultant materials to build a larger form. In some projects the participants are involved in all phases of the project from initial open inquiry through research and fabrication to final installation.

In a project titled *Democracy* (2003), using bricks and mixed media, she developed studies in the classroom

LEFT: *Caroline Court.* **Penelopeia.** *Installation at the US Inspection Facility in Detroit, USA. Height: 4m (13ft). Photograph by T. Thayer.*

TOP: *Caroline Court and Mr. Einstein's alternative 8th grade class at the Berkshire Middle School, Beverly Hills, MI.* **Democracy,** *2003.*

BOTTOM: *Caroline Court, students and teachers from Brethren High School, Edmonson Elementary School,and Young Detroit Builders.***Complements: Hands Hearts Cars Carts,** *(detail), 2003. Dimensions: 2 x 9 x 5m (6 ½ x 29½ x 16½ ft). Photograph by C. Court.*

focusing on the Bill of Rights of the US Constitution. The alternative 8th grade class at the Berkshire Middle School, Beverly Hills, MI, took part in all phases of design and fabrication in this project. They drew, carved, modelled and made plywood models several times.

In the project titled: *Complements: Hands Hearts Cars Carts* (2003), measuring 2 x 9 x 5m (6½ x 29½ x 16ft) students and teachers of Crandell, Thomas and Jager, the three school groups involved in this project, Brethren High School, Edmonson Elementary School and Young Detroit Builders, participated from the initial open inquiry through the design process and fabrication to installation. They had input into every phase of the project including, but not limited to, naming, subject research and laying the foundation.

> In *Penelopeia*, a permanent installation located at the US Inspection Facility in Detroit, USA, I brought together research in significant form with bricks and my community work, that is, brick carving. Many workshops were held in which customs inspectors, neighbours, school-children, foreign exchange students, brickmakers and others made their marks on unfired bricks. These highly textured small individual works of art form the interior of the arch. They dominate at night when the interior lights are lit. During the day, the exterior form is more noticeable – a 4m (12½ft) tall canted arch, seated in a 5m (15ft) circle of boxwood, lemon thyme and recycled Belgian Blocks.

In an article in *Ceramics Technical 16*, Caroline Court discusses her belief that brick is overdue for recognition as a significant aesthetic material. She involves the community in her work and uses local materials so that there is a relationship built up that is commemorative of both the work and the people who helped build it. She writes:

> Colours, structural arrangements, patterning, firing, local clays and community – all of these factors feeding into a brick structure can lead to a rich and diversified visual metaphor. There are no false fronts. Indigenous materials, traditional methods and metaphorical truths come together in the best of brickwork to enrich our environments and our involvement with each other.

MICHAEL KEIGHERY is a ceramic artist and teacher from Sydney, Australia. Currently Head of Fine Arts at the University of Western Sydney, he has been involved in a number of projects in the environment. Of particular interest to him is the integration of advanced manufacturing technologies in the production of limited-edition works, particularly tiles. He works with his colleague at the university, Denis Whitfield, who is also interested in using industrial waste as alternative raw materials for making ceramic bodies and glazes.

In another collaborative project, this time with the artist Kate Dunn, Keighery was approached by a local government agency to provide artwork for a small park precinct that had already been landscaped. 'It was a rather "twee" Victorian style work in keeping with that area of Sydney.' After a long resident action campaign, the park (called Green Bans Park) had been kept rather than sold for development. In keeping with the landscaped park, Dunn and Keighery decided to make ceramic tiles or friezes in a traditional and rather sedate style. On the 24 friezes the artists screen-printed images from the demonstrations and combined them with excerpts from the diary of one of the main union organisers.

Another environmental project was part of Sculpture by the Sea, an annual event showing the work of nearly 100 sculptors from around the world. The work, selected by jury, is displayed outdoors for two weeks in the sand and on the rocks and cliffs of one of Australia's most popular and dramatic 3km (1.8 miles) of coastal walks, starting from Bondi Beach in Sydney.

The event is hugely popular and attracts large crowds. For the event in 2002, Michael Keighery and Denis Whitfield proposed the temporary installation *Terra Terra Madonna Madonna* that was built *in situ* with 15 student volunteers from the University of Western Sydney. The 35cm^2 tiles were laid to follow the contours of the land, flowing into a space provided by a cliff overhang. The image used was from one of Michelangelo's Madonnas, which was digitally rendered as a relief map.

This map was used to make a model in foam and this model was then used to make four working moulds on to which clay tiles were pressed. Over the period of the

ABOVE: *Michael Keighery and Kate Dunn,* **Residents' Action Diary,** *2000. Tiles 32 x 60cm (12 ½ x 23 ½ in.), earthenware, screenprinted and press-moulded. Entrance to Green Bans Park, Sydney.*

RIGHT: *Detail of a tile.*

exhibition the work was affected by wind and water, gradually being returned to the sand and sea.

Michael Keighery has held many executive positions in craft organisations and has been invited to give papers at conferences internationally. He has exhibited his work consistently since 1982. Known for his innovative and multi-faceted styles, he has been one of the leaders in contemporary Australian ceramic practice.

*Michael Keighery and Denis Whitfield, **Terra Terra Madonna Madonna**, 2002. Installation in situ for Sculptures by the Sea, 35cm² (5 ½ sq. in.).*

OPPOSITE
*Madola, **Pergam**, 1990. Fired to 1280°C (2336°F). Dimensions: 100 x 100 x 35cm (39 x 39 x 13 ¾ in.).*

In **CONCLUSION**, I wish to say that the compilation of the works of these nearly 100 internatonal artists, their statements and reviews about their work, has given me a rewarding insight into the work of ceramic artists making sculptures for placing in the environment. Although I have been working with ceramics for 40 years as a potter, and for the past 25 years as an editor of ceramic magazines, I have made few works that could be classified as specifically environmental – there are some wood-fired stoneware seats made in Kecskemét, Hungary, during a salt-glaze symposium in 1988 that are still to be found in the courtyard of the International Ceramic Studio; and floor tiles for a house in Paddington, Sydney. The architect who commissioned the tiles insisted that they be fired to a low temperature saying that if they were soft then the habits of the people who lived and worked in that house could be seen – there would be the mark of time and use on the floors. In the same way we can evaluate the life and times of the artists depicted in this book and the influence they have had on those who have commissioned, lived with or viewed these works.

The text about each artist differs, in content and length. Their responses to my requests were varied: some practical, some theoretical, some poetic, and all valuable. I thank them all.

If environmental art is seen as the social and aesthetic pulse of a society, expressing its beliefs and values, and we do have these dedicated and responsible artists working in many countries, 26 nations represented here, there is hope for the future. We can be inspired by the works of these artists, and need to encourage and support them even more.

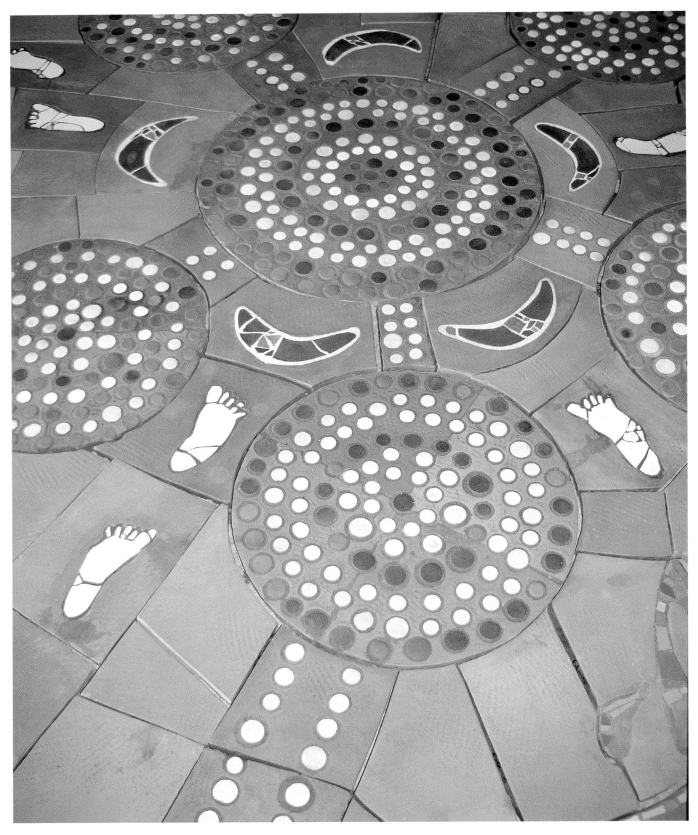

Diogenes Farri and Susie Downie, ceramic pavement and mural, 1998.

RECOMMENDED READING

Andrews, Tim. *Raku* (A&C Black, 1994)

Banfman, Steve. *Raku* (A&C Black/Krause, 1991)

Beard, Peter. *Resist and Masking Techniques* (A&C Black/University of Pennsylvania Press, 1996)

Birks, Tony. *Pottery* (A&C Black, 1988)

Blandino, Betty. *Coiled Pottery* (A&C Black, 1984)

Blandino, Betty. *The Figure in Fired Clay* (A&C Black 2001/Overlook Press, 2002)

Caiger-Smith, Alan. *Lustre Pottery, technique, tradition and innovation in Islam and the Western World* (Herbert Press/Faber & Faber, 1985)

Cochrane, Rosemary. *Salt-glaze Ceramics* (Crowood Press, 2001)

Coiclough, J. *Mould Making* (A&C Black/Gentle Breeze Publishing, 1999)

Daly, Greg. *Glazes and Glazing Techniques* (A&C Black 1998/Kangaroo Press, 1995)

Flynn, Michael. *Ceramic Figures* (directory of artists) (A&C Black/Rutgers University Press, 2002)

Fournier, Robert. *llustrated Dictionary of Practical Pottery* (A&C Black, 1992)

Fraser, Harry. *Ceramic Faults and their Remedies* (A&C Black, 1986)

Fraser, Harry. *Ceramics Handbook: The Electric Kiln* (A&C Black 1994/University of Pennsylvania Press, 2000)

Fraser, Harry. *Glazes for the Craft Potter* (A&C Black/The American Ceramic Society, 1998)

Frith, David. *Mould Making for Ceramics* (A&C Black/Krause, 1992)

Gault, Rosette. *Paper Clay* (A&C Black/University of Pennsylvania Press, 1998)

Gibson, John. *Pottery Decoration* (A&C Black 1987/Overlook Press/G&B, 1997)

Green, L. *Painting with Smoke: David Roberts – Raku Potter* (Smith Settle, 2000)

Gregory Ian. *Kiln Building* (A&C Black/Gentle Breeze Publishing, 1995.

Gregory, Ian. *Sculptural Ceramics* (A&C Black/Krause 1992)

Hamer, Frank and Janet. *The Potters Dictionary 5th Edition* (A&C Black/University of Pennsylvania Press, 2004)

Hardy, M. *Handbuilding* (A&C Black/University of Pennsylvania Press, 2000)

Heeney, Gwen. *Brickworks* (A&C Black, 2004)

Hessenberg, Karen. *Ceramics for Gardens and Landscapes* (A&C Black/Krause/G & B, 2000)

Jones, David. *Raku, Investigations into Fire* (Crowood Press, 1999)

King, Peter. *Architectural Ceramics for the Studio Potter* (Lark Books, 2000)

Lane, Peter. *Contemporary Porcelain* (A&C Black/Krause, 1995)

Leach, Bernard. *A Potter's Book* (Faber and Faber, 1940)

Levin, Elaine. *History of American Ceramics* (Abrams, 1988)

Lightwood, Anne. *Paperelay* (Crowood Press, 2000)

Lungley, Martin. *Gardenware* (Crowood Press, 1999)

Mansfield, Janet. *Contemporary Ceramic Art in Australia and New Zealand* (Craftsman House, 1995)

Mansfield, Janet. *Salt-glaze Ceramics* (A&C Black, 1991/Krause, 1992)

Minogue, Coll and Sanderson, Robert. *Wood-fired Ceramics* (A&C Black/University of Pennsylvania Press, 2000)

Minogue, Coll. *Impressed and Incised Ceramics* (A&C Black/Gentle Breeze Publishing, 1996)

Olsen, Frederick. *The Kiln Book* (A&C Black/Krause, 1983)

Ostermann, Matthias. *The New Maiolica* (A&C Black/University of Pennsylvania Press, 1999)

Panciolo, D. *Extruded Ceramics* (A&C Black, 2000)

Perryman, Jane. *Smoke-fired Pottery* (A&C Black, 1995)

Jorgen Hansen, constructing sculpture, Denmark.

Peterson, Susan. *Smashing Glazes* (North Light Books, 2001)

Peterson, Susan. *The Craft and Art of Clay 4th Edition* (Laurence King, 2003)

Rhodes, Daniel. *Clay and Glazes for the Potter* (A&C Black, 1973)

Robison, Jim. *Large-scale Ceramics* (A&C Black/The American Ceramic Society, 1997)

Rogers, Phil. *Ash Glazes* (A&C Black/Krause, 1991)

Scott, Paul *Ceramics and Print* (A&C Black 1994/ Kangaroo Press, 1995)

Scott, Paul. *Painted Clay* (A&C Black, 2001)

Troy, Jack. *Salt-glazed Ceramics* (Watson–Guptill, 1977)

Troy, Jack. *Wood-fired Stoneware and Porcelain* (Krause, 1995)

Tudball, Ruth-Anne. *Soda Glazing* (A&C Black/University of Pennsylvania Press, 1995)

Wardell, Sacha. *Slipcasting* (A&C Black/G & B, 1997)

Wood, Nigel. *Chinese Glazes* (A&C Black/University of Pennsylvania Press/G & B, 1999)

Young, Alistair: *Setting up a Pottery Workshop* (A&C Black/American Ceramic Society, 1999)

Zakin, Richard. *Electric Kiln Ceramics* (A&C Black 1994/Krause, 1981)

PERIODICALS

American Ceramics
15 W. 44th Street
New York, NY 10036
USA

American Craft
The American Crafts Council
72 Spring Street
New York, NY 10012-4019
USA

Arts and Crafts Magazine
180-21D PO Box 2532
Seoul
South Korea

Ceramica Revista
Guardiana 38
Ajalvir Madrid 28864
Spain

Ceramic Review
25 Fouberts Place
London, WIF 7QF
UK

Ceramics: Art and Perception
120 Glenmore Road, Paddington
Sydney, NSW 2021
Australia

Ceramics in Society
2 Bartholomew St West
Exeter EX4 3AJ
UK

Ceramics Monthly
735 Ceramic Place, Suite 100
Westerville, OH 43081
USA

Ceramics Technical
120 Glenmore Road, Paddington
Sydney, NSW 2021
Australia

Ceramics 1280°
59 Holland Street Haifa
3498 Israel

CraftArts International
PO Box 363
Neutral Bay NSW 2089
Australia

Crafts
Crafts Council
44a Pentonville Road
London NI 9BY
UK

Keramiek
Eendenbrink, 2492 DE
s'Gravenhage
The Netherlands

Keramik Magazin
Steinfelder Strasse 10
D-8 770 Lohr am Main
Germany

Kerameiki Techni
PO Box 76009
171 10 Nea Symyini
Greece

Keramika A Sklo
AS Heyrousketto 1178
500 03 Hradec Kralopve
Czech Republic

**La Revue de Ia Céramique
et du Verre**
61 Rue Marconi
62880 Vendin-le-Vieil
France

National Ceramics
PO Box 2980
Knysna 6570
South Africa

Neue Keramik
Steinruschweg 2
Höhr Grenzhausen 56203
Germany

Object
Centre for Craft and Design
415 Bourke Street
Sydney 2000
Australia

Pottery in Australia
PO Box 105
Erskineville NSW 2042
Australia

Studio Potter
Box 70
Goffstown
NH 03045
USA

Studio Potter Network Newsletter
69 High Street
Exeter, NH 03833
USA

*Maria Therese
Kusczinska. **The
Anaesthetist**.
Porcelain.*

GLOSSARY

AIR BRUSHING: the use of a fine spray to build up layers of colour pigments or glaze on a surface

ANAGAMA KILN: an Oriental style kiln called by a Japanese word meaning hole or cave, it consists of a single chamber, often 5m (16½ft) or more in length and placed on a slope, so that the chamber creates a draught. These kilns are fired for extended periods (up to 10 days) to give full vitrification of the clay and natural ash deposited glazes

BISQUE OR BISCUIT: an intermediate state of clay after it has been fired to a permanent form but still retains porosity

BURNISHING: a method of polishing the surface of a leather-hard clay vessel to provide a shiny smooth surface. This is usually done with a smooth stone or the back of a metal spoon. This polishing assists in sealing the surface of the piece

CAD/CAM: computer-aided design used by ceramic artists and designers to plot forms and textures

CLAY BODY: a mixture of clays and other minerals ready for using. This mixture varies according to the purpose of the potter and can be defined by temperature, earthenware, stoneware or porcelain or by other desired qualities such as coarse, smooth, dense, etc.

CNC MILLING: computer-controlled numerical controlled milling is an automated lathe technology enabling a designer to reproduce identical objects

COILING: a method of building up the side walls of a vessel using rope-like strands of clay. The coil can either be left as texture or smoothed over with the fingers or a scraping tool
CONE: a small triangular cone of fusible material formulated to bend at a certain temperature. The ceramist uses these to judge the temperature in the kiln

EARTHENWARE: a clay that will vitrify in the temperature range 1000° to 1100°C (1832° to 2012°F)

ENAMELS: a low temperature melting glass or glaze, usually applied over a glaze for coloured surface decoration

FIBRE BLANKET: an alumino-silicate refractory blanket used for insulation and coming in various grades according to insulating capability required

FIRECLAY: a variety of clay that has refractory properties and can be used to add texture to a clay body or as a mortar in kiln building

FIRING: the heating to vitrification of clay objects in a kiln

FRIT: a combination of minerals prepared for use in glaze or clay bodies by fusing and milling

GLAZE: a surface coating, usually glossy, applied to the clay for purposes of sealing or decoration. The coating is made from a mixture of minerals or frits and is designed to melt at a specific temperature according to its recipe

GOLD AND SILVER LEAF: an overglaze decoration using fine sheets of metallic leaf which are fired on to the surface of the glaze

GREEN WARE: the state of a clay object before firing

HANDBUILDING: a method of constructing vessels and other ceramic pieces by hand techniques such as coiling, slabs, or pinching the clay

KILN: a chamber for firing/vitrifying clay pots and other ceramic pieces to make them permanent. Kilns use fuels such as wood, gas, electricity or coal to gain temperatures across the range of earthenware, stoneware and porcelain, and are classified as to their style and purpose

LEATHERHARD: a stage in the drying process when the clay has lost its malleability but is still possible to carve. If clay is left in the air it will dry out completely

LOW-FIRED GLAZES: refers to the temperature at which the glaze will melt in the kiln usually in the 750° to 900°C (1382° to 1652°F) range

MOULDS: made from plaster, wood, clay or plastic, these are usually negative forms for pressing plastic clay into or over or for pouring in liquid clay to filla mould creating a positive object

OXIDATION: the atmosphere in a kiln during firing may be said to be oxidising or reducing or neutral depending on the amount of oxygen present. The condition of the atmosphere will alter the various components in the clay or glaze

PORCELAIN: a fine white clay body which is fired to 1300°C (2372°F) or more which, if potted thinly enough will be translucent and ring like a bell

RAKU: a style of ceramic wares, originating in Japan and fired at temperatures of around 1000°C (1832°F), which often involves the extraction of the pieces from the kiln at top temperature for further effects of smoking in combustible materials to alter the surface colour and texture

RESIN LUSTRES: made from oils and coloured pigments, these overglaze lustres will melt in the temperature range of 650° to 800°C (1202° to 1472°F) and are used for surface decoration

SALT GLAZE: a glaze formed on the surface of ceramic wares by the introduction of common salt at temperatures in excess of 1250°C (2282°F). The glaze has a typical texture resembling the surface of an orange. Sodium carbonate will react in a similar manner and this is called soda-glazing

SAWDUST FIRING: a method of firing pots. As the sawdust burns, the clay in the pots sinters and becomes hard. It is possible to reach temperatures of 1000°C (1832°F) from this method of firing

SLAB-BUILDING: a process of using flat plates of clay to build vessels by hand

SLIP: a liquid form of clay or clay body which is used for decorative or forming purposes

SMOKE FIRING: using the reduction effects of smoke from burning paper or grasses to alter the surface of ceramic wares

STONEWARE: a clay or mixture of clay used by potters to make permanent vessels that have the hardness of stone. Firing is usually in the 1200° to 1300°C (2192° to 2372°F) range

THROWING: a method of making pottery with the use of a turning wheel known as a potters' wheel. The hands of the potter shape the clay while the wheel is turning to give a symmetrical pot

TRANSFER PAPER: paper which is used to transfer a printed pattern to a clay surface

UNDERGLAZE: colours formulated for use in ceramics are available in a variety of colurs and strengths and applied to the surface of the clay before firing

Jacques Kaufmann. **Eroded Blocks.** *2001.*

INDEX

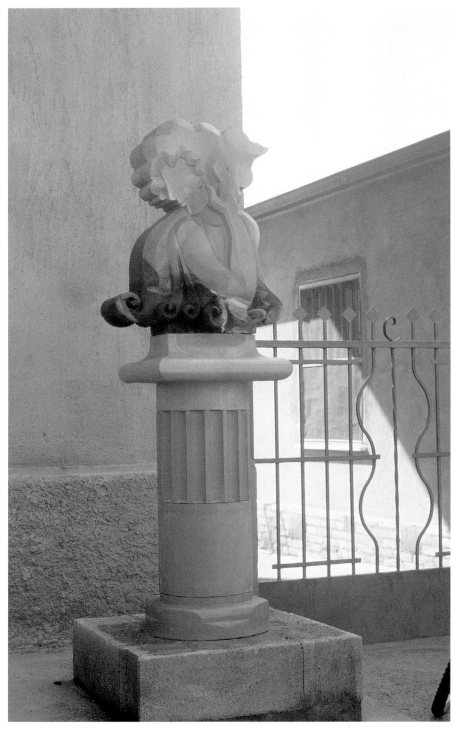

Nino Caruso, **Monument**. *Terracotta.*